Bad Predictions

Laura Lee

Elsewhere Press
Rochester, MI

©2000, Laura Lee

Bad Predictions
©Copyright 2000 by Laura Lee
All rights reserved.

Some images copyright www.arttoday.com.

Elsewhere Press
1326 Gettysburg
Rochester, MI
48306
248-652-9427

ISBN 0-9657345-9-5

Publisher's Cataloging in Publication Data

Lee, Laura 1969-
Bad Predictions
Includes Index
1. Forecasts 2. Forecasting 3. Quotations, English.
I. Title.

Library of Congress Card Number: 00-190255

Table of Contents

Introduction............................ 7

Society...................................... 17
Transportation......................... 59
The Final Frontier.................... 85
Science and Technology............ 95
Health and Medicine................. 119
Communications and Media..... 131
Movies...................................... 145
Arts 159
Music....................................... 163
Literature................................. 171
Sports...................................... 183
Business................................... 191
U.S. History and Politics........... 207
World History........................... 231
Military.................................... 239
The End of the World................ 257

We Predict................................ 286
Author Index............................ 287
Subject Index........................... 294

Introduction

"A thorough knowledge of the past could lead a profound scholar to predict the future course of history with great accuracy, provided that it did not turn out quite differently." —author Aubrey Menen

There is a story that my parents like to tell. When I was four years old, my family lived in a small house with an even smaller yard. To extend my play area I would often venture into the road. When my parents saw me out there they would shout, "Get out of the road— you'll get hit by a car." My reply was invariably, "but I didn't get hit by a car!" This is a book I was clearly born to write. From my earliest days I have had a keen ear for bad predictions.

I had to wait a while to write it, though. There was that whole business about growing up, of course, but there was another important reason. It takes a while for a normal prediction to ripen into a bad one. Something has to happen, or not happen first. If I predict, for example, that you will buy this book, and you fail to buy it today, it is still a valid prediction. You could still buy it tomorrow. Or the next day. As long as you are still around and the book is still around, there is a possibility my prediction will come to pass. Eventually though, you will die (unless some of the predictions about immortality in this book come true) or the book will disappear completely, in which case we would have a failed forecast on our hands.

That is why I chose this time to compile this book. Thanks to its round numbers, the year 2000 has held a special place in the world of forecasting. For the past century, scientists, writers, philosophers and social scientists— everyone, it seems, but computer programmers who thought two digits were enough to represent a year until about 1995— have been looking forward to the big 2-0. Between 1888 and 1900 alone there were 150 novels set in the year 2000. Now, here we are, living in the future so many envisioned. Is it all we imagined it would be?

In some ways, yes. Scientists of the past predicted widespread use of fax machines, personal computers and credit cards. Today there are televisions and telephones in almost every American home. Supersonic jets cross the Atlantic in three hours. Forecasters envisioned it all many years ago.

But this book is not about them. This book is about the people who got it wrong. It is about the prophets who said man could not fly, that nuclear war would destroy the world by 1980, that no one would sit still for television, and to the people who rejected The Beatles because guitar bands were on the way out. This is a book about bad predictions, and the world has no shortage.

There may be those who will criticize this book for being unfair to the people who are included. The quotes are taken out of context. When a railroad executive says airplanes will never work— shouldn't you explain the obvious vested interest he has in the status quo? And is it really a "bad prediction" when a politician in a time of war or depression tells the people what they need to hear to avoid a panic? ("The economy's fine, there's nothing to worry about, go out and invest now...")

All I can say in response is you're absolutely right! There are many good reasons to make a bad prediction. My parents, for example, had a purpose in predicting I would be hit by a car— to get me out of the street. As Paul Dickson wrote in his 1977 book *The Future File*: "A prediction that does not come true is not necessarily a bad prediction. For instance, predictions that have foretold environmental catastrophe may be avoided in the long run because of those very predictions." The terrible effects of the Y2K bug may have been avoided because people were frightened into action by doomsday predictions. Pollution legislation, caution over the use of nuclear weapons and environmental protection efforts may be similarly fueled.

My intention in compiling this book is not to make the prognosticators look foolish (even if some do). Some of the pronouncements are isolated mis-steps in otherwise insightful books and articles. You may even, as I did, look at some of the things that didn't happen and wonder why such good ideas were abandoned. But I leave it to others to explain why it made sense to say some of the things people have said. My only criterion for including a quote in this book was whether the prediction came true or not. If it did not, you'll find it here.

I have the greatest affection for the experts whose clouded crystal balls allowed them to be included here. During the course of my research I have read hundreds of articles on what the future would bring. Many scholars make their forecasts in a hedging prose full of "perhaps" and "statistics seem to indicate... if we assume current trends.. there are several possible scenarios..." Such experts employ language as though their greatest fear in the world is being proven wrong. Their careful pronouncements kept them out of these pages, but I stand in admiration of the scientists, the authors, the visionaries who were imaginative and bold enough to make statements that were absolute— unafraid that they might be proved absolutely wrong.

No one is immune to being a bad predictor. As scentist Neils Bohr put it, "It is difficult to make predictions, especially about the future." Some of the greatest minds in history have fallen prey to the various traps of prediction. There are the overly pessimistic forecasters— the doomsayers and alarmists who shout "the sky is falling" in the hopes that we will change our behavior and keep the sky up there.

There are those that assume the future will continue on a logical path based on what is happening today. This kind of "safe" prediction fails to take surprise into account. They generally say more about the time in which they were made than they do about the future. You will notice, for example that scientists of the 1950s, when bomb shelters, nylon and Styrofoam were news, predicted that the people of the 1990s and early 21st Century would enjoy better living through atomic energy and synthetics— plastics, nylon, Styrofoam— when, in fact, the buzzword of the 1990s was "natural." In the late 1960s, as we planned to send a man to the moon, scientists envisioned lunar colonies by 2000.

Then there are the overly optimistic. Some are lovers of technology who propose mechanical solutions to problems that don't really exist. For example, M. W. Thring's 1973 prototype household dish-clearing robot was designed to tackle what is arguably the least taxing of household chores.

Some inventions have been anticipated for years, yet they haven't caught on with the public. Case in point: the video telephone. First introduced by AT&T at the 1964 New York World's Fair, the picture phone allows callers to see as well as hear each other. Its use in homes seemed inevitable. Clearly, today, we have the technology to make home video phones an even sharper and affordable reality. So far, however, consumers have shown a reluctance to have them. When the phone rings and you've just gotten out of the shower, you may not want to be visible to the other party. The video phone would also put an end to one of the benefits of running a home office— the ability to talk to corporate clients while in your pajamas. The product may still be on the horizon, but many people, this author included, are not looking forward to that improvement in technology.

While many of the visions of life in 1999 and 2000 are theoretically possible for the future, many forecasters were premature in their timing. So far we do not have self cleaning clothes, push-button pre-fab houses, computerized food storage, or home hovercraft.

That said, technology has been moving so quickly

in the past decade that, in some cases, I was not entirely sure whether a prediction was bad or not. A 1971 prediction of self-repairing computers by the year 2000, for example, left me shaking my head. My laptop does not have this feature, but it is a possibility that there are computers out there somewhere with the ability to repair themselves in some way. When I wasn't sure if a prediction was bad or not, I left it out of the book. I assumed that any prediction that required a great deal of research to discover if it was actually wrong would probably not be particularly entertaining.

Before we get to the predictions themselves, let me reflect on a few specific predictions for our time that come up again and again.

Where is all the leisure time we were supposed to have? Most futurists imagined a year 2000 in which technology shortened work weeks and gave each American virtually unlimited time at home. In contrast to these predictions, a 1999 issue of *American Demographics Magazine* predicted that: "The cry of the needy in the new millennium may well be 'Brother, can you spare some time?' Harried baby boomers will create a time famine for themselves by working more hours and committing to more family and community obligations...Marjorie Valin of the Washington, D.C.-based American Advertising Federation says advertisers of the future will need to capitalize on what she calls 'the frenetic sense of lost time' and the life-out-of-control angst that permeates modern culture. "

The forecasters were right about one thing— we now have technology in the workplace that relieves us of the burden of many routine tasks, but instead of using the extra time for leisure, Americans see the tools as a way to get more done. We take on more tasks and raise our expectations of what we should accomplish in a short period of time.

Nor have computers eliminated paperwork, newspapers or printed books, as many people believed they

11

would. Despite some incursions by so-called E-books, the printed word still rules as witnessed by the fact that Internet bookseller Amazon.com was one of Wall Street's most successful stocks in the late 1990s. The number of books has done nothing but increase as computers have become commonplace. Until the middle of the 15th century, Europe was unlikely to have produced more than 1,000 hand-written books a year. In 1950, Europe produced 120,000 books, meaning a library that would once have taken a century to assemble could be collected in 10 months. Ten years later, the output of books had risen to 1,000 titles a day. In 1995, *Book Industry Trends* reported almost 2.3 billion books were sold in 1994. There are now more than 1,000,000 books titles in print, and the United States alone produces about 65,000 new titles a year.

As for the paperless office, the thousands of computers we own have one thing in common. They are all hooked up to printers. The quantity of paper shipped by U.S. producers almost doubled from 1980 to 1995, from 16.1 million tons to almost 30 million tons, according to the American Forest and Paper Association. Copier paper alone rose by 500,000 tons in just a year, from 1996 to 1997.

According to the International Data Corporation's Giga Information Group, when E-mail is introduced into an office, the percentage of printed documents actually goes up by 40 per cent. As a company's revenues increase, so does the amount of paper consumed— by 8.8 million sheets per $100 million in revenue. The organization went on to make a few short-term projections based on current use. By 2001, they predict, the amount of paper consumed by office copiers and printers will stretch around the world six times. The number of paper pages is projected to balloon to 1.1 trillion sheets for copiers and 1.2 trillion for laser printers. So much for the paperless office of 2000.

While observers reflected on the technological revolution, few envisioned much change in traditional sex roles. The 1964 educational film *1999* produced by the Ford Motor Company shows the woman of the future minding a fully automated kitchen, shopping on a computer terminal... and sending the bills to her husband's terminal so he can take care of the finances. The book *1999 Our Hopeful Future* by journalist Victor Cohn likewise imagines a world where the husband spends his time working with his cordless power tools while his wife switches the colors on the walls of the automated home. "And the kitchen? 'Ah!' One can hear the future housewife already..."

The only exception seems to be people who were specifically asked to consider the future of gender roles. Maybe this is simply because most of the writers and scientists of the past were men. Or perhaps, as Eleanor Burns and the Women's Collective speculated in *Motive Magazine* in 1971, women have not spent as much time contemplating the future as men. "It's really hard to dream of a future when the present demands so much of our attention," she wrote. "Maybe it's harder for us because as women we've learned that it's up to us to provide for immediate needs— like what to have for supper. We have a hard time imagining a time when such things will be the concern of the whole society."

Those writers— primarily feminists— who did comment on the role of women in the future, however, tended to imagine a reversal of traditional roles. They wrote about a time when women earned the money and men took care of household chores.

As it turns out, neither vision of the future was entirely correct. A recent study of housework trends shows that American houses are simply getting messier. Women have entered the work place. The superwoman image of the 1970s and 1980s— the woman who could be a CEO by day and housekeeper of the year by night— has now been largely abandoned. Women are no longer worried about the dishes.

As Pat Mainardi wrote in *The Politics of House-*

work, "We women have been brainwashed more than even we can imagine. Probably too many years of seeing media women in ecstasy over their shiny waxed floors or breaking down over their dirty shirt collars. Men have no such conditioning. They recognize the essential fact of housework. Which is that it stinks." Women, the study says, are starting to figure this out. As a culture we are lowering our expectations of what constitutes a clean house as men and women alike struggle to make productive use of our precious off-hours.

Now on to the predictions! You will find the forecasts arranged by category and then in chronological order based on when the predictions were made rather than when they were expected to come to fruition.

With very few exceptions, even though some reporters chose to write some of their predictions in the form of stories, the visions of the future come from nonfiction books and magazines. *1999 Our Hopeful Future*, for example, began each chapter with an illustration of the developments scientists foresaw. The author used characters "John and Emily Future" to dramatize his points. When it comes to forecasting, the line between non-fiction and fiction is often blurred. No one can be said to be reporting on the future. Novelists and scientists alike use their imaginations to make a guess at what is to come.

Due to the limits of time and space, I have not included future visions from novels and television series such as *Space 1999*, *Lost in Space*, which was set in 1997, or *Star Trek*, which spoke of the Eugenics wars of 1992. I will leave science fiction predictions for another book.

I also tried to avoid predictions by psychics, astrologers and other mentalists. I broke this rule in a few cases— a 1939 look at Adolf Hitler's astrological chart that proved World War II would not happen, for example, and throughout the chapter on the end of the world.

There are scores of examples of critics panning books, movies, plays and actors who went on to great prominence. I included them only if they contained an element of prediction. If, for example, a critic said that *Alice in Wonderland* was a bad book, I considered that to be simply an opinion. The fact that most people disagreed and that the book is now considered a classic does not mean the critic was necessarily wrong in his opinion. On the other hand, if the same critic said children would not like the book— time has proven this to be wrong.

Rejection letters contain an implicit prediction. The publisher who rejects a manuscript or the Hollywood studio that turns an actor away is betting that the artist will not be successful enough to make any money for them. While I primarily chose rejections that made specific predictions (give up writing, you'll never make it), there were a few that I chose on the basis of the implicit prediction alone.

If you are a critic, and you would like to avoid ending up in someone's future compendium of bad predictions, here is a hint: never predict that someone will never amount to anything. If you are correct, no one will remember. No one will ever record that you said John Smith will remain in oblivion if he does. On the other hand, if you are wrong, no one will ever forget.

In the same way, you should avoid saying any technological achievement can't or won't happen. If you predict we'll put a man on Mars in five years and we don't, you've made a bad prediction, but people will mostly smile and call you "optimistic." If you say it can't be done, you can be sure your quote will be painted on the side of the first manned Mars lander.

To be completely safe, you could follow the example of presidential hopeful Gary Hart, who made a prediction in which he had total control of the outcome. "As a candidate," he said, "I can almost guarantee that I'm going to make some mistakes."

Bad Predictions

Or you could follow the example of Wilbur Wright, who said, "I confer that in 1901, I said to my brother Orville that man would not fly for 50 years. Ever since I have distrusted myself and avoided all predictions."

Society

Everyday Life

Jules Verne's 1863 novel *Paris in the Twentieth Century* envisioned a future world with such things as the telephone, fax machine, cars and traffic jams. When his publisher Pierre-Jules Hetzel read the manuscript he said, "You took on an impossible task, and you did not pull it off. Nobody will ever believe your prophecies." The book was accordingly stored away in a safe and was not published until 1994.

Jules Verne wrote another work of fiction set in 2000. It was called *An Ideal City*. He foresaw a number of technological advances including self-cleaning streets and machine-fed infants. Bachelors, he wrote, would be taxed to encourage them to marry and doctors would be paid for healthy patients instead of sick ones. Human vanity was not going to diminish, however. Verne imagined women's gowns would grow to such lengths that they would need little wheels to move them around.

"By the year 2000, there will be no C, X, or Q in our every-day alphabet...They will be abandoned because unnecessary. Spelling by sound will have been adopted, first by the newspapers. English will be a language of condensed words expressing condensed ideas, and will be more extensively spoken than any other. Russian will rank second."
— *Ladies' Home Journal*, December, 1900.

In 1903, Arthur Bird wrote a novel called *Looking Forward: A Dream for the United States of America*. It was set in 1999 and predicted: "The businessman in 1999 [will take] a soup-pill or a concentrated meat-pill for his noonday lunch... Houses built in that period had no stairs.. Every private house had its elevator. Press a button and up it went... No one in 1999 ever locked his house. Every house was provided with an electrical outfit. Those who desired to leave the house for a few hours attached electric gongs and alarm bells."

Bad Predictions

"The man of A.D. 2000 is sitting in his study. At his elbow is a pot of synthetic coffee, in his fingers a letter delivered by rocket. Outside the sun is shining brightly, the result of climate control. In the background, a radio plays exotic music from a distant land, relayed by a space satellite. Presently his small son enters bearing a questionable report card, although his education is the product of efficient teaching machines. The man rants at his son, but he isn't really responsible for what he says. His thinking is carefully prescribed by brain control."
—*Newsweek*, Sept. 28, 1959.

In 1967 futurist Herman Kahn told *U.S. News and World Report* that by 2000 we would develop, "a method that will let people decide, before they doze off, what they want to dream about."

"The main result of all these developments will be to eliminate 99 percent of human activity, and to leave our descendants faced with a future of utter boredom, where the main problem in life is deciding which of the several hundred TV channels to select."
—Arthur C. Clarke, *The World of 2001*, 1968.

"On the wall, above the laser-beam meat slicer, will be a hook, but no flyswatter will land on it in the kitchen of thirty years hence. The flyswatter will have joined the buggy whip in oblivion, for the common housefly will have been eliminated by new techniques in black light, infrared magnetic waves, or perhaps bred out of existence by sterilization of the population."
—Henry Still, *Man: The Next 30 Years*, 1968.

"[By the year 2000] electric heating elements embedded in driveways will melt snow the instant it hits. Roadways, including alleys and interstate highways, will be brilliantly lit, cutting accidents and crime. The coldest weather won't stop the home owner from barbequing on his patio, protected from the elements by curtains of heated air."
—*Wall Street Journal*, 1969.

20

In 1974, Stanford University nuclear physicist Glenn Seaborg said the 1990s would be the decade "in which all waste and scrap become our major resources and our natural untapped resources become our back-up supplies." Although recycling has gone up from 6.6 percent of all waste in 1970, currently only 28 percent of the nation's trash is recycled.

The Woman, The Man and [their daughter] Millenny would bathe together, splashing, scrubbing and playing with things that fill and spill and float and sink. Sometimes friends would come and join them in the tub. Everyone enjoyed washing each other's bodies and feeling their slippery, soapy skins. Adults and children were relaxed about nudity, and a good group bath was considered more fun than a backyard barbeque."

> —*Ms. Magazine* editor Letty Cottin Pogrebin, "Born Free: A Feminist Fable," *Women in the Year 2000*, 1974.

"Adhesive tape will be strong enough to take care of all household repairs, and shoes will last a human lifetime [by 2000]."

> —scientist Desomond King-Hele, 1975.

"A familiar old gadget which has been around for hundreds of years is just about to get pensioned off forever—the key. Already you can obtain electronic locks which open when you punch in the appropriate combination, though they do rely on you remembering what the combination is... By the mid-1980s no one will ever need to hide a key under the doormat again."

> —computer scientist Christopher Evans, *The Micro Millennium*, 1979.

The Post Office

"The citizens who live in the next century are not going to pay two cents for a letter postage stamp. The price will be reduced to one cent."
> —Thomas L. James, Postmaster General, 1893.

"Free [mail] delivery will be universal."
> –merchant John Wanamaker, on life in 100 years, 1893.

"It would not be surprising to see . . . the extension of the pneumatic tube system to every house, thus insuring the immediate delivery of mail as soon as it arrives in the city,"
> —New York Postmaster General Charles Emory Smith, *The Brooklyn Eagle*, Dec. 30, 1900.

"However rapidly and however frequently the trains or airships of the period may travel, the process of making up van loads of mail matter for despatch to remote centres, and redistribution there, is far too clumsy for what commerce will demand a hundred years hence. No doubt the soil of every civilized country will be permeated by vast networks of pneumatic tubes: and all letters and parcels will be thus distributed at a speed hardly credible today."
> —T. Baron Russell, *A Hundred Years Hence*, 1905.

"Before man reaches the moon your mail will be delivered within hours from New York to Australia by guided missiles. We stand on the threshold of rocket mail."
> — Arthur Summerfield, U.S. Postmaster General under Eisenhower in 1959.

"By 1984, or maybe 1994, we won't need a post office."
> —Richard N. Farmer, *The Real World of 1984*, 1973.

"By the year 2000 most postal systems, separated from their respective national telephone and data systems, will have become expensive luxuries and sending and receiving physical mail, as opposed to the kind which arrives direct in the home via a special black box, will have become rather like home visits from the doctor or the direct delivery of coal or milk, a slightly archaic luxury."

—Anthony Smith, Director of the British Film Institute, 1983.

Fashion

"I regard the present date as the climax of fashion in dress... Woman will keep right on until every one of her suits costs a million dollars apiece, but man is bound to return to the simplicity of Biblical days. Sandals, a toga, and a cheap straw hat will replace the costumes now worn."

—columnist M. Quad, 1893.

"When the first cellophane raincoat was made, the textile industry entered a new era. Both the making of the yarn and the weaving of the cloth were eliminated. The goods were made as paper is made. During the next fifty years most of our clothes will be made in this way. The weaving process will largely be eliminated. The entire suit or dress may be turned out on great presses like those now printing, folding and mailing our color-illustrated magazines."

—economist Roger W. Babson, Looking Ahead Fifty Years, 1950.

The man of 1999's "suit was a one-piece belted job. No neck-tie, tight collar, lapels or other old-fashioned doo-dads. Color: a pale yellow. John Future had to dress conservatively."

— journalist Victor Cohn, 1999 Our Hopeful Future, 1954.

Bad Predictions

"Your clothing will be informal, lightweight, easily adaptable to changes in climate [in 1982]. Even men will lean to bright and comfortable apparel in the office. Some clothing will be made of paper products and priced so low that you will be able to dispose of it after a couple of wearings."
—*Changing Times Magazine*, 1957.

"Disposable clothing, made of paper but not looking like paper, will be available at low prices for children, garage men, factory workers, housewives and home handymen."
—Arnold B. Barach and the *Kiplinger* Washington Editors, *1975: and the Changes to Come*, 1962.

"We see other children, and even some adults [on the beach in 1984] covered from head to foot in plastic suits of a peculiar design. These are special swimming suits constructed to translate normal human leg motion into the highly effective wavy motions used by marine mammals for swimming. With these suits it is possible for a child, after a few lessons, to swim faster and farther than an Olympic champion who is using the traditional crawl stroke."
—Dr. Roger Revelle, *New Scientist*, 1964.

"It's a bad joke that won't last. Not with winter coming."
—fashion designer CoCo Chanel on the miniskirt, 1966.

"All baby clothes of the future will probably be disposable... The future will undoubtedly see many variations of clothing that glows in the dark and flashes on and off. Already striped op-art outfits flash in random patterns caused by electroluminescent plastic sewn into fabric and powered by tiny batteries. Tomorrow may see illuminated emergency night crews, glowing airport runway attendants, flashing civil defense crews or luminous tuxedos for 'candle-less dining'.. Instant make-up and hairdos will be available in vending machines and a woman (or man) may be able to make his or her own wig with a machine. Tomorrow's belle of the ball may spray

24

her hair with a substance that attracts butterflies, and then release her own butterflies from a plastic bag so that they can hover around her head during the evening."
—Henry Still, *Man: the Next 30 Years*, 1968.

"Clothing of the non-disposable variety will be stored in cleaning closets where a chemical vapor atmosphere and an ultrasonic vibrator will remove dirt particles."
—"Year 1999 A D.," a 1967 film by the Ford Motor Co.

Fashion designer Rudi Gernreich predicted that by the end of the 1970s both men and women would have no hair or eyebrows. Men and women would both wear bowl shaped wigs. "Tomorrow's woman will divest herself of her jewelry and cosmetics and dress exactly like tomorrow's man... women will wear pants and men will wear skirts interchangeably. And since there won't be any squeamishness about nudity, see-through clothes will only be see-through for reasons of comfort. Weather permitting, both sexes will go about bare-chested, though women will wear simple protective pasties... We will train the body to grow beautifully rather than cover it to produce beauty."

Farming, Food, Feast and Famine

Cyrus McCormick is remembered for inventing a reaper that revolutionized 19th Century agriculture. The inventor lost all his money in the panic of 1837 and his creditors had the right to take the patent for his reaper, but they didn't. They didn't believe it was worth anything.

"All such luxuries as silver serviette-rings, silver teapots and coffeepots, silver milk-jugs, silver toast-racks, silver candlesticks, silver salvers, silver cups and, in

short, silver plate generally, are mere expensive frivolities and wasteful excrescences of modern life that will probably disappear presently."
—"A Free Lance," *Towards Utopia*, 1894.

In 1889, at a conference of the British Association for the Advancement of Science, Sir William Crookes reported that with the world rapidly running out of fertile, easily cultivable virgin land, population growth would lead to mass famine by 1930 unless the production of nitrate fertilizer could be increased dramatically.

"Animal foods will to a large extent disappear [during the next hundred years] for it will be more economical to use the plant direct than to utilize it in an indirect way through the animal."
　　　—B.T. Galloway, a botanist for the U.S. Agriculture Department, *The Brooklyn Eagle*, 1900. Americans now eat 64 pounds of beef and 49.8 pounds of chicken per person each year, according to U.S. Department of Agriculture statistics. In the same newspaper, entomologist Dr. L.O. Howard predicted that within the next hundred years most insect pests would be destroyed, while people would most likely start cultivating insects for food. Americans today eat very few pounds of insects.

The man of 2000 "will not be a sportsman, because there will be no sport. At the present rate of killing, the wild animals, except the New Jersey mosquitoes, will have disappeared by 1950, and such a thing as a bird will be found only in the histories. Farming will be carried on in large glass houses, and those who live in them will be careful not to throw fits. For in the open air the insects, encouraged by the disappearance of the birds, will devour every green thing, except the men who live in Western Kansas, and the once forests and gardens will be as dreary as the middle of Fulton Street.../Teeth will disappear in about seventy-five years from now, because the food of the future will be concentrated and made directly from chemicals so that there will be no strain on the

digestion, or gums. It will be put up in pills, so many atoms of hydrogen, so many of carbon, so many of lime, and when you give a dinner party you will sit around and take these pills, gayly quaffing ice water to wash them down/and instead of smoking, which is a harmful practice, you will put a small nicotine wafer on your tongue for half a minute then go to the window."
— Editor C. M. Skinner, *Brooklyn Daily Eagle*, December 30, 1900.

"Such a wasteful food as animal flesh cannot survive: and even apart from the moral necessity which will compel mankind, for its own preservation, to abandon the use of alcohol, the direct and indirect wastefulness of alcohol will make it impossible for beverages containing it to be tolerated. Very likely tobacco will follow it."
—T. Baron Russell, *A Hundred Years Hence*, 1905.

"We shall escape the absurdity of growing a whole chicken in order to eat the breast or wing [within the next 50 years] by growing these parts separately under a suitable medium."
—Winston Churchill, "Fifty Years Hence," *Popular Mechanics*, 1930.

"You may dump the contents of a can of beans into the saucepan— and then chop up the can and toss it in, too. If it were a corn-flavored can, [you] could have a tasty bowl of succotash... and edible whipped-cream flavored can to go with preserved strawberries...And a tomato ketchup-flavored container to surround canned baked beans should appeal to a wide public."
—Norman V. Carlisle and Frank Latham, *Miracles Ahead!*, 1943.

"Housewives will use more concentrates and enrich their foods with electric waves and chemicals such as those of the amino group... Food in glass jars will be cooked by radio; dishes will float in mid air; automatic kitchens will wash dishes, throw out garbage, etc, by the spoken word... electronic waves in a room will make everyone

27

feel warm although the thermometer is only 40 degrees; sound will be turned into light, and light into sound; gravity and sunlight will be harnessed for heat, light and power; actual fruit juices will be made artificially from sun, air, water, and minerals; and many products will be grown, fed only on air and water without any soil, fertilizer or care."

> —economist Roger W. Babson, *Looking Ahead Fifty Years*, 1950.

"Pink snow covered the ground in 1999. Farmers sprinkled dye to absorb sunlight, speed melting and advance planting... For lunch the Futures ate wood steak, planked and loved it— all except Billy, who bawled, 'I want an oil-cream cone.'... 'Where's Susan?' said John. 'Oh here she comes.' 'Hi,' said the teen-ager. 'Gosh, I'm not very hungry tonight. The gang stopped at Joe's Fly-in for plankton-burgers."

> —Victor Cohn, *1999 Our Hopeful Future*, 1954.

"With really cheap energy, one might heat the flower or vegetable garden, so the growing season could start sooner... Lawn grass is due for some great strides forward, of which the Asiatic grass zoysia is a forerunner. Radiation—genetics may play a big part here— perhaps beef cattle the size of dogs will be grazed in the average man's backyard, eating specially-thick grass and producing specially-tender steaks."

> —*Science Digest*, "Your Life in 1985," 1955.

"Man in [2000] may be eating 'water flea' steaks as a part of his daily diet. Dr. John R. Olive of Colorado State University said the 'water flea,' Daphnia, is not really a flea at all but a bedbug-sized, soft-shelled crustacean that looks a bit like a tiny clam. Preliminary experiments have shown that a water flea-algae mixture is palatable as soup either cooked or uncooked. The mixture can also be dehydrated into a paste or into dried cakes. It has a taste somewhat similar to shrimp,' Dr. Olive said. With just a small amount of flavoring the mixture can be made to taste like eggs or steak."

> —*Science Digest*, 1961.

"It is a big expensive cookbook of elaborate information and might well prove formidable to the American housewife. She might easily clip one of these recipes out of a magazine but be frightened by the book as a whole."
> –publisher rejecting *Mastering the Art of French Cooking* by Julia Child, Simone Beck, and Louisette Bertholle. The 684-page cookbook was published in 1961. It was successful enough to get one of the authors, Julia Child, a television series called The French Chef. The combination of cookbook and cooking show made Child a nationwide celebrity.

"I think it likely that before 1984 we shall see huge steam or diesel or perhaps nuclear 'artificial whales' gathering the krill by the shipload to add to the larders of the world... By 1984 the krill may be making the greatest addition to man's food supply of the century."
> —Professor Sir Alister Hardy, *New Scientist*, 1964.

In 1966, the BBC in England aired a program, "Tomorrow's World," which predicted that by 1996 we would no longer be eating food at all. Instead we would take pills for an "all chemical meal."

"Huge fields of kelp and other kinds of seaweed will be tended by undersea 'farmers' - frogmen who will live for months at a time in submerged bunkhouses [by 2000]. This will provide at least a partial answer to doomsdayers who worry about the prospect of starvation for a burgeoning world population."
> —A Rand Corporation scientist, *Time Magazine*, 1966.

"By 2000, sawdust and wood pulp [will be] converted into sugary foods. Discarded paper table 'linen' and rayon underwear will be bought by chemical factories and converted into candy."
> —John Smith, *Science Digest*, 1967.

Bad Predictions

"Split second lunches; color keyed disposable dishes; a society rich in leisure and taken for granted comforts. At the turn of the next century, most food will be stored frozen in individual portions. The computer will keep a running inventory on all foodstuffs and the nutritional needs of the family."
> –"Year 1999 A D." a 1967 film by the Ford Motor Co.

"In his air-conditioned office on the ground, the Iowa farmer will check the daily status report on each hundred-acre field... Noting that one hillside acreage shows beginning drought symptoms, he picks up the telephone, dials the county airfield and orders a thundershower."
> —Henry Still, *Man: The Next 30 Years*, 1968.

"Mrs. American Homemaker at the end of the century will decide she likes the new square tomatoes— bred that way in the field for ease of handling and shipment— because they fit so compactly in her refrigerator and offer charming new salad arrangements. Mr. America, although he takes for granted the series of scientific marvels which led to square tomatoes, will eat a steak made of bacteria— and like it. The bacteria steak will not only taste like meat, but its shape, consistency, and texture will be so much like a slice of beef off the haunch of a real steer that the consumer won't be able to tell the difference. For dessert he may have green cookies made with high-protein flour from algae grown at the sewage disposal plant... By the end of the century, however, a large part of the world's protein may come from petroleum."
> —Henry Still, *Man: The Next 30 Years*, 1968.

"The battle to feed all of humanity is over. In the 1970s the world will undergo famines— hundreds of millions of people are going to starve to death in spite of any crash programs embarked upon now."
> —Paul Ehrlich, *The Population Bomb,*1968 He predicted that even England "will not exist in the year 2000."

30

"Agricultural experts state that a tripling of the food supply of the world will be necessary in the next 30 years or so if the 6 or 7 billion people who may be alive in the year 2000 are to be adequately fed... Millions of people are going to starve to death, and soon. There is nothing that can be done to prevent it."
        —Paul Ehrlich, *Sanford Today*, Winter, 1968.

"By the year 2000 animal meat may have become so uneconomical to produce as a regular source of protein that it will be eaten only in small quantities, as a condiment, as the Chinese use it now."
        —M.W. Thring, *Man, Machines and Tomorrow*, 1973.

The Producer's Council of Delphi in 1974 predicted that by 1980 the nation would be in the grips of a severe water shortage.

"By 2000 soil throughout the world will have been inventoried. Crops will be grown on the soils best suited for them."
        —former U.S. Secretary of Agriculture Orville Freeman, 1975.

"We hope that in the year 2000, when the world will have six billion people to feed, we can make sensible use of the protein fractions and other useful products from tobacco that will otherwise literally be going up in smoke."
        —Dr. T.C. Tso of the U.S Department of Agriculture's Agricultural Research Service, 1978.

"Because of water shortages, which will become so severe in the 1990s there could be 'water wars' between the western states. Look for much of the world to suffer water shortages...Look for the United States to begin the practice of towing glaciers out of the Arctic to East and West Coast ports where they'll be tapped for their water. The glaciers will serve a second purpose. They'll be used as floating islands where the country can locate breeder

31

power reactors, using the melting glacial ice to cool down the reactors while they produce enough electricity to light up entire costal regions."
—Marvin Cetron and Thomas O'Toole,
Encounters with the Future, 1982.

"At McDonald's you will say to a very friendly-looking machine, 'I'd like a Big Mac, please, and I'd like it cooked to order'... The machine will say to you in a very pleasing voice, 'That will be $1.59. Would you like anything to drink?' And you say, 'Oh yes, I'd like a Diet Coke.' And the machine says, 'That will be $2.35. You deposit your money in any kind of denomination, or you can write it a check...And by the time it has finished recording the information, your cooked to order Big Mac, microwaved, will be delivered out the slot, and you'll say, 'Thank you,' and the machine will say, 'Thank you,' in a very pleasant voice, and you'll go away. That's in ten years."
—Michael K. Hooker, *Christian Science Monitor*,
1987.

Home Sweet Home

"Modern rooms, equally with those of all time, seem to have been constructed so as to make it as difficult as possible to keep them clean. Square corners and rectangular junctions of wall and floor, wall and ceiling, will certainly before long be replaced everywhere by curves."
—T. Baron Russell, *A Hundred Years Hence*,
1905.

"In the construction of the house [of 1988] the use of wood, bricks and plaster had practically been superceded by panels of beryllium and magnesium alloys; low-grade silicas, or glass-like material; sheet materials such as asbestos, cement and occasionally plastic... A considerable use was made of moving partitions which made it possible to enclose a small space when privacy was required, and still provide a large space when it was not... In various rooms many of the pieces of furniture were

made of plastic molded as a unit, while others were made of magnesium alloy. In place of cushions, sponge like synthetic upholstery was used."
—Arthur Train, Jr., "John Doe in the year 1988," *Harper's Monthly*, 1938.

"We are entering the Plastics Era... Your entire house— walls, woodwork, stairs, doorknobs and almost everything else could be built of plastics [after the war]."
–John H. Walker, "War's End Will Bring a Better Life," *Popular Science*, November 1942.

"Emily had the ladies out in the garden bubble— the new enclosed part of the yard... where the climate was kept the same year round. And the snow was beautiful through the clear plastic bubble... 'Oh wait,' said Emily. 'I'll turn up the freshness.' She touched a knob at her chair side control board. The air became woodsy— Emily had added a bit of pine scent."
—journalist Victor Cohn, *1999 Our Hopeful Future*, 1954.

"As you and your family sit down to breakfast, you decided it would be sensible this wintry morning to turn the house around so the sun will come into the breakfast nook... Your house rests on a giant turntable, like a doll-house on a lazy Susan. Of course it takes a bit of trouble— you have to shift gears in order to start and stop the house gently. The house next door has an automatic transmission and your wife nags you about getting it for yours— but you claim there's too much risk of breaking glassware with sudden starts and stops. You claim your wife is a very poor house driver."
--*Science Digest*, "Your Life in 1985," 1955.

"A morning in 1982. You may wake up in a bedroom that is round instead of square. If it's summer, you'll use a blanket that keeps you cool. If it's winter you'll use no blanket at all— a dome over the bed will emit warming rays. In your shower you will push a button to get the right water temperature. Breakfast will consist of bacon and eggs that you've kept around the house for

Bad Predictions

weeks (fresh as ever thanks to atomic sterilization)... A
new kind of house is on the way. Its designers say it
may be round instead of square. It will blend into the
outdoors and bring nature inside. Its materials will be
plastic and aluminum and steel and glass. Partitions
will be moveable and rooms detachable. Walls will slide
or fold up like an accordion. Walls, ceilings and foun-
dations will be prebuilt in a mass-production factory.
Color will be everywhere, and if you get tired of the color
of an interior wall, you will replace the wall with one of
another shade. Technical wonders will include luminous ceilings so that you can alter the interior lighting
to suit your mood. Windows will be operated with push
buttons, and if it rains, they will close automatically.
TV screens...will provide baby-watching service...A few
lucky people will have closets designed for cold storage
or dry cleaning of clothing... Bathrooms may have foam
plastic floors and walls— if you slip you will fall onto a
cushion."
    --*Changing Times Magazine*, 1957.

"These two plastic houses... demonstrate how plastic
might be used in housing of the seventies. Both are
chemically-welded, using practically no nails, need almost no pointing or other outside maintenance, and offer exciting opportunities for dramatic design and lighting. Curved surfaces are easily created with the plastic
material... Five years from now, electroluminescence is
expected to come into its own as a light source for home
decoration. GE says you will be able to 'paper your walls'
with it. Other companies say there is no reason why
draperies could not be illuminated in soft, colored tones
at the turn of a switch... glass walls will be available;
transparent or opaque, as the occupants desire. Transparent, they would have the merit of making the house
look spacious and open. But by turning a dial, the occupants will be able to make the glass partly or completely opaque, thus providing privacy and, in the case
of bedrooms, protection from outside or interior light."
    —Arnold B. Barach and the *Kiplinger* Washing-
    ton Editors, *1975: and the Changes to Come*,
    1962.

"Houses will be able to fly [by 2000]... The time may come when whole communities may migrate south in the winter, or move to new lands whenever they feel the need for a change of scenery."
—Arthur C. Clarke, *Vogue*, 1966.

"In the year 2000, we will live in pre-fabricated houses light enough for two men to assemble... cook in our television sets and relax in chairs that emit a private sound-light-color spectacular."
—*New York Times*, 1968.

Housework

"It is hardly necessary to inform you that life [a hundred years hence] will be as nearly a holiday as it is possible to make it. Work will be reduced to a minimum by machinery. Everything will be brought to your hand by deaf and dumb waiters and sliding shelves, operated by electricity supplied to the entire country by the power of the sea."
—Editor C. M. Skinner, *Brooklyn Daily Eagle*, December 30, 1900.

"Housewives in 50 years may wash dirty dishes right down the drain. Cheap plastic [will] melt in hot water."
—*Popular Mechanics*, 1950.

"When [the housewife of 2000] cleans house she simply turns the hose on everything. Why not? Furniture— (upholstery included) rugs, draperies, unscratchable floors— all are made of synthetic fabric or waterproof plastic. After the water has run down a drain in the middle of the floor (later concealed by a rug of synthetic fiber) [she] turns on a blast of hot air and dries everything."
—Waldemar Kaempfert, *Popular Mechanics*, 1950.

Bad Predictions

"Let's say it's 1975... The house has no wires. A small transmitter broadcasts radio waves to operate cordless appliances... Housekeeping is changed radically. The vacuum cleaner, for example, is self-operating too, guided by a tiny electronic computer with a magnetic memory. This cleaner has no dustbag, and in fact, it is not a 'vacuum' cleaner at all any more. It collects the dirt electrostatically, and packs it into one bar of solid matter than need be removed only once in four or five years... Bed making is a push-button task, with soft, disposable paper sheeting drawn from a roller at the foot of the bed."

> — journalist Victor Cohn, *1999 Our Hopeful*
> *Future*, 1954.

"Nuclear powered vacuum cleaners will probably be a reality within 10 years."

> — Alex Lewyt, President of the Lewyt vacuum
> cleaner company quoted in *The New York Times*,
> June 10, 1955.

"What about housekeeping and home care [in the 1980s]? Girls, here is the ultimate, a kitchen sized Univac into which the house wife will insert a coded card, push a button, and voila, the food will be prepared...How will you keep your home dust free? Just pull out your electrostatic dust catcher; presto, the dust will be gone. Floor scrubbing? Self operating scrubbers and polishers will do the work. But, boys, this will match it. Plans are already drawn for a lawn mower that stays in a little shed. Then when the grass grows to a set height, out comes the lawn mower, automatically cuts the lawn, then returns to the shed."

> —James W. Armstrong addressing the
> Henderson County High School class of 1959.

"Within ten to twenty years' time we could have a robot that will completely eliminate all routine operations around the house and remove the drudgery from human life."

> —mechanical engineering professor M. W.
> Thring, 1964.

36

"By the year 2000, housewives...will probably have a robot 'maid'...shaped like a box (with one large eye on the top, several arms and hands, and long narrow pads on the side for moving about.)"
—*New York Times*, 1966.

"By the year 2000, we'll have eliminated the pot and pan."

—a representative of Swift and Company, explaining that microwaves would eliminate the need for such items, 1966.

"Keeping house will be a breeze by the year 2000. Sonic cleaning devices and air-filtering systems will banish dirt and just about eliminate dusting, scrubbing and vacuuming. Combination freezer-microwave ovens will take care of the cooking automatically. Dishwashing will be a thing of the past, since disposable dishes will be made from powdered plastic for each meal by a machine in the kitchen."
—Staff of the *Wall Street Journal*, *Here Comes Tomorrow*, 1966.

In a 1967 speech to the Women's National Democratic Club, Nobel laureate Glenn Seaborg, then head of the U.S. Atomic Energy Commission, spoke of the box-shaped, multi-armed robot that would be programmed for the specific needs of the housewife. The mechanical maids of 2000 would be capable of simultaneously sweeping, vacuuming, dusting, washing, "and picking up your husband's clothing," he said.

The house of 1999 will be virtually maintenance free—a central atmospheric system will maintain constant year round temperatures and control humidity, bacteria, pollen and dust."
—"Year 1999 A. D." a 1967 film by the Ford Motor Co.

Bad Predictions

"Chicago firm begins marketing [in 1972] robot 'house-keepers': mechanical mice to vacuum rugs and clean floors, automated kitchens that prepare hot meals according to consumer specifications."

> —Billy Rojas, "Headlines of the Near Future," printed in *Futures Conditional* by Robert Theobald, 1972.

"Although we already have various forms of garbage-compacting machines for home use, which you can see at many department stores, we need something still more useful, such as a gadget that compacts ordinary garbage into useful items, like building bricks. We already have prototypes of such machines. By 1984, we may have a home version."

> —Richard N. Farmer, *The Real World of 1984*, 1973.

"Every family in [the year 2000] would be able to afford a domestic robot... Like all other machines made in the Creative Society, the robot would be built to last at least twenty-five years, instead of being designed for obsolescence..."

> —M.W. Thring, *Man, Machines and Tomorrow*, 1973.

"Nobody carries keys [in the year 2000] and robberies are infrequent— but, since the night she came home bombed at two in the morning and struggled for two hours unable to remember any combination other than that to her parents' brownstone, she has carried the combination in code right next to her Completecreditcard, the only card she, or anyone else for that matter, carries."

> —Carol Rinlzer, "Femininity: 2000," *Woman in the Year 2000*, 1974.

In the Name of the Law

"Criminals will be prevented from propagating their kind. This will take the place of capital punishment. And, after a few generations, this will do away with crime, because no criminals will be born."
—poet Ella Wheeler Wilcox, 1893.

"Law will be simplified and brought within the range of the common people. As a result, the occupation of two-thirds of the lawyers will be destroyed [in the next century]."
—minister Thomas Dixon, Jr., 1893.

"Prisons and poorhouses will decline, and divorces will not be considered necessary. The system which makes criminals of men and women— and at the same time makes millionaires of the others— will have disappeared. As a consequence, the confinement and punishment of criminals will occupy but little of the thought or time of the men of 1993."
—labor leader T.V. Powderly, 1893.

"Law will be simplified [over the next century]. Lawyers will have diminished, and their fees will have been vastly curtailed."
—journalist Junius Henri Browne, 1893.

Thanks to electric lighting, "our picturesque friend of the nineteenth century, the burglar and his associate criminals, will pass away with that other picturesque criminal, the highwayman of the eighteenth century."
—Ralph W. Pope, Secretary of the American Institute of Electrical Engineers, *The Brooklyn Daily Eagle*, December 1900.

Bad Predictions

"There are not enough society cream-puffs, political grafters, underworld gunmen or social morons in the land to prevent the fulfillment of...prohibition."
>— Wayne B. Wheeler, General Counsel of the Anti-Saloon League of America, September, 1925.

"There is as much chance of repealing the 18th amendment prohibition of alcohol as there is for a hummingbird to fly to the Planet Mars with the Washington Monument tied to its tail."
>—Senator Morris Sheppard, TX, author of the 18th Amendment.

"I will never see the day when the Eighteenth Amendment is out of the Constitution of the United States."
>—Utah Senator William E. Borah, 1929. The amendment was repealed in 1933. Borah lived until 1940.

In 1931, the National Education Association predicted that, thanks to educational advances, "crime will be virtually abolished" in 20 years.

On August 2, 1931, the New York Times ran an article with the headline "Attica Prison to be Convict's Paradise."

"The woman barrister looks and is ridiculous; and has been so since Portia. Neither should the sex sit on juries; no woman will believe that a witness wearing the wrong hat can be giving the right evidence."
>—James Agate, *Ego 6*, 1944.

"It was almost impossible to commit burglary in 1999."
>—Victor Cohn, *1999 Our Hopeful Future*, 1954.

"The prison teachers and wardens [by 1976] will be the highest paid and most skilled part of our educational system. The principal of a reformatory will rank as high as a college president."
>—Morris Ernst, *Utopia 1976*, 1955.

"New Jersey becomes the first state to legalize marijuana [in 1973]."
>—Billy Rojas, "Headlines of the Near Future," printed in *Futures Conditional* by Robert Theobald, 1972. The same article envisioned the following headline for December 1979: "U.S. court system reformed. New features in clude... 'obsolete statute law'—any law on the books is retired after 20 years unless specifi cally renewed by legislative act."

"If we make such kinds of projections with regard to our criminal justice processes, there is only one outcome, namely, the total breakdown of the system. This break-down must take place before the year 2000."
>—Leslie T. Wilkins, professor of the State University of New York's Graduate School of Criminal Justice at Albany, 1973.

"I don't need bodyguards."
>—Jimmy Hoffa shortly before he disappeared on July 30, 1975.

"By the middle of the '80s, when most [credit] cards are fed directly into a scanning computer terminal at the point of purchase and each card receives an automatic screening check, their theft will become even more pointless...Obviously crime is going to be squeezed in a variety of ways, and the shift away from cash is just one of these."
>—computer scientist Christopher Evans under-estimating the ingenuity of criminals in *The Micro Millennium*, 1979.

"The U.S. legalizes cocaine. The government has fully enjoyed a windfall of revenue from the sale of marijuana and recognizes the ability of adults to use recreational drugs intelligently... It is sold in beautiful snuffboxes in liquor shops under names such as Peruvian Flake and Bolivian Rock."
>—prediction for the year 2000 from Shelley Levitt, editor of *High Times*, 1980.

41

Bad Predictions

"The case is a loser."
    —Johnnie Cochran on the prospects of winning the O.J. Simpson murder case, July 1994.

"Race is not, and will not be an issue in this case."
    —Robert Shapiro to Judge Lance Ito on the O.J. Simpson case, October, 1994.

"It will take [the jury] weeks to sift through he evidence and reach a verdict. Every one of them will want to try on the gloves."
    —jury consultant Robert Hirschorn on the O.J. Simpson jury, USA Today, October 2, 1995. The jury came back with a "not guilty" verdict in only a few hours.

Population and Related Probabilities

"I have found that there is scarcely one tenth as many people on the earth as in ancient times. What is surprising is that the population of the earth decreases every day, and if this continues, in another ten centuries the earth will be nothing but a desert."
    —philosopher Montesquieu, 1721.

"The population is constant in size and will remain so right up to the end of mankind."
    —L'Encyclopedie, 1756.

"Long before the 1990s, America will have no very rich or very poor. And the family will be restricted to the capacity of the parents to maintain and educate it."
    —editor T.V. Powderly, 1893.

In 1900 Ladies' Home Journal predicted the U.S. population of about 76 million would go as high as 500 million by the year 2000. Current estimated U.S. population: 274 million

42

In 1943, just before the soldiers returned from World War II, a panel of social scientists presented President Franklin Roosevelt with a population estimate for the rest of the century. At the time, there were 132 million Americans. In 1990, the panel said, "the maximum population [will be] almost 168 million." The actual population in 1990 was 249 million.

"The population will begin to get smaller and smaller."
—author Cyril Bibby in 1947, at the beginning of the Baby Boom.

"Scientists Predict Population Peak in 1950. Shrewd statisticians and far-seeing economists and sociologists claim to foresee a maximum population of 150,000,000 for this country within another generation or so."
—Dr. Herman Rubin, M.D., 1939.

In 1972, the Club of Rome's *The Limits to Growth* suggested that at exponential growth rates, the world would run out of gold by 1981, mercury by 1985, tin by 1987, zinc by 1990, petroleum by 1992, and copper, lead, and natural gas by 1993.

Urban Living

A futurist in the 1890s once predicted that New York City would be abandoned as unfit for habitation by the 1930s. He correctly estimated that population would grow from 4 million to over 7 million in 40 years. Therefore it was obvious, he said, that with the number of horses necessary to provide transportation for that many people, there would be horse manure piled up to the third floor windows everywhere in Manhattan, and the city would have to be abandoned for health reasons.

Bad Predictions

"One of the greatest cities in the United States [by 1993] will be found to occupy the area between Buffalo and Niagara Falls... It will be one of the greatest manufacturing cities in the world."
—diplomat Albert D. Shaw, 1893.

"The powers of the wind, the sea, the rivers and the sun will be chained so that the air will no longer be fouled with smoke for which men have worn out their lives in coal mines."
—William Randolph Hearst's prediction for the 20th Century.

In 1902 *Life Magazine* printed a cartoon with the caption "Sightseeing in 1920." It showed a group of tourists floating in a balloon while a guide pointed downwards saying, "That depression down there is where New York City stood. But with all its skyscrapers and underground tunnels it suddenly sunk one day and they haven't been able to find it since."

"The people of New York will practically live in the sky... there will be avenues of aerial gardens and sky golf courses. Instead of going up to the country, people will go 'up' for country air. There will be aerial hangars and airplanes will be as common as flivvers."
—architect and "urban visionary" Hugh Ferriss, 1925.

"Safe from bomb attacks— free from disease and changing temperatures— living in cities a mile beneath the surface of the earth— such is the dream of science for the man of the future, a not impractical dream which may doom the towers of Manhattan and every other large city to destruction... With habitable space growing more scarce every year in the crowded centers, architects and scientists freely predict that vertical cities, built from the earth's surface downward, may eventually supplant the skyscrapers of today."
—William Jennings, *Mechanix Illustrated*, 1930s.

"Smoke and noise— so easy to overcome— will be held in decent check by legislation..."
—Morris L. Ernst, *Utopia 1976*, 1955.

"Scientists will be seriously considering mobile floating cities, which by 2000 will have been built in prototype." *1/24/02*
—research scientist Lloyd V. Stover, 1975.

In 1980, anthropologist Magoroh Maruyama told the editors of *The Book of Predictions* that between 1985 *1/25/02* and 1995 underwater cities would be built in tropical and arctic regions. In desert regions, subterranean cities would be built.

Women's Place

"Extend now to women suffrage and eligibility; give them the political right to vote and be voted for, render it feasible for them to enter the arena of political strife... and what remains of family union will soon be dissolved."
—*The Catholic World*, 1869.

"The love of liberty and the desire of being governed by law alone appears to be characteristically male... If power were put into the hands of the women, free government, and with it liberty of opinion would fail."
—*The Eclectic Magazine*, 1874.

"As for women taking the place of men in the work of active life, and becoming either sailors, soldiers, surgeons, barristers or other occupations or professions, the thought is unworthy of serious consideration."
—advice author Samuel Smiles (1812-1904).

"Women beware. You are on the brink of destruction: You have hitherto been engaged in crushing your waists; now you are attempting to cultivate your mind... Beware!! Science pronounces that the woman who studies is lost."
—Dr. R. R. Coleman, late 1880s.

Bad Predictions

"Hereafter this outbreak will stand in history as an instance of national sickness, of moral decadence, of social disorder."
　　—journalist Eliza Lynn Linton on the push for women's suffrage, *The Nineteenth Century*, 1892.

"Women will never want the right of suffrage— that is, there will not be enough of them that want it to even encourage the menfolks to give it to them."
　　—humorist Bill Nye, 1893.

"Woman's participation in political life... would involve the domestic calamity of a deserted home and the loss of the womanly qualities for which refined men adore women and marry them... Doctors tell us too that thousands of children would be harmed or killed before birth by the injurious effect of untimely political excitement on their mothers."
　　—Henry T. Finck, *The Independent*, 1901.

"Sensible and responsible women do not want to vote."
　　—President Grover Cleveland in 1905.

"Brain work will cause [the 'new woman'] to become bald, while increasing masculinity and contempt for beauty will induce the growth of hair on the face. In the future, therefore, women will be bald and will wear long mustaches and patriarchal beards."
　　—Berlin University professor Hans Friedenthal, 1914.

"That she will fly to her job in a plane we cannot well doubt, but we shall be foolish if we assume that she will therefore wear an aviator's costume... As the inhabitants learn to fly safely, they will realize that they have neglected too long that vast acreage of roofs, and our narrow little island will bloom out a real city of the sky to our flying business girl."
　　—Josephine Daskam Bacon, in "1979: The American Woman-A Prophecy", *Century Magazine*, 1929.

46

"The girl who leaves the farm to work in an office or factory in the city has far fewer chances of meeting eligible young men than had her grandmother who stayed at home."
> —Gregory Mason, *Scribner's Magazine*, 1931.

The Associated Press' 1950 predictions on life in the year 2000 included Amazon women. The average woman, it forecasted, would be more than 6 feet tall, with muscles like a truck driver, and would consume food capsules instead of meat and potatoes.

"While I am not saying that there is a necessary connection between baboon patterns and human patterns... I am proposing that 'human nature' is such that it is 'unnatural' for females to engage in defense, politics, and, by implication, high politics."
> —Lionel Tiger, *Men in Groups*, 1969.

"[Expect] all 50 states to ratify the Equal Rights Amendment... in 1989."
> —Marvin Cetron and Thomas O'Toole,
> *Encounters with the Future*, 1982.

Education and Child Rearing

"The school houses [of the 20th Century] will be models in architecture and in sanitary arrangement and they will be filled with everything in the way of decoration and equipment that a cultured and refined taste can suggest. Pictures of the best artists and models of the world's great sculptures will here have their true home. Much that is now buried in inaccessible museums will be transferred to the schools simply because there they can be most effective for good."
> —Principal Walter B. Gunnison, *Brooklyn Daily Eagle*, December 30, 1900.

Bad Predictions

"A university education will be free to every man and woman [by the end of the 20th Century]. Several great national universities will have been established. Children will study a simple English grammar adapted to simplified English and not copied after the Latin. Medical inspectors regularly visiting the public schools will furnish poor children free eyeglasses, free dentistry, and free medical attention of every kind."
    —John Watkins, 1900.

"I believe that the motion picture is destined to revolutionize our educational system and that in a few years it will supplant largely, if not entirely, the use of textbooks."
    —Thomas Alva Edison, 1922

"The birth of war will be the death of education as we have known it...School hours will be shortened to permit war work by the children which will release more men for the fighting. 'Useless' subjects, which will mean everything that does not train for war, will gradually be dropped from the curricula....Colleges will become no more than finishing schools for officers... And in its place will be a specialized system under which robot minds will be put through their paces with military precision... All liberal books, all books giving 'the other side of the question,' will be banned and very likely burned as they have been in other countries. A book like this would be the first to go."
    —W.W. Chaplin, *What Will Happen and What to do When War Comes*, 1939.

"As I visualize the next fifty years, I see the number of teachers increase as the number of agriculturists, skilled laborers and industrial workers decrease. Future generations will use their spare time to educate their children themselves, or else employ more people to develop their children physically, intellectually and spiritually."
    —economist Roger W. Babson, *Looking Ahead Fifty Years*, 1950.

48

"Schools will be open 12 months a year [by 1982]. Courses will be speeded up; instead of a four-year high school education, three-year plans may be in effect. Another variation will be staggered semesters— some students studying while others are vacationing."
—*Changing Times Magazine*, 1957.

"Brightly coloured illustrations in a reading primer may attract the pupil to the text they accompany, but they entertain the pupil before he reads; a page of black-and-white text offers him a much greater opportunity to enjoy the consequences of reading. The audio-visual aids of 1984 will be less concerned with attracting and holding attention."
—B.F. Skinner, *New Scientist*, 1964.

"Dr. John I. Goodlad, dean of the Graduate School of Education at UCLA says that by the start of the twenty-first century 'the school as a physical entity will either change drastically or won't even exist.' He predicts that children will begin school at the age of two and will continue throughout their lives, what he terms 'total lifetime learning for the total community.' School classes, according to Dr. Goodlad, will be replaced by 'some kind of generating mechanism which will enable a youngster to pick up his own program and follow it at his own speed.'"
—Henry Still, *Man: The Next 30 Years*, 1968.

"Education will still be a concern of the [Catholic] Church, but adult religious education will be of much more importance than in the past. Recall that we can expect three-day weekends and 13-week vacations by the year 2000. The familiar summer bible schools of decades past will, I think, be replaced by new religious education ventures, not for children but for vacationing adults. Moreover, public school education will probably move close to a 12-month year."
—William Byron, professor of economics at
Loyola College, 1969.

Bad Predictions

"No longer will Johnny or Susie go to schools that teach everyone at the same age the same thing with the same words found in the same books [in 2000]— or heard from the same teacher according to the same schedule. Nor will pupils live by the dictatorial rule of the clock on the wall that today requires them to grasp the new math, the new economics, the new chemistry, within uniform 45-minute sessions."
   —Professor Patrick S. Collins, 1969.

According to the Hawaiian Education Task Force's preliminary report for the Governor's Conference on the Year 2000, conducted in the late 1960s, school will no longer be compulsory, but because everyone receives a guaranteed income, most people will want to use their ample leisure time taking classes. Schools, the report said, "will not be at all like the present complexes of classrooms and offices and playgrounds. They will not be segregated by ages into elementary, middle, intermediate, secondary or higher education. The school of the future will be an educational center where the people of all ages gather to learn together or individually... Some people will want to study at night, on week-ends, during holidays or vacations. Others will want to be absent between nine in the morning and three in the afternoon Monday through Friday. That may be their time to work— or the surf may be up!"

The 1972 book *Futures Conditional* included an article by Billy Rojas entitled "Headlines of the Near Future." He envisioned the following headline for October 1977: "Sexual intercourse allowed in Yale sex ed. classes. Harvard follows suit."

"Cribs and playpens went out about the time automobiles converted from gasoline to batteries [sometime before 2000] . It was considered simply barbaric to put babies behind bars when they could crawl and roll about freely on the sleep-and-play mat... When [Millenny, born in 2000] did start to speak, at about two and a half, her first words were 'Oh, shit'... (Needless to say, no one was shocked. There was no longer any double standard

50

for linguistic propriety as practiced by adults or children, or boys and girls. If people permitted such words to themselves, they permitted them to their children)."
—*Ms. Magazine* editor Letty Cottin Pogrebin, "Born Free: A Feminist Fable," *Woman in the Year 2000*, 1974.

"Much of our formal education in the past was designed to prepare us for a world in industrial revolution. We went to school on specific days at specific times, just as our parents went to work. By 2000 that will have changed and education will be as unregimented as our lives at that time."
—David Saperstein, "Your Time, Your Station," in the 1974 book *Woman in the Year 2000*.

In 1974 the U.S. Forest Service published a study on "Future Leisure Environments." The authors believed that by 1989 American public schools would be open year-round, and vacations would be staggered throughout the year.

"The middle of the 1990s will probably see the disappearance of formal, group education along traditional lines, and the transformation of the present school system will be apparent a decade earlier. The third great barrier to universal education— the lack of any true understanding as to how teaching should be most efficiently done— will also fall."
—computer scientist Dr. Christopher Evans, "Computers and Artificial Intelligence" in *Science Fact*, 1978.

"There will be a deterioration in large-scale public institutions. One which will collapse entirely will be the public school system. In its place, one-room schools associated with particular neighborhoods and communities and local and small schools catering to every sort of interest will spring up. There will be a flowering of literacy, art and science."
—author Karl Hess, in 1980 on life in the 1980s.

51

Bad Predictions

"People will increasingly live in extended families of up to a dozen people, in order to afford high mortgages and rents. They will work shorter hours. Their pay will buy about two thirds as many objects as in 1980, and they will watch much less TV and engage in much more gardening, participant sports, adult education, political activity, and friendly partying. They will be thinner, more active, less frantic, more secure and physically and emotionally healthier than we are."
>—author Ernest Callenbach, 1980.

"By 1990, the [television] cable will touch all parts of human life: It will allow students to attend school three days a week, letting them learn at home on the other days over two-way television."
>—Marvin Cetron and Thomas O'Toole,
>*Encounters with the Future*, 1982.

Religion

When the Quebec Act recognized Catholic rights in Canada in 1774, a New England pamphlet warned, "If Gallic Papists have a right to worship in their own way, then farewell to the liberties of poor America!"

"I think the territorial parish is dead. I think, too, that we will have a married clergy [in the Catholic church] by the year 2000...Pastoral counseling centers located in suburban shopping plazas or downtown office buildings will be as common as medical arts centers are today."
>—William Byron, professor of economics,
>Loyola College, 1969.

"The Lord is going to call me back to heaven."
>—Television evangelist Oral Roberts in 1987, who said he would die if he did not raise $8 million in donations. He fell short of his goal but is still living.

52

"I think he will step out of the ministry at this point."
—Reverend Don George on Jimmy Swaggart after the latter was given three traffic tickets while riding in a car with a prostitute, 1991. He did not leave the ministry.

Culture and Society in General

In 1789, author Nicolas-Edme Restif de la Bretonne wrote a play called "The Year 2000." In his vision of the future, marriages are arranged with bridegrooms chosen by a council of elders according to merit. Married couples are kept apart for years to ensure the survival of their passion. There are no lawyers, and society as a whole, ruled by a fair and virtuous king, is Utopian. One of the King's lines: "In the year 2000, virtue never goes unrewarded!"

"There is a physical difference between the White and Black races which I believe will forever forbid the two races living together on terms of social and political equality."
—Abraham Lincoln, speech, 1858.

"Undoubtedly, harlotry and intemperance are sore evils, and starvation is hard to bear, or even to know of; but the prostitution of the mind, the soddening of the conscience, the dwarfing of manhood are worse calamities. It is a greater evil to have the intellect of the nation put down by organized fanaticism, to see its political and industrial affairs at the mercy of a despot whose chief thought is to make that fanaticism prevail... How far does the Salvation Army differ from a Sicilian Mafia?"
—T.H. Huxley, *The Times of London*, ca. 1890.

"All marriages will be happy [in the 1990s], for the law will put to death any man or woman who assumes conjugal position without the proper physical, mental and financial qualifications."
—author John Habberton, 1893.

Bad Predictions

"All Americans will have happy homes [in the next century] Vice and immorality will have largely, if not altogether, ceased to exist. There will be not only great intellectual advancement, but also very great moral advancement."
— politician Sidney G. Brock, 1893.

"In less than thirty years time... there will be only two races left of any real account in the world... namely the Anglicans or Anglo Saxons and the Slavs."
— *Living Age Magazine*, 1896.

"Drinking in excess is plainly on the decrease. And with every step in this direction the self-respect of the people must grow, pauperism decrease, and an enlightened conception of public duty develop. Whatever else the twentieth century brings about, we may reasonably look for a great revolution in the political status of the world."
— Charles Morris, *The Marvelous Record of the Closing Century*, 1899.

Senator Chauncey Depew, a New York Republican, said in 1899 that he feared the productive energies released by the power of invention, steam engines and electricity would create a massive surplus "which endangers the health, happiness and lives of the people of Europe and America."

In 1902 *Atlantic Monthly* published a "look back" on the 20th Century by economist John Bates Clark. War and poverty had been eliminated. So had traffic jams, thanks to electricity and aerial navigation. Slums had long been gone, replaced with "abodes of happiness and health" made merrier by parks and playgrounds many stories in height. Such progress allowed "society [to] take its present shape from one that was as far below it as a tree-climbing ape is inferior to a cultured man."

"Men will live for each other, and war will stop after 1983... There will be no bad rich men, for they will take men who work for them into their business... Nothing will be wasted and nobody will go hungry. People will not live in crowded towns. Big towns are not natural. Nobody likes them. Everybody will live in a little house of his own, maybe go to the city to work, but not live there. Hospitals will go out of business because everybody will be well. Sick people will be gone. When a man gets sick, neighbors will shame him. Nobody will feel sorry for a sick man as much as now because it will be his own fault."

> —*Gin Chow's First Annual Almanac*, 1932. (Note: this passage was originally written in stylized broken English.)

"Sex [by 1982] will have become much less a theme for either poetry or analysis. Much of the romanticism and all of the hypochondria on the subject will be over."

> —philosophy professor Irwin Edman, 1932.

"If we are to begin to try and understand life as it will be in 1960, we must begin by realizing that food, clothing and shelter will cost as little as air... By 1975 sexual feeling and marriage will have nothing to do with each other."

> —John Langdon-Davies, *A Short History of the Future*, 1936.

In 1939 *Life Magazine* wrote an article about "Furutama," a General Motors exhibit at the World's Fair that looked at life in 1960. Future people, it said, "do not care for possessions... they are not attached to their homes and hometowns, because trains, express highways (and of course planes) get them across America in 24 hours...they have their choice of all of America for their two month vacations."

"There is [sic] not enough troops in the army to force the Southern people to break down segregation and admit the Negro race into our theaters, into our swimming pools, and into our churches."

> —Senator Strom Thurmond, 1948.

Bad Predictions

The 1962 World's Fair in Seattle took a look forward at life in the 21st Century. By the 21st Century, they predicted, people would be able to control the weather and would have eradicated disease and solved the world's population problem by providing food for all. Homes would rotate to take advantage of the sun and other weather conditions. Walls would be replaced by curtains of air, clothes would be made entirely of plastic, and foods would be made from cotton and wood debris. Commuters would fly in convertiplanes or take helicopters to work from their own private helicopter pads.

"The increase in wealth and leisure should, by 1984, have forced us to abandon, as a major source of human effort, the one-against-all competitiveness which we have relied on so much hitherto. We shall have come to regard an individual as a cooperating element in society, and society itself as part of a functioning system of nature. That can, I think, fairly be considered a step forward in the increase of wisdom."
>   —Professor C. H. Waddington, *New Scientist*,
>   1964.

In 1966, the director of Harvard University's Center for Population Studies estimated that in 2000 as there would be two Americans for every foot of coastline, only a fraction of the coastline would be available for public recreation. He suggested building artificial offshore islands for 21st Century swimming.

"Untold adventure awaits him. He is the man who will land on the moon, cure cancer and the common cold, lay out blight-proof, smog-free cities, enrich the underdeveloped world and, no doubt, write finis to poverty and war. With his skeptical yet humanistic outlook, his disdain for fanaticism and his scorn for the spurious, the Man of the Year suggests that he will infuse the future with a new sense of morality."
>   —*Time Magazine*, Jan. 6, 1967, from Man of the
>   Year profile of the "25 and Under" generation.

In 1967, a group called the Committee on the Year 2000 led by Herman Kahn and Anthony J. Wiener speculated on what life would be like in 2000. The majority of their careful projections were uncannily accurate. Here are a few of the misses: The use of nuclear explosives for excavation and mining, permanent inhabited undersea installations and perhaps even colonies, greater use of underground buildings, human hibernation for extensive periods, individual flying platforms and artificial moons for lighting large areas at night.

In February, 1971, *Life Magazine* ran a feature on Buckminster Fuller. "Fuller himself has such faith in his visionary insights that it often seems as though he were a visitor from the year 2000, looking back on the years that lie ahead." And what did he say was in store for us in 2000? "Technology will eliminate scarcity, and nations and classes will disappear as the new era of awareness creates a race of World Men whose allegiance is universal."

As for sex in 2000, Shere Hite, director of Hite Research International, believed that by 2000, "Men will no longer speak of their 'sex drive' as a biological phenomenon. Male sexuality will change radically from the way we know it today. Masculinity will no longer be universally equated with intercourse, and there will be more open discussion of sex and sex roles among men."

"A lasting reminder that America remains the land of opportunity... and we must continue to promote the American dream and encourage all Americans to freely pursue life, liberty and happiness."
> —Commemorative Corn Flake box featuring the first African-American Miss America, Vanessa Williams. The "lasting reminder" was recalled immediately after *Penthouse* published nude photos of Williams.

Howard Rheingold, author of the 1988 book *Excursions to the Far Side of the Mind* had a different view of sex in the next century: "Men of the year 2000 could enjoy exotic extras like orgasmic earlobes, replaceable sex organs, electronic aphrodisiacs, ultra-sensory intercourse, and a range of ecstasy options that would make current notions of kinkiness look sedate by comparison."

Transportation

Bad Predictions

"It is scarcely possible that the twentieth century will witness improvements in transportation that will be as great as were those of the nineteenth century."
—*Brooklyn Daily Eagle*, December 30, 1900 (three years before the Wright Brothers' flight).

Ships and Travel by Water

Sir Joseph Banks, English explorer-naturalist and President of the British Royal Society, said of a proposal to apply steam to ships. "...a pretty plan; but there is just one point overlooked that the steam engine requires a firm basis on which to work!"

"What, sir, would you make a ship sail against the wind and currents by lighting a bonfire under her deck? I pray you excuse me. I have no time to listen to such nonsense."
-- Napoleon Bonaparte to Robert Fulton, inventor of the steamship.

Sir William Symonds, Surveyor of the British Navy on an 1837 proposal to drive a steamboat by screw-propeller: "Even if the propeller had the power of propelling a vessel, it would be found altogether useless in practice, because of the power being applied in the stern it would be absolutely impossible to make the vessel steer."

In November, 1837, British physicist and astronomer Dionysius Lardner demonstrated mathematically that it was impossible to build a steamship capable of a non-stop voyage to New York from Britain. He presented his findings in a lecture, and copies were printed. Some of the copies arrived in Manhattan on April 24,1838... aboard the first boat to cross the Atlantic entirely under steam.

60

"Men might as well project a voyage to the moon as attempt to employ steam navigation against the stormy north Atlantic Ocean."
> —a rare two-for-one bad prediction from astronomer Dionysius Lardner, 1838.

"A most futile attempt and totally impossible to be carried out."
> —Benjamin Disraeli, then British Chancellor of the Exchequer on the proposed Suez Canal, 1858.

"All mankind has heard much of M. Lesseps and his Suez Canal. I have a very strong opinion that such a canal will not and cannot be made; that all the strength of the arguments adduced in the matter are hostile to it; and that steam navigation by land will and ought to be the means of transit through Europe."
> —novelist Anthony Trollope, *The West Indies and the Spanish Man*, 1860.

"...Without going into the consideration of many minor objections to the general adoption of [electric] light on board ship, it may be sufficient to call attention to the following serious drawbacks, viz.: That whether fixed, revolving, or intermittent, a powerful light, such as is referred to, could not fail to interface very considerably with the distinctive arrangements for lighting the coasts by means of light-houses and light vessels. That such powerful lights would be almost certain to detract very much from the value of the smaller lights which the law compels all ships to show by night, and the risks of collision would be increased. That the glare of such powerful lights in crowded channels would be perplexing, and would probably cause such confusion that the risks of collision would be increased."
> —Remarks of Mr. Farrer, Minutes of Evidence Taken before the Select Committee on Lighting by Electricity in Report from the Select Committee on Lighting by Electricity. London, House of Commons, 1879.

61

Bad Predictions

"The Panama Canal is actually a thing of the past, and Nature in her works will soon obliterate all traces of French energy and money expended on the Isthmus."
—*Scientific American*, 1891.

There is a story, perhaps apocryphal, about how Colonel George Washington Goethals, the man who successfully completed the Panama Canal, dealt with the criticism of those who predicted the project was doomed to fail. "Aren't you going to answer these critics?" asked a friend. "In time," Goethals is said to have replied. "How?" asked the friend. "With a canal," he said.

"I do not believe that Robert Fulton's invention of the paddle wheel will ever be improved on for inland navigation."
—Alfred van Santvoord, shipping executive, 1893.

"I cannot imagine any condition which could cause this ship to founder. I cannot conceive of any vital disaster happening to this vessel. Modern shipbuilding has gone beyond that."
—Capt. E.J. Smith of the Titanic, 1906.

"God himself could not sink this ship."
—Deckhand on the Titanic, April 10, 1912.

"P.A.S. Franklin, Vice President of the International Mercantile Marine Company, said this morning that... there was no cause for alarm regarding the safety of the passengers or the ship, as they regard the Titanic as being practically unsinkable... The Titanic is well able to withstand almost any exterior damage and could keep afloat indefinitely after being struck... Franklin was most emphatic in his assurances regarding the safety of the passengers and the steamer."
—Press release by the International Mercantile Marine Company, which owned Titanic's White Star Line, April 15, 1912. (The ship had already gone down with 1,500 passengers.)

"My imagination refuses to see any sort of submarine doing anything but suffocate its crew and floundering at sea."
—H. G. Wells, 1902

Railroads

"Rail travel at high speeds is not possible because passengers, unable to breathe, would die of asphyxia."
—British scientist Dionysius Lardner, 1823.

"I see no reason to suppose [steam locomotives] will ever force themselves into general use."
—Arthur Wellesley, first Duke of Wellington
(1769-1852)

"...We are not the advocates for visionary projects that interfere with useful establishments; we scout the idea of a general rail-road, as altogether impracticable; or, as one, at least, which will be rendered nugatory in lines, where the traffic is so small that the receipts would scarcely pay for this consumption of coals. As to those persons who speculate on making rail-ways general throughout the kingdom, and superseding all the canals, all the wagons, mail and stage-coaches, post-chaises, and, in short, every other mode of conveyance by land and by water, we deem them and their visionary schemes unworthy of notice....The gross exaggerations of the powers of the locomotive steam-engine, or, to speak in plain English, the steam-carriages, may delude for a time, but must end in the mortification of those concerned. ...It is certainly some consolation to those who are to be whirled at the rate of eighteen or twenty miles an hour, by means of a high pressure engine, to be told that they are in no danger of being seasick while on shore; that they are not to be scalded to death nor drowned by the bursting of the boiler; and that they need not mind being shot by the scattered fragments, or dashed in pieces by the flying off, or the breaking of a wheel, But with all these assurances, we should as soon expect the people of Woolwich to suffer themselves to be fired off upon one of Congreve's ricochet rockets, as trust themselves to the mercy of such a machine, going at such a rate;...we will back old father Thames against the Woolwich rail-way for any sum."

—*Quarterly Review* (Great Britain),
March 1825

"What can be more palpably absurd than the prospect held out of locomotives traveling twice as fast as stage-coaches."

—*The Quarterly Review*, 1825.

Samuel Smiles, in his 1859 biography of George Stephenson, *The Life of George Stephenson, Railway Engineer*, described the reaction when a bill to build a railway between Liverpool and Manchester, England, was introduced in Parliament in 1825: "...pamphlets were written and newspapers were hired to revile the railway. It was declared that its formation would prevent cows grazing and hens laying. The poisoned air from the loco-motives would kill birds as they flew over them, and render the preservation of pheasants and foxes no longer possible. Householders adjoining the projected line were told that their houses would be burnt up by the fire thrown from the engine-chimneys, while the air around would be polluted by clouds of smoke. There would no longer be any use for horses; and if railways extended, the species would become extinguished, and oats and hay unsalable commodities. Traveling by road would be rendered highly dangerous, and country inns would be ruined. Boilers would burst and blow passengers to at-oms. But there was always this consolation to wind up with— that the weight of the locomotive would completely prevent its moving, and that railways, even if made, could never be worked by steam-power!"

"The most ridiculous ideas have been formed and circulated of [railroad engines'] powers; and though I am of the opinion, when made the subject of attention amongst engineers, they will advance in improvement like other machines.. It is far from my wish to promulgate to the world that the ridiculous expectations, or rather professions, of the enthusiastic speculist will be realised, and that we shall see them traveling at the rate of 12, 16, 18 or 20 miles an hour: nothing could do more harm towards their adoption, or general improvement, than the promulgation of such nonsense."

    —Nicholas Wood, *Practical Treatise on Rail-roads*, 1825.

"The canal system of this country is being threatened by the spread of a new form of transportation known as 'railroads.' The federal government must preserve the canals for the following reasons: One: If canal boats are supplanted by 'railroads,' serious unemployment will result. Captains, cooks, drivers, hostlers, repairmen, and lock tenders will be left without means of livelihood, not to mention the numerous farmers now employed growing hay for the horses. Two: Boat builders would suffer and tow-line, whip and harness makers would be left destitute. Three: Canal boats are undoubtedly essential to the defense of the United States. In the event of the expected trouble with England, the Erie Canal would be the only means by which we could move the supplies so vital to waging modern war. As you may well know, Mr. President, 'railroad' carriages are pulled at the enormous speed of 15 miles per hour by 'engines' which, in addition to endangering life and limb of passengers, roar and snort their way through the countryside, setting *fire to crops*, scaring the livestock and frightening women and children. The Almighty certainly never intended that people should travel at such breakneck speed."

    —Martin Van Buren, then governor of New York, in a letter to President Andrew Jackson, 1829.

Bad Predictions

"That any general system of conveying passengers would...go at a velocity exceeding ten miles an hour, or thereabouts, is extremely improbable."
—Thomas Tredgold, British railroad designer, *Practical Treatise on Railroads and Carriages*, 1835.

"Railways can be of no advantage to rural areas, since agricultural products are too heavy or too voluminous to be transported by them."
—F.J.B. Noel from an 1842 pamphlet entitled: "The Railroads will be Ruinous for France and Especially for the Cities Through Which They Go."

In 1899, *Life Magazine* featured a cartoon by F. W. Read which depicted a bridge the artist predicted would cross the Atlantic in the 20th Century providing trolley service between New York and London.

That same year the *British Home Journal* predicted that in Britain in the 20th Century "railway travel will be free all over the country."

"It may, however, be safe to assume that it will hardly be possible to apply electricity to haul great passenger trains."
—George H. Daniels, railroad executive, *Brooklyn Daily Eagle*, 1900.

"'Levecars,' a creation of Ford Motor Company engineers, are expected to be in use between major cities within the next 15 years... Their gas turbine or turbojet engines would provide power for both levitation and propulsion at speeds of 200 miles per hour and up. The trains would ride on a thin film of air a fraction of an inch above the rails, with huge airplane-type propellers at either end for propulsion."
—Arnold B. Barach and the *Kiplinger* Washington Editors, *1975: and the Changes to Come*, 1962.

66

Roads and Automobiles

"We must not be misled to our own detriment to assume that the untried machine can displace the proved and tried horse."
>—John K. Herr, 1878-1955, major general,
>U.S. Army.

"One [result of the automobile] will be the passing of the housefly... If there are no stables in the city and no horses on the streets, there will be no flies. A good portion of the filth of the city will go with the horse... With the passing of the horse will be a very material lessening of the noise of the city."
>—Ralph W. Pope, Secretary of the American Institute of Electrical Engineers, *Brooklyn Daily Eagle*, December, 1900.

"All traffic will be below or high above ground when brought within city limits. In most cities it will be confined to broad subways or tunnels, well lighted and well ventilated, or to high trestles with moving-sidewalk stairways leading to the top. These underground or overhead streets will teem with automobile passenger coaches and freight wagons with cushioned wheels. Cities, therefore will be free from all noises."
>—John Watkins, predicting what life would be like in 100 years in the pages of *The Ladies' Home Journal*, 1900.

"It is possible that within a few years our native woods will be so treated with antiseptic preservatives that they will be successfully used for street pavements, or that vegetable fiber will be compressed and cemented into blocks for this purpose. The fact that such a pavement is more quiet than asphalt will be a strong argument in its favor."
>—Nelson P. Lewis, Engineer of the Department of Highways of Brooklyn, *Brooklyn Daily Eagle*, December 1900.

67

Bad Predictions

Cartoonist E. W. Kemble predicted in a cartoon in *Life Magazine* that the automobile would pass out of existence by 1905. His comic depicted a man planting flowers in a horseless carriage with the caption, "Of course there will always be some use for the automobile."

"The actual building of roads devoted to motor cars is not for the near future, in spite of the many rumors to that effect."
> —*Harper's Weekly*, August 2, 1902

"The horse is here to stay, but the automobile is only a novelty, a fad."
> —President of the Michigan Savings Bank advising Henry Ford's lawyer, Horace Rackham, not to invest in the Ford Motor Company, 1903.

"Nothing has come along that can beat the horse and buggy."
> —U.S. Senator Chauncey Depew advising his nephew against investing $5,000 with Henry Ford.

The book *Monopoly on Wheels* by William Greenleaf recounts the story of how Henry Ford, in 1903, asked that membership in the Association of Licensed Automobile Manufacturers be granted to the Ford Motor Company. Frederic L. Smith, President of A.L.A.M. at that time, later recalled giving this reply: "I remember solemnly telling Henry Ford that his outfit was really nothing but an 'assemblage plant', poison to the A.L.A.M., and that when they had their own plant and became a factor in the industry they would be welcome..."

"There will never be a mass market for motor cars, about 1,000 in Europe, because that is the limit on the number of chauffeurs available."
> —Spokesman for Daimler Benz

In 1908 a writer within the automobile industry proved that the wealth of the United States was insufficient to support more than 200,000 new cars every year.

"The improvement in city conditions by the general adoption of the motor car can hardly be overestimated. Streets clean, dustless and odorless, with light rubber-tired vehicles moving swiftly and noiselessly over their smooth expanse, would eliminate a greater part of the nervousness, distraction, and strain of modern metropolitan life."
—*Scientific American*, July 1899

"That the automobile has practically reached the limit of its development is suggested by the fact that during the past year no improvements of a radical nature have been introduced."
—*Scientific American*, January 2, 1909.

"In 15 years, more electricity will be sold for electric vehicles than for light."
—Thomas Alva Edison, 1910   10/23

In 1920, the Federal Trade Commission's report on fuel led to the general conclusion that the motor fuel supply would be exhausted in about six years.   10/24

"...my gas-engine experiments were no more popular with the president of the company than my first mechanical leanings were with my father. It was not that my employer objected to experiments— only to experiments with gas engines. I can still hear him say: 'Electricity yes, that's the coming thing. But gas— no.' The Edison Company offered me the general superintendency of the company, but only on condition that I would give up my gas engine and devote myself to something really useful."
—Henry Ford, *My Life and Work*, 1922

"It certainly seems to be a reasonable conclusion that the possible maximum for automotive passenger cars cannot exceed one to every family."
—*Forbes Magazine*, November 24, 1923.   10/25

Bad Predictions

"In less than 25 years... the motor-car will be obsolete, because the aeroplane will run along the ground as well as fly over it."
>—British journalist Sir Philip Gibbs, *The Day After Tomorrow: What is Going to Happen in the World*, 1928.

"The question has been raised whether the cost of manufacture in a country like Germany might reach the point where, through evolution, motor cars could be produced and sold in competition in the American market... In my opinion it is impossible to reach the conclusion that competition from without can ever be any factor whatsoever."
>—General Motors President Alfred P. Sloan, *New York Times*, September 12, 1929.

"Cars will cost as little as $200. People will have two-month vacations. They will care little for possessions. The happiest people live in one-factory villages."
>—Predictions for 1960 in a 1939 Futurama exhibit sponsored by General Motors at the New York World's Fair.

"Next year's cars should be rolling out of Detroit with plastic bodies."
>—L.M. Bloomingdale, "The Future of Plastics," *Yale Scientific Magazine*, 1941.

In the 1941 book *The Story of Everyday Things*, author Arthur Train, Jr. explained how a businessman would travel in 2000: "He will not be obliged to handle the controls by himself. He may well be able to doze or read, while, from a distant point, his car or plane will be held on its course by short-wave impulses."

"Automobiles will start to decline almost as soon as the last shot is fired in World War II... Instead of a car in every garage there will be a helicopter."
>—Aviation writer Harry Bruno, 1943.

"Japan should not resume passenger car production, since it would be more economically practical to rely on foreign supply as an international division of labor— especially in view of the overwhelming dominance of the Big Three auto makers."
>—Hisato Ichimada, the head of the Bank of Japan, early 1950s.

1/29/02

"As long as there is a man left to own one there will be a Packard for him."
>—a prominent automotive historian in 1953, quoted in *Car and Driver Magazine*. Packard merged with Studebaker a year later, and in two years it was out of business.

1/30/02

"When accidents do happen [in 1999], death and injury will be rarer, for we will wake up at last and require cars to have control levers replacing the steering wheel, with its deadly harpoon, the obsolete steering shaft... Helicopters will swoop down on freeways to remove disabled cars... New synthetic tires will last 100,000 miles and come in colors to match our cars."
>—Victor Cohn, *1999 Our Hopeful Future*, 1954.

"I find it difficult to believe that the seat belt can afford the driver any great amount of protection over and above that which is available to him through the medium of the safety-type steering wheel if he has his hands on the wheel and grips the rim sufficiently tight to take advantage of its energy absorption properties and also takes advantage of the shock-absorbing action which can be achieved by correct positioning of the feet and legs."
>—General Motors vehicle safety engineer Howard Gandelot, 1954.

9/1/02

"The Edsel is here to stay."
>—Henry Ford II, December 7, 1957

7/25

Bad Predictions

"The megalopolis centers of the year 2000 will probably not feel the rubber tread of anything but feet."
> —Vincent F. Caputo, director for transportation and warehousing policy in the Office of the Secretary of Defense, 1964.

"The first floor of future homes will be turned over to cars."
> —A General Motors official to the *Wall Street Journal*, 1966.

"Private passenger vehicles will be barred from most city cores by 1986."
> —*The Futurist*, 1967

"[Commuters will] rent small four-seater capsules such as we find on a ski lift. These capsules will be linked together into little trains that come into the city. As the train goes towards the perimeter of the city, the capsule will become an individual unit. One can then drive to wherever he may want to go."
> —Ulrich Frantzen, *Prophecy for the Year 2000*, 1967.

"The electromobile will rescue an industry already struggling with the saturated market. The traffic problem in cities will be solved by the new vehicle. The probability is that private cars will no longer be permitted; in their place there will be small cars for hire, all standardized and capable of being activated for a certain time by the insertion of a coin. Once the occupant has arrived at his destination he simply leaves the car where he is... To prevent accidents a kind of radar installation will be built in and powered by the engine current. Programmed driving in 1984 will mean the driver inserts a punch card into the vehicle's electronic computer. If he is in New York and wants to go to Boston, the card is punched accordingly and the vehicle makes the journey by the shortest route without the driver needing to concern himself further."
> —nuclear physicist Jaques Bergier, *Impossible Possibilities*, 1968.

72

"Although it would be pleasant to contemplate the end of the automobile by the turn of the century, this vehicle is likely to be much with us just as it is today. It is likely, however, that gasoline and diesel power systems, at least for city and suburban driving, will have been replaced by quieter and cleaner methods of propulsion... Combining the electric car and the freeway, 2000 may see freeway lanes which transmit power directly to the automobile passing overhead and thus control its speed and position."

—Henry Still, *Man: The Next 30 Years*, 1968.

"The reciprocating piston engine is as dead as a dodo."
—*Sports Illustrated*, 1969

"The smelly engines at present used in cars and heavy vehicles will either be banned in cities or be redesigned so that they do not pollute the air [before the 21st Century]. Small publicly-owned electric cars may play a major part in personal transport in cities. Inserting a coin would give, say, three miles of driving, and the car could be left free at any parking meter... On some roads these cars might run automatically at a fixed speed, guided by wires in the road... The traveler gets in, writes his destination on a card, inserts this card with a personal credit card in a slot, and presses the starting-button. The car, which may be self-powered or pick up power from a roadside rail, will proceed at a steady speed to the destination, the journey being charged to the traveler's account."

—professor Desmond King-Hele, *The End of the Twentieth Century?*, 1970.

"The year is 2000 and you have to get from the airport to downtown Honolulu in five minutes... You step into a small, automatically controlled capsule which takes you on your way at a rate of 15 miles per hour on tracks high above the streets... By 2000, downtown Honolulu—like cities on the Mainland— will be off-limits to private automobiles..."

—reporter William Helton, *Honolulu Advertiser*, July 27, 1970.

73

"Every time some expert predicts that the automobile industry has reached the saturation point and is going downhill from now on, I reach around and look for the famous story about how, in 1908, William C. Durant, then head of Buick, told George W. Perkins of J.P. Morgan and Co. that 'the time will come when 500,000 automobiles will be manufactured and sold in this country every year.' The banker, incensed by what he took to be Durant's effrontery and stupidity, left the room."

>—Frank S. Hedge, vice-president of American
>   Motors Corp., 1971.

"The modern gasoline-powered car will disappear, but not by 1984. Around the turn of the century, we will indeed run out of a few key things, like fuel... Atomic cars? Ridiculous— just like the gas-drive engines in 1880... Hence, in 1984 or 2000 we will still be running around in cars— but not the type we now use."

>—Richard N. Farmer, *The Real World of 1984*,
>   1973.

"A road sign of the future is likely to read 'No wheeled vehicles on this highway.' Cars without wheels will float on air, bringing about the passing of the wheel."

>—scientist and author Arthur C. Clarke's
>   1975 vision of transportation in 2000.

"By the end of the period [1982-2000] most main highways in developed countries will have built-in vehicle guidance devices, smaller than the cats' eyes of today, which will control the speed and course of robot trucks and cars."

>—computer scientist Dr. Chris Evans, "Computers and Artificial Intelligence" in *Science Fact*, 1978.

"With over 50 foreign cars already on sale here, the Japanese auto industry isn't likely to carve out a big slice of the U.S. market."

>—*Business Week*, 1979

"A car which refuses to start when its driver has ingested too much alcohol has often been joked about, but it could well be the only type on the road in the late 1980s. By then most cars will be virtually theft-proof."
— computer scientist Christopher Evans, *The Micro Millennium*, 1979.

9/20

"Ultra-high-speed, magnetic-levitation, linear-motor trains (probably imported from Japan or Germany because of lagging U.S. technology) will become standard means of intercity transportation, displacing airplanes for distances up to around 1,000 kilometers. (We will finally have switched to the metric system!)"
— author Ernest Callenbach, 1980.

1/20/03

Aviation

"Other difficulties I do not foresee that could prevail against this invention [the "flying canoe"] save one only, which to me seems the greatest of them all, and that is that God would never surely allow such a machine to be successful."
— "flying canoe" designer Father Francesco de Lana-Terzi, 1670.

"What can you conceive more silly and extravagant than to suppose a man racking his brains, and studying night and day how to fly?"
— English author William Law, *A Senior Call to a Devout and Holy Life*, 1728

"It is entirely impossible for man to rise into the air and float there. For this you would need wings of tremendous dimensions and they would have to be moved at a speed of three feet per second. Only a fool would expect such a thing to be realized."
— Joseph de Lalande of the French Academy, 1782.

Bad Predictions

"We know a method of mounting into the air, and, I think, are not likely to know more."
> —Dr. Samuel Johnson, author, after
> the Montgolfier balloon flight of 1783.

Victor Hugo believed that lighter-than-air flight would have the following impact. "No more hatreds, no more self-interests devouring one another, no more wars, a new life made up of harmony and light prevails."

"It has been demonstrated by the fruitlessness of a thousand attempts that it is not possible for a machine, moving under its own power, to generate enough force to raise itself, or sustain itself, in the air."
> —M. de Marles, *Les Cents Merveilles des
> Science et des Arts*, 1847.

"An entirely new profession— that of airmanship— will be thoroughly organized, employing a countless army of airmen... Boundaries will be obliterated... The great peoples of Christendom will arrive at a common understanding; the Congress of Nations will no longer be an ideal scheme... Troops, aerial squadrons, death-dealing armaments will be maintained only for police surveillance over barbarous races, and for instantly enforcing the judicial decrees of the world's international court of appeal."
> —*Century Magazine*, 1878.

"One: There is a low limit of weight (of about) 50 pounds beyond which it is impossible for an animal to fly. Two: The animal machine is far more effective than any we can hope to make. Three: The weight of any machine constructed for flying, including fuel and engineer, cannot be less than three or four hundred pounds. Is it not demonstrated that a true flying machine, self-raising, self-sustaining, self-propelling, is physically impossible?"
> —University of California Professor Joseph Le
> Conte in 1888

"The railway and the steamship will be as obsolete as the stagecoach. It will be as common for the citizen to call for his dirigible balloon as it now is for him to call for his buggy or his boots."
　　　—Kansas political leader John J. Ingalls, 1893.

"[Within 100 years] Airships will facilitate travel, and the pneumatic tube will be the means of transporting goods."
　　　—poet Ella Wheeler Wilcox, 1893.

"Heavier than air flying machines are impossible."
　　　—physicist William Thompson, Lord Kelvin, 1895.

"It is apparent to me that the possibilities of the aeroplane, which two or three years ago was thought to hold the solution to the flying machine problem, have been exhausted, and that we must turn elsewhere."
　　　—Thomas Alva Edison quoted in
　　　The New York World, November 17, 1895

An 1895 cartoon in *Life Magazine* took a look forward to the status of airplanes in 1950. "Why there goes a flying machine!" the illustration was captioned. "So it is. It's the first one I've seen in ten years. I can remember when the sky used to be covered with them. Curious how these fads die out."

"I have not the smallest molecule of faith in aerial navigation other than ballooning, or of the expectation of good results from any of the trials we hear of."
　　　—William Thompson, Lord Kelvin, 1896

"Should man succeed in building a machine small enough to fly and large enough to carry himself, then in attempting to build a still larger machine he will find himself limited by the strength of his materials in the same manner and for the same reasons that nature has... There is no basis for the ardent hopes and positive statements made as to the safe and successful use of the dirigible balloon or flying machine, or both, for commer-

77

cial transportation or as weapons of war, and that, there-fore, it would be a wrong, whether wilful or unknowing, to lead the people and perhaps governments at this time to believe in the contrary."

   —Rear Admiral George W. Melville,
   North American Review, 1901.

"It was confidently predicted 100 years ago that in the century then coming man would learn to fly... He has not made any striking advance in the direction of his hopes... Possibly, the next 100 years of experiment teach us that we will never fly in the air as do the birds, or if we do so, it will be merely for the pleasure of the thing. Flying in so variable an element as the air can never, we think, be reduced to a science."

   —*The Daily Register*, Mobile, Alabama,
   January 1, 1901.

"Men will never fly, because flying is reserved for an-gels."

   —The Wright Brothers' father,
   Episcopalian Bishop Milton Wright.

"Man will not fly for 50 years."

   —Wilbur Wright to his brother Orville in 1901.
   (Their famous flight at Kitty Hawk took place two
   years later)

"Flight by machines heavier than air is unpractical, and insignificant, if not utterly impossible."

   —astronomer Simon Newcomb, 1902.

"The example of the bird does not prove that man can fly. The hundred and fifty pounds of dead weight which the manager of the machine must add to it over and above that necessary in the bird may well prove an in-surmountable obstacle to success. The practical diffi-culties in the way of realizing the movement of such an object are obvious. The aeroplane must have its propel-lers. These must be driven by an engine with a source of power. Weight is an essential quality of every engine. The propellers must be made of metal, which has its weakness, and which is liable to give way when its speed attains a certain limit. And, granting complete success, imagine the proud possessor of the aeroplane darting through the air at a speed of several hundred feet per second. It is the speed alone that sustains him. How is he ever going to stop? Once he slackens his speed, down he begins to fall. He may, indeed, increase the inclination of his aeroplane. Then he increases the resistance necessary to move it. Once he stops he falls a dead mass. How shall he reach the ground without destroying his delicate machinery?"

—Simon Newcomb, "Outlook for the Flying Machine," *The Independent*, October 22, 1903.

"We hope that Professor [Samuel] Langley will not put his substantial greatness as a scientist in further peril by continuing to waste his time, and the money involved, in further airship experiments. Life is short, and he is capable of services to humanity incomparably greater than can be expected to result from trying to fly...For students and investigators of the Langley type there are more useful employments."

—*The New York Times*, December 10, 1903, exactly one week before the first successful flight at Kitty Hawk.

"The flying machine will eventually be fast; they will be used in sport, but they are not to be thought of as commercial carriers... [it] will not be enough to carry much greater extraneous loads, such as a store of explosives or big guns to shoot them. The power required will always be great, say something like one horse power to every hundred pounds of weight, and hence fuel can not be carried for long single journeys."

—aviation pioneer Octave Chanute, 1904.

"As it is not at all likely that any means of suspending the effect of air-resistance can ever be devised, a flying-machine must always be slow and cumbersome."

—T. Baron Russell,
A Hundred Years Hence, 1905.

Bad Predictions

From the really, really bad predictions file: "The demonstration that no possible combination of known substances, known forms of machinery and known forms of force can be united in a practical machine by which men shall fly long distances through the air, seems to the writer as complete as it is possible for the demonstration of any physical fact to be."

> —Simon Newcomb, American astronomer in 1906, three years *after* the flight at Kitty Hawk.

"All attempts at artificial aviation are not only dangerous to human life, but foredoomed to failure from the engineering standpoint."

> —Engineering Editor, *The Times*, 1906.

"No flying machine will ever fly from New York to Paris."

> —Orville Wright, 1908.

"I do not think that a flight across the Atlantic will be made in our time, and in our time I include the youngest readers."

> —Rolls-Royce co-founder Charles Stewart Rolls, around 1908. Rolls-Royce engines eventually powered trans-Atlantic flights.

"It is idle to look for a commercial future for the flying machine. There is, and always will be a limit to its carrying capacity. Some will argue that because a machine will carry two people, another may be constructed that will carry a dozen, but those who make this contention do not understand the theory."

> —W.J. Jackman and Thomas Russell, *Flying Machines: Construction and Operation*, 1910.

"The popular mind often pictures gigantic flying machines speeding across the Atlantic and carrying innumerable passengers in a way analogous to our modern steamships... It seems safe to say that such ideas must be wholly visionary, and even if a machine could get across with one or two passengers the expense would be prohibitive."

> —astronomer William H. Pickering, 1910.

"Over cities... the aerial sentry or policeman will be found. A thousand aeroplanes flying to the opera must be kept in line and each allowed to alight upon the roof of the auditorium in its proper turn."

> —Editor Waldemar Kaempfert, *Scientific American*, 1913. Kaempfert also predicted that the aeroplane "is not capable of unlimited magnification. It is not likely that it will ever carry more than five or seven passengers. High-speed monoplanes will carry even less."

"The aeroplane will help peace in more ways that one... it will have a tendency to make war impossible. Indeed, it is my conviction that, had the European governments foreseen the part which the aeroplane was to play [in World War I]... they would never had entered upon the war.... Civilized countries, knowing this in advance, will hesitate before taking up arms— a fact which makes me believe that the aeroplane, far more than Hague conferences and Leagues to enforce peace, will exert a powerful influence in putting an end to war."

> —Orville Wright, 1917.

"An impractical sort of fad, and has no place in the serious job of postal transportation."

> —Second Assistant U.S. Postmaster General Paul Henderson on airmail, 1922.

"This fellow Charles Lindbergh will never make it. He's doomed."

> —millionaire Harry Guggenheim, 1927.

"Within a few years passenger-carrying aeroplanes will be traveling at over 300 m.p.h, the speed record today... [but] the commercial aeroplane will have a definite range of development ahead of it beyond which no further advance can be anticipated."

> —novelist and pilot Nevil Shute, 1929. He believed the maximum limits, which would probably be reached by 1980, were a speed of 110-130 mph and a range of 600 miles with a payload of 4 tons.

Bad Predictions

"[It is] physically impossible for a pilot to withstand a speed much over 400 miles per hour."
> —aeronautical engineer Dr. Starr Truscott, 1929.

"Aircraft will be provided with sleeping compartments and dining saloons."
> —Norman Bel Geddes, "Ten Years From Now," *Ladies' Home Journal*, 1931.

"The idea is that the flying machine will rise rapidly until it gets into the stratosphere, which is, approximately, fifteen miles above the earth. Once there... it would, in fact, stand still and allow the earth to revolve beneath it."
> —J.P. Lockhart-Mummery, *After Us*, 1936.

"The use of aircraft over water has much to be said for it. They present, however, one tremendous difficulty. To get off the ground with the weight of passengers, freight, mail and fuel with which they would be loaded requires a landing field of gargantuan proportions. Certainly there are no fields today in either the U.S. or Europe which could accommodate such a plane. And it may be impracticable ever to build them."
> —*Forbes Magazine*, July 1, 1938.

"There will never be a bigger plane built."
> —a Boeing engineer after the first flight of the Boeing 247 in 1932. The twin engine plane had a capacity of 10 people.

In 1940, Theodore von Karman, of the National Academy of Science, said jet engines and rockets would be of no future use because there was no material tough enough to stand up under their high combustion temperatures. Karman changed his mind five years later. In 1955 he said of his 1940 prediction, "What I did wrong was to write it down."

"In about three years commercial planes will fly from New York to California in one hour."
—Dr. Alexander W. Lippisch, U. S. Air Force researcher, 1948.

"[In 2000] commuters will go to the city in huge aerial buses that hold 200 passengers. Hundreds of thousands more will make such journeys twice a day in their own helicopters."
—Waldemar Kaempfert, *Popular Mechanics*, 1950.

"Nuclear energy may bring back the dirigible... When you move to the country for the summer, you will not call a moving van, you'll call the atomic dirigible— to lift an entire wing of your house and carry it to the mountains."
—*Science Digest*, "Your Life in 1985," 1955.

"Since the aircars of the future need to stick to the traffic lanes only when their drivers feel like it, the chief motoring offense at the turn of the century will not be speeding, but trespass... There are few spots that a skillful aircar driver could not reach, and the breakdown vans of the future are going to receive S.O.S. calls from families stranded in some very odd places."
—Arthur C. Clarke, on life by 2000 in *Profiles of the Future*, 1962.

"Man of the future will be eager to return to his home at the end of the day. Perhaps he will commute to his job in his own gyrocopter... There are no traffic jams nor crowded subways [in 2000]. No smokestacks to pollute the air. The factories of tomorrow are located in landscaped industrial parks, producing more of everything for less in material, time and money."
—1962 Seattle World's Fair Century 21 exhibit.

Henry G. Edler, a staff member of the National Aviation and Space Council in 1967 proposed a vertical take off and landing vehicle for each garage. A commuter at the turn of the century would, in the words of Henry Still, author of *Man: The Next 30 Years*, "leave the front door of his home, step into a VTOL type of vehicle parked in his driveway and dial the number of his office roof landing pad. Then he will sit back to read his morning paper, or watch a telecast, while he takes his five to ten minute ride to the office by computer control. The aircraft will be guided automatically through separate levels of traffic at speeds comparable to uncongested highway travel today."

"The 747 will operate just below the speed of sound and will carry up to 490 passengers— three times the capacity of the jets which have dominated the airways for the past 10 years. As large inside as a small ocean liner, the 747 will offer more luxurious seating space, entertainment for all ages of passengers (including play areas for youngsters) and not least of all, the jumbo jet will bring a sharp break in passenger fares."
—Henry Still, *Man: The Next 30 Years*, 1968.

"The supersonic airliner illustrates the dilemma: 'Should millions be subjected to the noise of sonic booms just to allow a few privileged travelers to cross the Atlantic in two hours?' The millions will answer 'No.'"
–science and mathematics professor Desmond King-Hele, *The End of the Twentieth Century?*, 1970.

In 1974 the U.S. Forest Service published a study on "Future Leisure Environments." By 1989, it predicted, private aircraft would be banned from metropolitan airports and only non-polluting vehicles would be allowed on the streets.

According to the *Chicago Tribune* in the late 1980s, The Skycar, a vertical take off and landing aircraft, "could be flying commuters to work in the millions by the year 2000."

84

The Final
Frontier

Bad Predictions

"People give ear to an upstart astrologer who strove to show that the earth revolves, not the heavens or the firmament, the sun and the moon. Whoever wishes to appear clever must devise some new system, which of all systems is of course the very best. This fool wishes to reverse the entire science of astronomy."
  —Martin Luther on Copernicus, 1543.

Dutch astronomer Christiaan Huygens invented a new, more accurate telescope in 1655 and with it discovered Saturn's largest moon Titan. The known solar system then consisted of six planets and six moons. Huygens believed that the number of moons could not logically exceed the number of planets, so he stopped searching the solar system

According to Amabel Williams-Ellis' *Men Who Found Out*, after Galileos discovered Jupiter's moons by telescope, his contemporaries scoffed: "Jupiter's moons are invisible to the naked eye, and therefore can have no influence on the earth, and therefore would be useless, and therefore do not exist."

"The proposition, that the sun is the centre and does not revolve about the earth, is foolish, absurd, false in theology and heretical."
  —The Inquisition, on Galileo's proposals.

"Comets are not heavenly bodies, but originate in the earth's atmosphere below the moon."
  —Augustion de Angelis of the Clementine
   College, Rome, 1673.

Reformer Mary E. Lease, in 1893, predicted that within the next 100 years: "We will hold communication with the inhabitants of other planets, and Sunday excursions to the mountains of the moon will not excite comment."

"That Professor Goddard and his 'chair' in Clark College and the countenancing of the Smithsonian Institution does not know the relation between action and reaction, and of the need to have something better than a

vacuum against which to react — to say that would be absurd. Of course, he only seems to lack the basic knowledge ladled out daily in high schools."
    — 1921 *New York Times* editorial about Robert Goddard's revolutionary rocket work. (The *Times* printed a formal retraction of this comment some 49 years later, on July 17, 1969, just prior to the Apollo landing on the moon.)

"This foolish idea of shooting at the moon is an example of the absurd length to which vicious specialisation will carry scientists working in thought-tight compartments. Let us critically examine the proposal. For a projectile entirely to escape the gravitation of the earth, it needs a velocity of 7 miles a second. The thermal energy of a gramme at this speed is 15,180 calories... The energy of our most violent explosive— niroglycerine— is less than 1,500 calories per gramme. Consequently, even had the explosive nothing to carry, it has only one-tenth of the energy necessary to escape the earth... Hence the proposition appears to be basically impossible."
    —British scientist William Bickerton, 1926.

"No rocket will reach the moon save by a miraculous discovery of an explosive far more energetic than any known. And even if the requisite fuel were produced, it would still have to be shown that the rocket machine would operate at 459 degrees below zero— the temperature of interplanetary space."
    —scientist and inventor Nikola Tesla,
    November 1928.

"There is no hope for the fanciful idea of reaching the moon, because of insurmountable barriers to escaping the earth's gravity."
    —University of Chicago astronomer
    Dr. F.R. Moulton, 1932.

"The acceleration which must result from the use of rockets, or from being fired out of a gun by explosion, inevitably would damage the brain beyond repair. The exact rate of acceleration in feet per second that the human

Bad Predictions

brain can survive is not known. It is almost certainly not
enough, however, to render flight by rockets possible."
>-J.P. Lockhart-Mummery,
>*After Us*, 1936.

"I would much prefer to have Goddard interested in real
scientific development than to have him primarily interested in more spectacular achievements which are of
less real value."
>—Letter from Charles A. Lindbergh to Harry
>Guggenheim of the Guggenheim Foundation,
>May 1936.

"It must be said at once that the whole procedure
sketched in [*Rockets through Space* by P.E. Cleator] presents difficulties of so fundamental a nature that we are
forced to dismiss the notion as essentially impracticable,
in spite of the author's insistent appeal to put aside
prejudice and recollect the supposed impossibility of
heavier-than-air flight before it was actually accomplished. An analogy such as this may be misleading,
and we believe it to be so in this case."
>—book review in *Nature*, March 14, 1936.

"While it is always dangerous to make a negative prediction, it would appear that the statement that rocket
flight to the moon does not seem so remote as television
did less than one hundred years ago is over-optimistic."
>—Professor A. W. Bickerton,
>*Philosophical Magazine*, 1941.

"Landing and moving around on the moon offer so many
serious problems for human beings that it may take science another 200 years to lick them."
>—*Science Digest*, August, 1948.

The 1954 book *1999 Our Hopeful Future* was not hopeful enough when predicting the future of space exploration. Author Victor Cohn predicted we would make our
first manned landing on the moon in 1999. Cohn's timetable for space exploration: By 1963 a United States
Space Exploration Commission would be organized. In

1964 the first three-stage rocket would be launched. "Not all further attempts succeeded," he wrote, "and further expansion was still too costly. It was 1976 before an unmanned missile was built to circle the moon and report back by space television. It was thus that man first saw the back side of the moon. In 1989 came a huge further step— a highly developed unmanned craft was landed intact on the moon to look around with TV eyes and inspect and analyze the terrain." The first manned space flight, Cohn predicted, would be launched in 1996.

"Space travel is utter bilge."
> — Astronomer Royal Sir Richard van der Riet Wooley,1956. This prediction was so infamous that in 1961 when the Soviets launched Yuri Gagarin into space the British Interplanetary Society announced that the cosmonaut had been launched "into utter bilge." Humorist Douglas Adams included a "bilge room" in his recent CD-ROM game "Starship Titanic."

"Man will never reach the moon, regardless of all future scientific advances."
> — radio pioneer Lee De Forest, February 25, 1957. He also said, "To place a man in a multi-stage rocket and project him into the controlling gravitational field of the moon, where the passenger can make scientific observations, perhaps land alive, and then return to earth— all that constitutes a wild dream worthy of Jules Verne."

"No matter what we do now, the Russians will beat us to the moon... I would not be surprised if the Russians reached the moon in a week."
> —John Rinehard of the Smithsonian Astrophysical Observatory, October 1957.

Bad Predictions

"With the first moon colonies predicted for the seventies, preliminary work is moving ahead on the types of shelter that will be required to maintain men on the moon."

> —Arnold B. Barach and the Kiplinger Washington Editors, *1975: and the Changes to Come*, 1962.

"In all likelihood, the development of the moon as Space Research Base No. 1 will already be well advanced by the end of the 1970s... The moon, then will be the base for space exploration—/ the platform which will provide space vehicles with their communications, ranging from great wide-band systems for nearer craft engaged in measurements and detailed observations, to the delicately-controlled transmissions directed to craft venturing towards the farther limits of the solar system."

> —Professor Sir Harrie Massey,
> *New Scientist,* 1964.

"Man may have landed on the surface of Mars by 1984. If not, he will surely have made a close approach for personal observation of the red planet. Likewise, manned fly-bys to Venus will have been made... Astronauts will be shuttling back and forth on regular schedules from the earth to a small permanent base of operations on the moon."

> —Dr. Wernher von Braun, *New Scientist*, 1964.

"The odds are now that the United States will not be able to honor the 1970 manned-lunar-landing date set by Mr. Kennedy."

> —*New Scientist*, 1964.

"I'll have my first Zambian astronaut on the Moon by 1965."

> —Edward Mukaka Nkoloso, Director-General of the Zambia National Academy of Space Research, November 3, 1964.

"The most ambitious United States space endeavor in the years ahead will be the campaign to land men on neighboring Mars. Most experts estimate the task can be accomplished by 1985."
—*Wall Street Journal*, 1966.

"Space exploration has its limitations, and man has almost... achieved all that is humanly possible in his corner of the universe. This means that the Space Age, though it will undoubtedly witness other marvelous achievements, is actually coming to an end almost before it has begun. Scientists will soon be weeping, like Alexander, that they have no more worlds to conquer."
—religious author Arthur S. Maxwell,
This is the End, 1967.

"A manned lunar base will be in existence by 1986."
—*The Futurist*, 1967

"I predict that many in this room will live to see an excursion into space become as commonplace as were airplane rides when some of us were in our youth."
—Charles C. Tillinghast Jr. president of Trans-World Airlines at the Midwest Research Institute, 1967.

"And what of the so-called conquest of space? To some, including educator and writer Willy Ley, it promises the solution of most of our problems.... On the other hand, it is perhaps equally probable that the recognition of the economic burden, or even simple disillusion with the results, may, even before the year 2000, make the obsession with outer space remembered only as a temporary folly."
—Joseph Wood Krutch, "What the Year 2000 Won't Be Like," *Saturday Review*, January 20, 1968.

In 1968 during the flight of Apollo 8, Pan Am, then one of the country's top airlines, made the semi-tongue-in-cheek announcement that they would be accepting reservations for flights to the moon, which would begin in

Bad Predictions

2000. A company official estimated the cost of a round-trip ticket would be $28,000. By 1971, more than 30,000 people had signed up for the trip. Pam Am went out of business in 1991 and no moon flights are planned for 2000 or any other year.

"By the year 2000, we will undoubtedly have a sizeable operation on the moon; we will have achieved a manned Mars landing; and it's entirely possible we will have flown with men to the outer planets."
　　　　—NASA scientist Werner von Braun, 1969.

"I don't think we should be too timid to say that at the end of the century, we're going to put a man on Mars; somebody's going to do it."
　　　　—Vice President Spiro Agnew, 1969.

"Within a decade, the nuclear-powered pressurized covered wagons of the new pioneers will be trundling over the dusky lunar plains; a generation later, across the sands of Mars; and nuclear power is indeed the key to the solar system."
　　　　—Arthur C. Clarke, "The Odyssey Into Space,"
　　　　Look Magazine, February, 1969.

"Permanent bases will probably be established on the Moon before 1980: these bases will be small at first, but within twenty years we may well see the air-conditioned settlements envisaged by science-fiction writers, beneath domes or perhaps largely underground to avoid dangerous radiation from the Sun. Most of the building materials needed would be mined on the Moon, and food would be grown in air-conditioned transparent domes."
　　　　–mathematics and science professor Desmond King-Hele, *The End of the Twentieth Century?*, 1970.

In his article "Headlines of the Near Future," which appeared in the 1972 book *Futures Conditional* by Robert Theobald, Billy Rojas predicted that the U.S.S.R. would establish the first space hospital ("4 beds") in August, 1975.

Before its appearance, scientists predicted that Comet Kohoutek would be a stunning light show for the people of earth. *Newsweek* proclaimed "Comet Kohoutek promises to be the celestial extravaganza of the century." In fact, the comet's passing was all but invisible to earthlings.

"When they'd gone off for that long weekend to the Moon, there was no question that they were compatible under the worst circumstances— for three days, the air conditioning in their room was off and the depressurization was down to sixty percent."
    —Carol Rinzler, "Femininity 2000,"
    Woman in the Year 2000, 1974.

"Air-conditioned settlements on the moon will be situated under domes or below ground to avoid solar radiation [by 2000]. Food will be grown in air-conditioned domes, and building materials will be mined from the moon itself."
    —Arthur C. Clarke, 1975.

The Book of Predictions, a 1980 collection of forecasts by the authors of *The People's Almanac*, suggests that by the year 2000 we should be spending a lot of time in space. Rocket scientist Robert Traux predicted 50,000 people would be living and working in space by the turn of the century. Physicist Gerald Feinberg believed that around this time the first "O'Neill-type" space colony (named for Gerard O'Neill's *The High Frontier*) would be built and inhabited and that the first human children would be born off the earth. The colony, he said, would be an artificial planetoid made of lunar materials and powered by solar energy.

Science and Technology

Machines, Inventions and Gadgets

"Inventions have long since reached their limit, and I see no hope for further developments."
    —Roman Engineer Sextus Julius Frontinus,
    10 A.D.

"There is a young madman proposing to light the streets of London— with what do you suppose— with smoke!"
    —Sir Walter Scott, 1810 on gas lighting.

"The advancement of the arts from year to year taxes our credulity and seems to presage the arrival of that period when further improvement must end."
    —U.S. Commissioner of Patents
    Henry L. Ellsworth, 1844.

In 1989 a "lost" Jules Verne manuscript written in 1863 was discovered in a safe. The novel, *Paris in the Twentieth Century*, predicted a number of modern conveniences including horseless carriages, automated trains, electric lights and a 500 foot lighthouse standing only yards from where the Eiffel Tower stands today. Editor Pierre-Jules Hetzel rejected the novel because, "No one today will believe your prophecy."

"To fix fleeting reflections is not only impossible as has been shown by thorough-going German research, but to wish to do it is blasphemy."
    —*Leipzig City Advertiser* on Louis Jacques DaGuerre's announcement of his invention the Daguerrotype, an early form of photography.

A committee of the British Parliament in 1878 reported Thomas Edison's ideas of developing an incandescent lamp to be "good enough for our transatlantic friends... but unworthy of the attention of practical or scientific men"

Before viewing a demonstration of Edison's phonograph in 1878, Jean Bouillaud of the French Academy of Sciences had already dismissed it: "It is quite impossible that the noble organs of human speech could be replaced by ignoble, senseless metal."
Edison, himself, became discouraged with his invention. In 1880 he told his assistant Sam Insull, "The phonograph is not of any commercial value."

"Everyone acquainted with the subject will recognize it as a conspicuous failure."
> –Henry Morton, President of the Stevens Institute of Technology on Thomas Edison's first demonstration of the electric light, 1879.

"My recent studies have made me more adverse than ever to the new scientific doctrines which are flourishing now in England. This sensational zeal reminds me of what I experienced as a young man in Germany, when the physio-philosophy of Oken had invaded every centre of scientific activity; and yet, what is there left of it? I trust to outlive this mania also."
> —Louis Agassiz, professor of geology and zoology at Harvard University on Darwin's Theory of Evolution, 1893.

"Phrenology will prove to be the true science of the mind. Its practical uses in education, in self-disciplining, in reformatory treatment of criminals, and in the remedial treatment of the insane, will give it one of the highest places in the hierarchy of the sciences."
> —British naturalist and biologist Alfred Russel Wallace, 1898.

In 1899, it is said, the Director of the U.S. Patent Office advised President McKinley to close the office because everything that could be invented had been invented.

"Discoveries which seem approaching their ultimate condition are telephony, photography, illumination and apparently labor-saving machinery in some of its fields, since the performance of some machines appears to have practically reached perfection...We cannot, indeed, well conceive of a greater activity of invention and a more rapid unfoldment of new processes than we have had before us in the nineteenth century... One by one each of the varied lines of invention will reach its ultimatum and gradually the activity of man in this direction decrease. While the twentieth century may be as active in the development of mechanism as the nineteenth has been, it seems unlikely to be more so, and in succeeding centuries, inventive activity must decline for want of fields in which to exercise itself."

> —Charles Morris, *The Marvelous Record of the Closing Century*, 1899.

"We have sanitation, surgery, drainage, plumbing—every product of science and accessory of luxury. It seems impossible to imagine any improvement on what we have."

> —*Washington Post* editorial, 1901.

"Paper will be replaced by material which does not depend upon the slow growth of trees for its production."

> —Norman Bel Geddes, "Ten Years From Now," *Ladies' Home Journal*, 1931.

"Wherever he went Mr. Doe carried a camera hardly bigger than a watch and also a tiny sound-recording device, so that anything he saw or heard during the day he could conveniently remember by mechanical means."

> —Arthur Train, "Predictions: Fifty Years from now in 1988," *Harper's*, 1938.

"Famous in our circles is the story of the visiting English banker who in 1948 upon seeing our model 95 camera commented, 'Very interesting, but why would one want a picture in a minute?'"

> —Polaroid founder Dr. Edwin Land in the 1979 *Polaroid Annual Report*.

"Beams of atomic radiation, instead of saws, cut lumber [in 1999]"

> —Victor Cohn, *1999 Our Hopeful Future*, 1954.

Half a dozen firms, including Kodak and IBM, passed on the opportunity to buy Chester Carlson's patent on xerography before the Haloid company saw value in it and formed the Xerox Corporation.

"The island of Ceylon supplies a representative example of how life can be saved by the application of scientific methods. DDT spraying cut the mortality rate 34% in a single year."

> —Paul F. Douglas, Chairman of the National Advisory Committee on the Recruitment, Training and Placement of Recreation Personnel, 1957.

"Apart from the electromobile, there will [in 1984] be thousands of appliances similar to those of today; vacuum cleaners, electric drills, toasters, irons and so on. But they will be enormously different in one respect. They will no longer need to be plugged into the electric current, but will be driven instead by an independent source of energy."

> —nuclear physicist Jacques Bergier, *Impossible Possibilities*, 1968.

"Within five to seven years, we will have a lot of service robots cleaning buildings and toilets, or helping out in hotel kitchens. Within 10 years... every home will have them."

> —robotics researcher Line Kye, Young, 1991.

The *London Evening Standard*, in 1999, looked back and predicted for the year 2000: "The Millennium has long proved irresistible to TV pseudo-science programmes," it wrote. "Since the early Sixties, their presenters have been telling us, authoritatively, what to expect in 2000. Futuristic transport provision has been a hot topic. A young James Burke predicted Londoners would get work via the River Thames, safely tucked inside inflated plastic bags, and remote control cars were predicted for the Eighties. There were walking bikes with artificial feet, cars on stilts, and one looked like a slug on wheels, run by computer-aided navigation."

Powerful Predictions (Energy, Fuel and Natural Resources)

"We thankful are that sun and moon
Were placed so very high
That no tempestuous hand might reach
To tear them from the sky.
Were it not so, we soon should find
That some reforming ass
Would straight propose to snuff them out
 And light the world with Gas."
> —popular rhyme that ridiculed the idea of lighting English cities with gas in the early 1800s.

"[They] might as well try to light London with a slice from the moon."
> —William H. Wollaston, English chemist and natural philosopher on gas lighting.

"Thou knowest no man can split the atom."
> —physicist John Dalton, 1803.

"...a web of naked fancies."
"...he who looks on the world with the eye of reverence must turn aside from this book as the result of an incurable delusion, whose sole effort is to detract from the dignity of nature."
"...a physicist who professed such heresies was unworthy to teach science."
> —critics of George Simon Ohm's theory of electricity published in 1827 in *The Galvanic Chain, Mathematically Worked Out.*

In 1878, the Hartford Woman's Friday Club, one of the oldest women's organizations, published a paper which concluded that electricity, though an interesting experiment, was too uncertain and dangerous to be put to practical use.

"When the Paris Exhibition closes, electric light will close with it and no more will be heard of it."
— Oxford University professor Erasmus Wilson, 1878.

"Electric light will never take the place of gas."
—German inventor Werner von Siemens.

"I do not think there is the slightest chance of its [electricity] competing, in a general way, with gas. There are defects about the electric light which, unless some essential change takes place, must entirely prevent its application to ordinary lighting purposes."
—Remarks of Mr. Keates, Minutes of Evidence Taken before the Select Committee on Lighting, London, House of Commons, 1879.

"There is no plea which will justify the use of high-tension and alternating currents, either in a scientific or a commercial sense. They are employed solely to reduce investment in copper wire and real estate... My personal desire would be to prohibit entirely the use of alternating currents. They are unnecessary as they are dangerous...I can therefore see no justification for the introduction of a system which has no element of permanency and every elements of danger to life and property... I have always consistently opposed high-tension and alternating systems of electric lighting...not only on account of danger, but because of their general unreliability and unsuitability for any general system of distribution... The public may rest absolutely assured that safety will not be secured by burying these wires. The condensation of moisture, the ingress of water, the dissolving influence of coal gas and air-oxidation upon the various insulating compounds will result only in the transfer of deaths to man-holes, houses, stores, and offices, through the agency of the telephone, the low-pressure systems, and the apparatus of the high-tension current itself."
— Thomas Alva Edison, "The Dangers of Electric Lighting," *North American Review*, November, 1889.

101

Bad Predictions

Edison also made the following pronouncements on electricity in the home: "Fooling around with alternating currents is just a waste of time. Nobody will use it, ever. It's too dangerous...it could kill a man as quick as a bolt of lightning. Direct current is safe."

"Edison said he could light by electricity a room and even a whole town... I c id not think the device amounted to a row of pins."
— eminent Bostonian J. Murray Forbes.

In the 1890s, according to *Time Magazine*, it was widely predicted that the U.S. would be bare of trees by the 1920s because they would all have been chopped down to provide wood for heating and cooking.

"It is mathematically certain to me that another thirty years of energy-development at the rate of the last century, must reach an impasse."
— author and historian Henry Brooks
  Adams, 1902.

"The speculation... is interesting, but the impossibility of ever doing it is so certain that it is not practically useful."
— editor of *Popular Astronomy* in a letter to rocket pioneer Robert Goddard, who had proposed consideration of nuclear energy, 1902.

"There is no likelihood man can ever tap the power of the atom...Nature has introduced a few foolproof devices into the great majority of elements that constitute the bulk of the world, and they have no energy to give up in the process of disintegration."
— Robert Andrews Millikan, winner of the 1923 Nobel Prize for Physics.

"On thermodynamical grounds which I can hardly summarize shortly, I do not much believe in the commercial possibility of induced radio-activity."
— J.B.S. Haldane, biologist, *Daedalus*, 1923.

"There is by no means the same certainty today as a decade ago that the atoms of an element contain hidden sources of energy."
>—Sir Ernest Rutherford, called the "father of nuclear physics" for his studies on the structure atoms, 1923.

"Nothing is gained by exaggerating the possibilities of tomorrow. We need not worry over the consequences of breaking up the atom."
>—engineer Floyd W. Parsons, *Saturday Evening Post*, 1931.

"A new fuel of vastly increased power but of infinitesimal bulk will supersede gasoline [in the next 10 years]."
>—Norman Bel Geddes, "Ten Years From Now," *Ladies' Home Journal*, 1931.

"To us who think in terms of practical use, the splitting of the atom means nothing."
>—British science writer Lord Ritchie Calder, 1932.

"The energy produced by the breaking down of the atom is a very poor kind of thing. Anyone who expects a source of power from the transformation of the atom is talking moonshine."
>— British Physicist Lord Ernest Rutherford after the first experimental splitting of the atom from the *New York Herald Tribune*, September 12, 1933.

"I do not think it hazardous to predict that we will be enabled to illuminate the whole sky at night and that eventually we will flash power in virtually unlimited amounts to planets. I would not be surprised at all if an experiment to transmit thousands of horsepower to the moon were made in a few years from now... Motion pictures will be flashed across limited spaces by my system. The same energy will drive airplanes and dirigibles from one central base."
>–Scientist Nikola Tesla (1856-1943).

Bad Predictions

In the same article Tesla wrote, "The idea of atomic energy is illusionary but it has taken a powerful hold on the mind and there are still some who believe it to be realizable."

"Splitting the atom is like trying to shoot a gnat in the Albert Hall at night and using ten million rounds of ammunition on the off chance of getting it. That should convince you that the atom will always be a sink of energy and never a reservoir of energy."
–British physicist Lord Ernest Rutherford (1871-1937).

"Few scientists foresee any serious or practical use for atomic energy. They regard the atom-splitting experiments as useful steps in the attempt to describe the atom more accurately, not as the key to the unlocking of any new power."
—*Fortune Magazine*, 1938.

"If there are enough shovels to go around, everybody's going to make it."
—T.K. Jones, Deputy Under Secretary of Defense on the chances of surviving a nuclear attack.

"It is not too much to expect that our children will enjoy in their homes electrical energy too cheap to meter."
—Lewis L. Strauss, chairman of the U.S. Atomic Energy Commission, 1954.

"Atomic batteries will be commonplace long before 1980... It can be taken for granted that before 1980 ships, aircraft, locomotives and even automobiles will be atomically fueled."
—RCA founder David Sarnoff, *The Fabulous Future: America in 1980*, 1956.

"There is only enough natural gas for another 25 years or so...By the end of the century there will be practically no tungsten, copper, lead, zinc, gold, silver or platinum."
—Teddy Goldsmith, *Can Britain Survive?*, 1971.

"Plastic waste, by the year 2000, ought to be a compara- 4/30
tively minor problem since, in a Creative Society, non-
returnable containers of any kind would certainly be il-
legal."

–M.W. Thring, *Man, Machines and Tomorrow*,
1973.

2/25/03

In 1979 the film "The China Syndrome" was released.
In the film a reporter witnesses an accident at a nuclear
power plant. In a chilling case of life imitating art, the
famous incident at the Three Mile Island plant in Harrisburg, PA occurred only days after its release. Previous to that an executive of Southern California Edison
said the film "hasn't any scientific credibility and is, in
fact, ridiculous." Syndrome rendered an
unconscionable public disservice by using phony the-
atrics to frighten Americans away from a desperately
needed energy source."

"Under global sponsorship, the construction of solar
power stations in orbit around the earth will have begun [by 2000]."

—Isaac Asimov, 1980.

Computers

"Worthless."

— Sir George Bidell Airy, Astronomer Royal of
Great Britain on the "analytical engine" (theoretical computer) invented by Charles Babbage,
September 15, 1842. Baggage himself, in 1883,
said that his invention would never go beyond
"a theoretical possibility." While he was correct
in that the engine was never constructed, his
work did form the basis of later computer research.

105

Bad Predictions

"Where a calculator on the ENIAC is equipped with 18,000 vacuum tubes and weighs 30 tons, computers in the future may have only 1,000 vacuum tubes and perhaps weigh 10½ tons."
> — *Popular Mechanics*, March 1949.

"It would appear we have reached the limits of what it is possible to achieve with computer technology, although one should be careful with such statements; they tend to sound pretty silly in five years."
> — computer scientist John von Neumann, 1949.

"I have traveled the length and breadth of this country and talked with the best people, and I can assure you that data processing is a fad that won't last out the year."
> —The editor in charge of business books for Prentice Hall, 1957

"I think there is a world market for maybe five computers."
> —Thomas Watson, Chairman of IBM, 1958, attributed.

"Computers are multiplying at a rapid rate. By the turn of the century there will be 220,000 in the U.S."
> —*Wall Street Journal*, 1966. There are millions of computers in the US today.

"To maintain hundreds of complex electronic circuits [in the home computer of 1999] a monitor checks all circuits every few seconds, inserts a back-up circuit if and when trouble develops and alerts the communal service agency for replacement."
> —"Year 1999 A D.," a 1967 film by the Ford Motor Co.

"But what is [the microchip] good for?"
> — Engineer at the Advanced Computing Systems Division of IBM, 1968.

In 1952, IBM forecasted the total global market for computers as 52 units. In 1982, IBM forecasted the total global market for PCs as 200,000 units. In 1966 RCA forecasted that there would be 220,000 computers in the United States by the turn of the 21st Century. The figure is lower than current weekly shipments.

"Nor are computers going to get much faster..."
—Dr. Arthur L. Samuel, "The Banishment of Paper-Work," *New Scientist*, 1964.

"Computers will benefit even more than telephones from the development of integrated circuits in ever smaller 'chips,' and very small computers may emerge. Most computers will probably still occupy a large room, however, because of the space needed for the ancillary software— the tapes and cards to be fed in, the operating staff, and the huge piles of paper for printing out the results. But future computers, though no smaller, will be capable of doing far more than their predecessors."
—professor Desmond King-Hele, *The End of the Twentieth Century?*, 1970.

"There is no reason for any individual to have a computer in their home."
—Ken Olsen president of Digital Equipment, 1977.

"Access to computers is going to be less dependent upon public data lines as small local computers carry more of the relevant information. Of course it might be argued that with the new microcomputers all the criminal has to do is steal the whole device and crack it in the leisure of his own home, but the same argument applies to a filing cabinet. That latter, however, will yield to a jimmy and a bit of brute force, while the former only to a skilled and highly intelligent operator."
—computer scientist Christopher Evans underestimating the ingenuity of criminals, the extent to which computers would become user-friendly and the number of people who would be using the Internet in *The Micro Millennium*, 1979.

107

Bad Predictions

"So we went to Atari and said, 'Hey, we've got this amazing thing, even built with some of your parts, and what do you think about funding us? Or we'll give it to you. We just want to do it. Pay our salary, we'll come work for you.' And they said, 'No.' So then we went to Hewlett-Packard, and they said, 'Hey, we don't need you. You haven't got through college yet."
> —Apple Computer Inc. founder Steve Jobs on attempts to get Atari and Hewlett Packard interested in his personal computer.

"640K ought to be enough for anybody."
> —Bill Gates, 1981, attributed.

"When I am 30 I'll have a computer that has long arms that can clean the house and cook meals. And another computer that has a little slot that money comes out to pay for groceries and stuff."
> —A 6th grader in 1983 asked what her computer would do when she was 30. (She would be 30 in 2001 or 2002 depending on her age in 6th grade. Although that is a few years from now, I believe it is safe enough to assume our computers will not be dispensing free money by then, but I would be happy to be proven wrong.)

"By the year 2000, we will all be talking into our word processors instead of typing."
> —Jan Galvin, Director of Assertive Technology at the National Rehabilitation Hospital, 1991.

"I predict the Internet... will soon go spectacularly supernova and in 1996 catastrophically collapse."
> —Bob Metcalfe, *InfoWorld*, 1995.

Paul Saffo, a director of the Institute for the Future, in February, 1996, predicted the Web would mutate into "something else very quickly and be unrecognizable within 12 months."

"Microsoft has stretched itself so thin, within a couple of years it will experience serious reversals. We'll make the millennium my deadline."
        —Bob Lewis, *InfoWorld*, 1997.

8/8

The Dreaded Y2K Bug and other Millennial Madness

"I think we're in for a very rough ride. I just hope the constitutional boat holds together."
        –medieval historian Richard Lande on doomsday fears as 2000 grew near, 1996. In fact, the year 2000 was rung in with what President Bill Clinton called a "jubilant and peaceful" global celebration. British Prime Minister Tony Blair joined a giant millennium parade through the streets of London and said he wanted to "bottle and keep" the country's new sense of optimism.

"I'm saying that it's over. Right now. It cannot be fixed Whatever it does, the Millennium Bug will bite us."
        —writer Gary North, early 1997.

2/12/02

North also predicted that the Y2K bug would create "a disaster greater than anything the world has experienced since the bubonic plague of the mid-14th century."
"This is not a prediction, it is a certainty– there will be serious disruption in the world's financial services industry. I can't tell whether it's going to be 10% business failure, or a meltdown, but it's going to be ugly."
        —a banker quoted in *Y2K: Opportunity or Apocalypse?*, a promotional publication by the consulting firm Prep 2000, 1997.

"The more I read, the more convinced I am that some economic disruptions are inevitable. The year 2000 problem is a serious threat to the global economy. Yet it isn't being taken seriously enough."
        —economist Edward Yardeni in *Computer World*, 1997.

9/4

109

Bad Predictions

Not wanting to be alarmist about the whole Y2K issue, consultant Cory Hamasaki wrote in his *DC Y2K Weather Report* newsletter in January, 1998: "[You should cache] most of your arms and supplies, while this is still possible and legal. Preferably, you should have several smaller caches known only to you and to a highly trusted backup... someone who will pass supplies on to your family or group if anything happens to you... you need to convert most of your spare cash and paper investments into gold and/or silver coins."

"I recently sold our New York City apartment and bought a house in a small town in New Mexico... I've often joked that I expect New York to resemble Beirut if even a subset of the Y2K infrastructure problems actually materialize– but it's really not a joke... Y2K is so worrisome, in my opinion, that I'll make sure my family isn't there when the clock rolls over to Jan 1, 2000."
—Consultant Ed Yourdon, July 1998.

In October, 1998, Kathy Mulady, a writer for the *Spokane Spokesman-Review*, reported on a talk by Y2K guru Jim Lord: "Around next summer, there could be complete disaster and the effects could last a long time," he said.   Mulady then summarized Lord's specific predictions: "Expect blackouts and energy rationing, food shortages, bank and airport closures, unusable medical equipment, disruptions in Social Security, Medicare and Medicaid payments and the demise of the Internal Revenue Service."

"We must also prepare ourselves for the very real possibility that the outcome of this situation might well be the total extinction of the entire human race. It really could be worse than I am predicting, and I really am being optimistic. First, I would like to assure you that I am not some kind of nut anxiously waiting for the end of the world...."
—Cory Hamasaki, *DC Y2K Weather Report*, November 1998.

"Doomsayers predict nothing short of total collapse within the next two years... the mounting evidence was convincing enough to make us look for a place to ride out the turmoil. We have now found it in Arizona."
> —Russ Voorhees on his web page, www.heritagefarms2000.com, which described his planned community Heritage West 2000.

The Reverend Jerry Falwell produced a 1999 video on the millennium bug warning that it might be God's attempt "to confound our language, jam our communications, judge us for our sin ... ."

Diane Auston, author of a self-published guide to the Y2K bug, called it "the handwriting on the wall for the end times."

"[Y2K will be] the cause of the mother of all traffic jams on the information highway."
> —financial planner John Mauldin in his 1999 book *How to Profit From The Y2K Recession . . . By Converting the Year 2000 Crisis into an Opportunity for Your Investments and Business.*

"We're going to suffer a year of technological disruptions, followed by a decade of depression... We're likely to be living in an environment much like the Third World countries some of us have visited, where nothing works particularly well."
> —Consultant Ed Yourdon, February, 1999.

"We're in that same type of scenario as 1929. Y2K will be the straw that breaks the camel's back. The market will be imploding on itself, with everyone heading for the door, and it will be a very small exit."
> — Bill Muir, a Redding, California, businessman who sold his stocks and invested in gold in anticipation of the Y2K market collapse quoted in *USA Today*, March, 1999. The economy did not collapse, but the price of gold declined in early 2000.

111

Bad Predictions

"I can no longer say with any confidence that there is enough time to avoid a severe global Y2K recession."
—Edward Yardeni, June 1999.

"Plague will follow shortly. Most of the inhabitants of the northern hemisphere will die within a matter of a few weeks, from cold, disease, fires started in an attempt to keep warm, or violence. This is bad enough, of course, to qualify as a disaster ranking with the Black Plague, if not the extinction of the dinosaurs."
—Cory Hamasaki, *DC Y2K Weather Report*, July 1999.

"The most significant event on Jan. 1, 2000, will be the failure of the telephone and Internet infrastructure. It won't be due to any real failure but rather to the flood of telephone calls and hits to CNN.com to check on everybody else around the world. There will most likely be some areas where older utility infrastructures fail - perhaps seriously for some - and it is reasonable to assume that a very large and concerted effort may have to be undertaken on the part of the government/National Guard to help restore power, provide heating and food."
—columnist Fred McClimans, *Network World*, December, 6, 1999.

"The Year-2000 phenomenon is clearly such a jolt, and we believe that it will be much more pervasive and serious than most of the [disasters] we've experienced in modern history."
-Ed and Jennifer Yourdon in *Time Bomb 2000!*, 1999.

Along with *Timebomb 2000!*, Y2K books included: *Don't Panic! You Can Prepare for the Y2K Crisis, Crisis Investing for the Year 2000, The Hippy Survival Guide to Y2K, the Y2K Recipe Collection*, which featured recipes that could be made with "only canned, boxed, and dried items found in your Y2K food storage pantry," and the novel *The Millennium Bug* by George E. Grant and Michael S. Hyatt. The novel focused on a Fortune 500 executive who is fired after failing to convince his boss of the urgency of Y2K preparation. He then sets up his own Y2K consulting firm. The worst-case scenario, of course, occurs. The economy collapses, the power grid fails and people take to the hills to hide out with their rifles and rations. NBC television also aired a critically panned science fiction adventure called "Y2K" in which the protagonists tried to avert the meltdown of a nuclear plant caused by computer malfunctions.

Other Scientific Projections

"I utterly reject the atomic theory of Dalton."
—Sir Humphrey Davy (1778-1829) on
John Dalton's theory of the existence
of atoms.

"Mendel lacks the requisite clarity of thought to be a scientist."
–professor at the University of Vienna on Gregor
Mendel (1822-1884), the founder of genetics.

Thomas Edison did not show much promise as a student. His first teacher called him "addled," and another predicted he would "never make a success of anything."

"X-rays will prove a hoax."
–William Thompson, Lord Kelvin,
president of England's Royal Society.

"In the papers of Thomas Young I can find nothing which deserves the name either of experiment or discovery. I deem them destitute of every species of merit. The Royal Society is to be censured for printing such paltry and unsubstantial papers."
—Lord Henry Peter Brougham (1778-1868)
on the originator of the wave theory of light.

Bad Predictions

"The paper is nothing but nonsense, unfit even for reading before the Society."
>—A member of the Royal Society commenting on J.J. Waterson's paper which developed the foundations of the kinetic theory of gases and thermodynamics.

"In the nineteenth century the transmutation of metals will be generally known to be practiced. Every chemist and every artist will make gold; kitchen utensils will be of silver, and even gold, which will contribute more than anything else to prolong life, poisoned at present by the oxides of copper, lead and iron, which we daily swallow with our food."
>—Dr. Christoph Girtanner (1760-1800).

"I am strongly opposed to Charles going on this Beagle voyage. He is moving away from the Church, drifting irretrievably into a life of sport and idleness."
>—Charles Darwin's father, Robert Darwin.

"I doubt whether Darwin will have the determination to survive the difficult journey of several years. My studies of physiognomy indicate that people with a broad, squat nose like his don't have the character."
>—Robert Fitzroy, Captain of the H.M.S. Beagle. It was during his voyage on the Beagle that Charles Darwin first formulated his theory of evolution.

"1858 has not, indeed, been marked by any of those discoveries which at once revolutionize, so to speak, the department of science in which they occur."
>—Thomas Bell, president of the Linnean Society, speaking in the year in which Darwin read his papers on the origin of the species to the society.

"I trust to outlive this mania."
>—geology professor Louis Agassiz on Darwinism,
in an 1893 letter. It was published posthumously.

"The more important fundamental laws and facts of physical science have all been discovered, and these are now so firmly established that the possibility of their ever being supplanted in consequence of new discoveries is exceedingly remote....Future discoveries must be looked for in the sixth place of decimals."
>— British scientist Albert A. Michelson from
an 1894 lecture, reprinted in his 1903 book
Light Waves and Their Uses.

"It doesn't matter what he does, he will never amount to anything."
>—Albert Einstein's teacher to his father, 1895.

"Experimental evidence is strongly in favor of my argument that the chemical purity of the air is of no importance."
>—professor L. Erskine Hill of London Hospital,
1912.

"[Dr. Velikovsky's discoveries] may well rank him in contemporary and future history with Galileo, Newton, Planck, Kepler, Darwin, Einstein."
>—editor Ted Thackery, *New York Compass*, on
Dr. Immanuel Velikovsky (1895-1979), author of
Worlds in Collision. His theory that a series of
comets caused such Biblical events as the parting of the Red Sea is no longer taken seriously
by most scientists.

"Physics as we know it will be over in six months."
>—physicist Max Born, 1928.

Bad Predictions

"Einstein a scientist? It were difficult to imagine anyone more contrary to what a scientist should be... As a rational physicist, Einstein is a fair violinist... [By 1940] the relativity theory will be considered a joke... Einstein is already dead and buried, alongside Andersen, Grimm, and the Mad Hatter."
> —George Francis Gillette, creator of the
> "backscrewing theory of gravity," 1929.

"To me truth is precious... I should rather be right and stand alone than run with the multitude and be wrong... [My views have] already won for me the scorn and contempt and ridicule of some of my fellowmen. I am looked upon as being odd, strange, peculiar... but truth is truth and though all the world reject it and turn against me, I will cling to truth still."
> —Charles S. deFord, from the introduction to his
> 1931 book in which he proves the world is flat.

"The final proof of the whole cosmic ice theory will be obtained when the first landing on the ice-coated surface of the Moon takes place."
> —Hörbiger Institute pamphlet, 1953.
> In 1913, German philosopher Hans Hörbiger
> published a 790-page book called
> Glazial-Kosmogonie, which theorized that all
> the planets, except the earth, were covered in
> layers of ice that were several miles deep. Ice
> was also floating throughout space, causing
> sunspots and landing on earth as hail.
> Hörbiger had many proponents, including
> Adolf Hitler.

"California, 1984— To those of us who remember the hurricanes of the 1960s, with their grimly girlish names and their incredible viciousness, a certain excitement has gone out of life. It turned out that hurricanes could be prevented rather easily."
> —Dr. Roger Revelle, New Scientist, 1964.

116

"The popular notion that the Sun is on fire is rubbish, and merely a hoary superstition, on par with a belief in a flat earth, an earth resting on the back of a tortoise or an elephant, or a sun revolving around a stationary earth... If the sun is a hot body, it is improbable that life on earth will exist tomorrow."
>   —Reverend P.H. Francis, *The Temperate Sun,*
>   1970. (We're still here.)

"No one knows more about this mountain than Harry. And it don't dare blow up on him."
>   —Harry Truman (not the president), who owned
>   a lodge near Mt. St. Helens, which erupted a few
>   days later. Truman did not survive.

Bad Predictions

Health and Medicine

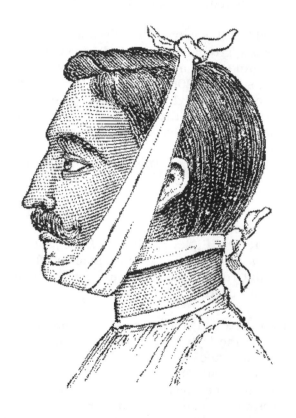

Health

"Listerian antisepsis is absurd in theory and impossible in practice."

> —George Bernard Shaw (1856-1950) on Joseph Lister's theories about the connection between poor surgical hygiene and the spread of germs.

"By [1993] longevity will be so improved that 150 years will be no unusual age to reach."

> —Reverend Thomas De Witt Talmage, 1893.

"Boards of health will have destroyed all mosquito haunts and breeding grounds, drained all stagnant pools, filled in all swamp-lands, and chemically treated all still-water streams [in the 20th Century]... Gymnastics will begin in the nursery, where toys and games will be designed to strengthen the muscles]... A man or woman unable to walk ten miles at a stretch will be regarded as a weakling."

> —John Watkins, *The Ladies' Home Journal*, 1900.

"I'm just in for a checkup, and I'll be out to the farm to see you tomorrow."

> —Robert Ripley, author of *Ripley's Believe it or Not*, in a May 27, 1949, phone call from his hospital room. He hung up, and fell back on his bed– dead.

"What do these statements have in common? 'Scrofula is cured by the laying on of royal hands; a good treatment for tuberculosis is horseback riding; gout is manifestly an affliction of the nervous system.' Answer: They were all believed correct by leading members of the medical profession at one time, but were later proved to be false. To this list may be added the statement that cigarette smoking causes lung cancer."

> --*California Medicine*, June 1963.

"A child born in the year 2000 has good prospects of not dying at all-ever... The immortals are necessary, but how can they be chosen from among mortals? That will be the big question of 1984."
> —physicist Jacques Bergier,
> *Impossible Possibilities,* 1968.

The 1969 *Delphic Study of the Future of Medicine* by Smith Kline and French Laboratories predicted that by 1995, human suspended animation would come into common use for medical treatment such as complicated surgical procedures.

"By 1980 we should have unraveled the chemical basis of sleep, and many of us, by adjusting our supplies of certain chemicals, may possibly be able to manage with much less sleep than at present, while feeling just as vigorous, or more so."
> —Desmond King-Hele, *The End of the Twentieth Century?*, 1970.

"I'm going to live to be one hundred."
> —Health writer Jerome Rodale, 1971.
> He died the next day at age 51.

The 1972 book *Futures Conditional* by Robert Theobald featured an article on "Headlines of the Near Future" by Billy Rojas. He predicted that in March, 1972, safe cigarettes would be invented and, Lorillard cigarette company stock would advance 20 points in one day.

"American medicine is by far the most costly in the world. American medicine at its best is also as good, or better, than anyplace else. The trouble is that we can't quite figure out how to get it all to our citizens—which is why there is so much controversy over medical plans and organizations. By 1984, we will have straightened out the mess."
> —Richard N. Farmer, *The Real World of 1984*,
> 1973.

Bad Predictions

A 1974 report by the Institute for the Future predicted that by 1985 no one would be overweight, thanks to special foods and supplements.

"Medical brainpower was rerouted and a few years [after 1984] doctors found a cure for sterility. Shortly thereafter, hormone researchers invented male and female contraceptives that were completely safe (and conveniently dispensed by the government at most post offices.)"
—Ms. *Magazine* editor Letty Cottin Pogrebin, "Born Free: A Feminist Fable" in the 1974 book *Women in the Year 2000.*

"With her drinks, the [push-button bar] console is also programmed to deliver three pills: weight control, beauty complex I, and brain stimulator... Thank God for weight-control pills, she thinks for the ten-thousandth time."
—Carol Rinzler, "Femininity 2000," *Woman in the Year 2000*, 1974.

At the 1984 annual meeting of the American Lung Association, Surgeon General C. Everett Koop predicted an end to smoking in America by 2000. "I know a smoke-free society is not just pie in the sky but an achievable goal," he said. Asked about his prediction in 1999 he said, "We believed that the high school graduating class of the year 2000 could be smoke-free. We were certain that by targeting young people that we would get the best return for our investment, and that rather than simply a vague goal, by focusing on the Class of 2000, we would get them young enough before they could become addicted." According to the federal Centers for Disease Control and Prevention, teenage smoking actually increased from 1991 to 1997. Thirty-three percent of ninth graders reported they smoked in 1997, a 10 percent jump in six years. By the time they become high school seniors, almost 40 percent say they have smoked. The graduating class of 2000 will not be smoke free. All together, 47 million adults are smokers.

Medicine and Disease

Amabel Williams-Ellis' book *Men Who Found Out* quoted John Aubrey, a contemporary of William Harvey whose 1628 book *De Motu Cordis* described his discovery of the blood's circulation: "...I heard Harvey say that after his book came out, he fell mightily in his practice. 'Twas believed by the vulgar that he was crack-brained, and all the physicians were against him. I knew several doctors in London that would not have given threepence for one of his medicines."

In 1796 Edward Jenner wrote a paper demonstrating his finding that serum taken from a person suffering from cowpox could be used to vaccinate individuals against the more deadly smallpox. The Royal Society rejected his paper on the grounds that it would damage his good reputation.

"This is the place to state my opinions with regard to that fearful disease the Small-Pox... I was always from the very first mention of the thing opposed to the Cow-Pox scheme. If efficacious in preventing the Small Pox, I objected to it merely on the score of its beastliness. There are some things more hideous than death, and more resolutely to be avoided. I always reckoned that of a parent causing the blood, and the diseased blood too, of a beast to be put into the veins of human beings. I therefore most strenuously opposed the giving of twenty thousand pounds to Jenner out of the taxes, paid in great part by the working people, which I deemed and asserted to be a scandalous waste of the public money. I contended that this beastly application could not, in nature, be efficacious in preventing the Small-Pox and that, even if efficacious for that purpose it was unnecessary."

— William Cobbett, *Advice to Young Men*, 1846.

"Louis Pasteur's theory of germs is ridiculous fiction."
—Pierre Pachet, Professor of Physiology
at Toulouse, France, 1872.

123

Bad Predictions

"However fascinating it may be as a scholarly achievement, there is virtually nothing that has come from molecular biology that can be of any value to human living."

—Nobel Prize-winning innumologist Frank MacFarlane Burnet (1899-1985), whose work made organ transplantation possible.

"Cancer and consumption will be as easily cured as influenza or [diarrhea]."

—Reverend Thomas De Witt Talmage, on the state of medicine in 100 years, 1893.

In 1898 Dr. Heinrich Dreser, head of the drug research laboratory at the Bayer Company announced that he had developed a nonaddictive substitute for morphine. His invention was called heroin.

"Scientists and inventors are forecasting [for the 20th Century]... the complete abolition of all contagious diseases... [and] the lengthening of human life so that centenarians will be the rule and not the exception."

—The Sun, Baltimore, January 1, 1901.

"There are numerous diseases which can be not merely cured, but ultimately abolished when we have once discovered how to use oxygen adequately... Liquefied oxygen will not doubt be our sole disinfectant."

—T. Baron Russell, A Hundred Years Hence, 1905.

"There will be no epidemics. There will be no incurable diseases. Medical and surgical treatment will reduce crime to a fraction of its present day proportion."

—Norman Bel Geddes, "Ten Years From Now," Ladies' Home Journal, 1931.

Newsweek, in 1955, predicted that within the next 20 years we would see "the end or near end for heart disease, cancer and the common cold."

124

"Jonas Salk, Yiddish inventor of a so-called polio vaccine, [is part of a Jewish plot to] mass poison American
children."
—Eustace Mullins, in the anti-Jewish
Women's Voice, 1955.

"There is strong hope that a drug, taken by mouth, will
be found to correct [diabetes] completely [by 1975]."
—Arnold B. Barach and the Kiplinger Washington Editors, *1975: and the Changes to Come*,
1962.

"Between changed environmental factors and better
drugs, coronary heart disease will be pretty well licked
by 2000."
—Dr. Irvine Page of the Cleveland Clinic, 1966.

"We just won't have arthritis in 2000."
—Dr. William Clark, president of the
Arthritis Foundation, 1966.

"Psychological chemical and physical techniques will give
man the ability to control the behavior of other men without force... We may see the pharmaceutical equivalent
of the liquor store in which chemicals can be obtained
to buy any mood, from euphoria to mystic contempla-
tion. Wives perhaps will slip anti-grouch pills into their
husbands' coffee."
—Dr. Theodore Gordon, 1967.

"In 1984 no week will go by without warnings from the
World Health Organization about pills supposed to increase intelligence but which in fact are useless and
likely to cause cancer. New pseudo religious cults and
pseudo hypnotic methods will make promises of raising
I.Q.s."
—nuclear physicist Jacques Bergier, 1968.

"By the year 2000, [Russian biochemist Vladimir
Englehardt] says, we will have pep pills which have no
after-effects and which banish fatigue entirely; cancer
will be no more serious than a nose cold; and defective

organs will be replaced by spare parts as routinely as is now the case with other machines."
> —Joseph Wood Krutch, "What the Year 2000 Won't Be Like," *Saturday Review*, January 20, 1968.

"All these new things that had come along in the last ten years... The hyp-pill, for example. She knew that they were physiologically harmless, but it was a bit frightening to think that a pill could induce a mild hypnosis which would insure total attention to the subject matter of the lecture, as well as total and permanent recall of the delivered information. Education scientists had calculated that a child could learn as much in two hours of hyp-lecture as he learned in a month of the old teacher-pupil haphazard process of information transfer."
> —Henry Still, *Man: The Next 30 Years*, 1968.

"Fuel, food, social poisons such as tobacco, etc.— all will be engineered to remove factors causative or contributory to disease patterns."
> —Task Force on Science and Technology in the Year 2000, 1970.

"I'm so healthy I expect to live on and on."
> —health guru Jerome Rodale moments before he dropped dead during a taping of the Dick Cavett Show, 1971.

"By the year 2000 [medical] diagnostic instruments should have been taken to the point where a doctor can seat his patient in a chair where a machine can scan his or her whole body, internally and externally, and give an immediate indication of any abnormality."
> —M.W. Thring, *Man, Machines and Tomorrow*, 1973.

"It should be possible to treat almost all illnesses, including battlefield trauma, electromagnetically. Cells of the body will be fooled into producing antibodies, coagulants, new tissue, chemicals, etc., by being exposed to certain kinds of electric and magnetic fields. This

type of drugless treatment will revolutionize military as well as other types of medicine."
> —engineer Eldon Byrd, 1980.

"All human infectious diseases [will be] successfully eradicated."
> —prediction for the year 1999 by economist Felix Kaufmann, 1980.

"Within a few more years, large numbers of terminally ill or hopelessly aged patients will be frozen prior to death and stored for reanimation in the future, when cures are developed for their illnesses or techniques of age reversal become available,"
> —Paul Segall, a graduate of the State University at Stony Brook doing postgraduate research at the University of California at Berkeley on the physiology of aging, 1980. He predicted that by 1992 "the first human will be successfully resuscitated after being frozen and thawed."

"By the year 2000... There will be pills that cure phobias. Fear of heights, crowds, strangers, elevators, closed-in places, even fear of flying will be a phobia of the past."
> —Marvin Cetron and Thomas O'Toole, *Encounters with the Future*, 1982.

"At this time the risk of contracting this immunosuppressive agent is minimal and C.D.C. is not recommending any change in blood-product use."
> —National Hemophilia Foundation on AIDS, July 1982. In fact, about 90 percent of severe hemophiliacs in the country were infected.

"That virus is a pussycat."
> —Dr. Peter Dusenberg, professor of Molecular Biology at the University of California at Berkley, on HIV, 1988.

Surgery and Hospitals

"The abolishment of pain in surgery is a chimera. It is absurd to go on seeking it today. Knife and pain are two words in surgery that must forever be associated in the consciousness of the patient. To this compulsory combination we shall have to adjust ourselves."
> — Dr. Alfred Velpeau, 1839. Anesthesia was introduced 7 years later.

"The abdomen, the chest, and the brain will forever be shut from the intrusion of the wise and humane surgeon."
> —John Eric Ericksen, Surgeon-Extraordinary to Queen Victoria, 1873

"I believe firmly that more patients have died from the use of gloves than have ever been saved from infection by their use."
> —Dr. W. P. Carr, 1911

In 1925, a French journal of surgery warned that blood transfusions would prove fatal.
"For the average [hospital] patient, life should be much more comfortable. Inflated beds which alternate pressure on different parts of the body will prevent bed fatigue and sores. Closed-circuit television will enable you to maintain contact with nurses, and also perhaps to talk with your children in a downstairs lobby. Rooms will be clean, light, airy and completely climate controlled with the exact temperature, moisture, air movements and barometric pressure you need for your condition. In fact, the throwaway room (consisting of a plastic liner which can be discarded after an infectious patient has used it) may be in the not-too-distant future...There is even the possibility that hospital food of the future will be edible."
> —Henry Still, *Man: The Next 30 Years*, 1968.

Health and Medicine

Communications
and Media

Newspapers and Print

"The trade of Advertising is now so near to perfection that it is not easy to propose any improvement."
—*The Idler*, 1759

"The twenty-first century [edition of this newspaper] which will issue about one hundred years from to-day will be different from this one... No more blazing headlines announcing the pleasant particulars of the last murder. Nothing but literature. Things not worth while will be condensed into a couple of lines, and the gentleman who now has his name and history and picture put into the paper because he kills or robs or cheats a citizen will pass into desutude, kicking and using bad language about it, because nobody except the police will pay any attention to him. No, the newspaper will appear on sheets of convenient size, instead of in blankets; the information will be classified on regular pages so that you will not have to hunt all over an acre of ink to find the notice of your daughter's surprise party... Typewriters will have almost disappeared from the city room, because it will then be merely necessary to talk into a machine containing the casts of phonogram. The vibrations of each sound will shake into place the letters or rather the symbols— because language will be sensibly phonetic then."
—Editor C. M. Skinner, *Brooklyn Daily Eagle*, December 30, 1900.

"The journal of the twentieth century will not be a newspaper. From the beginning of its development electricity has been tenderly cared for and one of its missions in the twentieth will be, in the graphic language of the ring, to 'knock out' its best friend as disseminator of news."
—Ralph W. Pope, Secretary of the American Institute of Electrical Engineers, *The Brooklyn Daily Eagle*, December 1900.

"The intrinsic nature of the vastly-extended advertising of the new age will be influenced by the new growth of public intelligence... Advertising will in the future world become gradually more and more intelligent in tone. It will seek to influence demand by argument instead of clamour, a tendency already more apparent every year. Cheap attention-calling tricks and clap-trap will be wholly replaced, as they are already being greatly replaced, by serious exposition; and advertisements, instead of being mere repetitions of stale catch-words, will be made interesting and informative, so that they will be welcomed instead of being shunned."
> —T. Baron Russell, *A Hundred Years Hence*, 1905.

"They [the modern generation] will not be affected by advertisements, no more than the priests and peasants of the Middle Ages would have been affected by advertisements. Only a very soft-headed, sentimental and rather servile generation could possibly be affected by advertisements at all."
> —G. K. Chesterson, *What I Saw In America*, 1922.

"A newspaper distributed by van or pushed though the letter-box will have become a preposterous anachronism [by 1984]." 5/16
> —Sir Gerald Barry, "Mass Communications in 1984," *New Scientist*, 1964.

Telegraph and Telephone

"Telegraphs of any kind are now wholly unnecessary... no other than the one now in use will be adopted."
> —John Barrow, secretary of the Admiralty, writing to Francis Ronalds in 1816.

133

Bad Predictions

"I watched his countenance closely, to see if he was not deranged... and I was assured by other Senators after we left the room that they had no confidence in it."
> —Senator Oliver Smith of Indiana on a telegraph demonstration by Samuel Morse, 1842.

"What was this telegraph to do? Would it transmit letters and newspapers? Jnder what power in the constitution did Senators propose to erect this telegraph? He was not aware of any authority except under the clause for the establishment of post roads. And besides, the telegraph might be made very mischievous, and secret information after communicated to the prejudice of merchants."
> —Senator George McDuffie, *Congressional Globe*, 28th Congress, 2nd session, 1845.

"A man has been arrested in New York for attempting to extort funds from ignorant and superstitious people by exhibiting a device which he says will convey the human voice any distance over metallic wires so that it will be heard by the listener at the other end. He calls the instrument a telephone. Well-informed people know that it is impossible to transmit the human voice over wires."
> —news item in an 1868 New York paper.

Western Union saw little use for the telephone when Alexander Graham Bell offered them exclusive rights for $100,000 in 1875. "What use could this company make of an electrical toy?" the President of Western Union is reported to have said. An internal memo that year elaborated: "This 'telephone' has too many shortcomings to be seriously considered as a means of communication. The device is inherently of no value to us." In 1882 Western Union went on to reject Bell's proposal to build the first municipal telephone network. "Bell's proposal to place his instrument in every home and business is, of course fantastic in view of the capital costs involved in installing endless numbers of wires... Any development of the kind and scale which Bell so fondly imagines is utterly out of the question."

134

"It's only a toy."
>—Gardiner Green Hubbard, a founder of the
>National Geographic Society and Alexander Gra-
>ham Bell's future father-in-law on seeing Bell's
>telephone in 1876.

"That's an amazing invention, but who would ever want
to use one of them?"
>—President Rutherford B. Hayes to Alexander
>Graham Bell after a trial telephone conversation
>between Washington and Philadelphia in 1876.

"One day there will be one in every city."
>— A town mayor who was impressed with
>the 1876 demonstration of the telephone.

"The Americans have need of the telephone— but we do
not. We have plenty of messenger boys."
>—Sir William Preece, chief engineer of the
>British Post Office.

"As far as I can judge, I do not look upon any system of
wireless telegraphy as a serious competitor with our
cables. Some years ago I said the same thing and nothing has since occurred to alter my views."
>— Sir John Wolfe-Barry at a 1907 meeting of
>stockholders of the Western Telegraph Company.

"Telephones [will] bring peace on earth, eliminate Southern accents, revolutionize surgery, stamp out 'heathen-
ism' abroad, and save the farm by making farmers less
lonely."
>—1895 pronouncements reprinted in the
>*Wall Street Journal* in 1995.

In 1984, AT&T rejected a free opportunity to enter the
cellular phone market because their forecasts indicated
only 900,000 units would be sold by 1995. It was considered too small a niche to bother with. The actual us-
ers in the U.S. today number more than 20 million.

Bad Predictions

According to Charles Townes, a Nobel Prize winner for his work on the laser, the attorneys for Bell Labs initially refused, in the 1960s, to patent the laser because they believed it had no applications in the field of telecommunications. Only in the 1980s, after extensive improvements in fiber optics technology, did the laser's importance for telecommunications become apparent.

A 1973 study "Florida 10 Million" by the Florida Division of State Planning predicted that by 1982 magazine subscriptions would be so costly that few individuals could afford them. The use of libraries would, therefore, increase. The performing arts would also be too expensive for all but the wealthiest patrons. Movie theaters would go out of business as people stayed home to watch rented movies. The same study forecasted medical visits via two-way electronic monitoring would be common by that year.

"The idea of everyone having a wristwatch-sized transmitter and receiver to communicate with other people anywhere in the world is still in the realm of science fiction and is unlikely ever to move out of it."
> —science writer Arthur Garratt, "Transport and Communication," in *Science Fact*, 1978.

Radio

"I do not think that the wireless waves I have discovered will have any practical application."
> —Heinrich Rudolf Hertz (1857-1894), on his discovery of radio waves.

"Radio has no future."
> –William Thompson, Lord Kelvin (1890-95).

In 1896, an English journal predicted that the idea of the wireless transmission of the human voice would be forgotten by the end of the year.

"...You could put in this room, de Forest, all the radiotelephone apparatus that the country will ever need!"
 —W. W. Dean, President of the Dean Telephone
  Company to Lee de Forest, 1907.

"DeForest has said in many newspapers and over his signature that it would be possible to transmit the human voice across the Atlantic before many years. Based on these absurd and deliberately misleading statements, the misguided public... has been persuaded to purchase stock in his company."
 —The U.S. District Attorney prosecuting
  inventor Lee DeForest for fraud, 1913.

"The wireless music box has no imaginable commercial value. Who would pay for a message sent to nobody in particular?"
 —David Sarnoff's associates in response to his
  urgings for investment in the radio in the 1920s.

"It is a matter of general advertising interest to record that the American Telephone and Telegraph Company is trying to establish a new advertising medium. Through its station WEAF, New York, it is permitting advertisers to broadcast messages... It is our advice to the American Telephone and Telegraph Company to 'stop, look and listen' before extending this new branch of its business. The plan is loaded with insidious dangers... Station WEAF has built up its reputation on the fine quality of its programs. Radio fans who tune in on this station are accustomed to get high-class entertainment. If they are obliged to listen to some advertiser exploit his wares, they will very properly resent it... An audience that has been wheeled into listening to a selfish message will naturally be offended."
 —trade journal *Printer's Ink*, 1923.

"It is inconceivable that we should allow so great a possibility for service to be drowned in advertising chatter."
 —Secretary of Commerce Herbert Hoover
  on radio advertising.

137

"Radio will serve to make the concept of Peace on Earth, Good Will Toward Man a reality."
—General James J. Harbord, 1925.

"I have anticipated [radio's] complete disappearance— confident that the unfortunate people, who must now subdue themselves to 'listening-in' will soon find a better pastime for their leisure."
—H.G. Wells, *The Way the World is Going*, 1925.

In 1983, radio station KMBZ in Kansas City fired a talk show host for his on-air behavior, which included jokes about what Geraldine Ferrarro would do every 28 days if she were elected president, conservative political rants and other material that was deemed inappropriate for the station's audience. The host took his act, virtually unchanged to a Sacramento station and eventually to a national audience. By 1992, Rush Limbaugh was carried on 500 stations.

Television

"Television? No good will come of this device. The word is half Greek and half Latin."
—editor of the *Manchester Guardian*, C. P. Scott 1846-1932.

"While theoretically and technically television may be feasible, commercially and financially I consider it an impossibility, a development of which we need waste little time dreaming."
—radio pioneer Lee De Forest, 1926.

"Television won't matter in your lifetime or mine."
—Rex Lambert, editorial in *The Listener*, 1936.

"The problem with television is that the people must sit and keep their eyes glued on a screen; the average American family hasn't time for it."
—*New York Times* after a prototype television was demonstrated at the 1939 World's Fair.

3/5/02

"Television won't be able to hold onto any market it captures after the first six months. People will soon get tired of staring at a plywood box every night."
—movie executive Darryl F. Zanuck.

10/5

"It is probable that television drama of high caliber and produced by first-rate artists will materially raise the level of dramatic taste of the nation."
—RCA CEO David Sarnoff, 1939

"Television won't last. It's a flash in the pan."
—Mary Somerville, pioneer in educational radio, 1948.

2/3/03

"People will never watch an hour-long drama on TV."
—radio writer and producer James Jewell, 1952.

9/28

"You can expect [within the next 15 years] three-dimensional television. The screen will give an appearance of depth to what you see, similar to the effect of wide-screen movies."
—Arnold B. Barach et al, *1975: and the Changes to Come*, 1962.

7/17/02

"The more channels and choices you have, the better. If you really want freedom, consider a telstar satellite parked over the United States, sending down eighty or more channels to choose from. It's possible, but it won't happen soon, largely because network executives, advertisers, government agencies, and lots of others are scared to death of the idea."
—Richard N. Farmer, *The Real World of 1984*, 1973.

6/6

139

Bad Predictions

"Television, probably following the lead of the cinema, may well by 1990 be offering three-dimensional programmes in colour, with smell, taste and touch added."
—Desmond King-Hele, *The End of the Twentieth Century?*, 1970

"For some years now there has been promise of a large, flat TV screen which would hang on the wall like a picture and provide a picture in full color. The hopes have not materialized yet and it may be that we shall never see such a system in operation."
—science writer Arthur Garratt, "Transport and Communication," in *Science Fact*, 1978.

"Today the three broadcast networks pretty much look alike. To stay in business they will have to find a way to be distinctive. [By the end of the decade], one may emphasize news programming, another sports, and another dramatic programming."
—Robert Pepper of the F.C.C., 1991.

Specific Television Programs and TV Stars

In 1951 CBS executives went to almost every ad agency in New York trying to get a sponsor for a new television show. They all passed on the opportunity to advertise on "I Love Lucy" until Phillip Morris finally took a chance.

"With your voice, nobody is going to let you broadcast."
—CBS producer Don Hewitt to Barbara Walters, 1958.

Executives at NBC were so sure "I Dream of Jeannie" was going to be short-lived that they decided to save money by shooting it in black and white. Jeannie's 1964 season was one of the last new shows to be produced by the network in black and white. The program ran from 1965-1970.

Actress Natalie Schaefer didn't want to be in a television series in 1964, but she decided to take a role in a pilot for a new series anyway. Her reasoning was that it would only be a few days work. "The script was so awful I didn't think it had a prayer," she said. But "Gilligan's Island" ran for three years, from 1964-1967, and has continued to run in syndication ever since.

"Dirty and un-American"
  — ABC executives turning down a 1965 television pilot from Mel Brooks and Buck Henry. The script, a parody on popular spy dramas, pitted a bumbling spy with the code name 86 against an organization called KAOS that was threatening to blow up the Statue of Liberty. After ABC passed, NBC picked up "Get Smart," and the episode in question was nominated for an Emmy.

"Get rid of the pointed ears guy."
  —NBC executive to Gene Roddenberry, 1966, on Star Trek's Mr. Spock.

When Paramount bought the Desilu production company in 1969, the studio reasoned it could make "Mission Impossible" a more profitable show, in part, by firing two of the show's most expensive stars, Martin Landau and Barbara Bain. The result was that what was once the #11 show in the nation dropped out of the top 25, never to return.

"Preempt Doris Day? Are you out of your mind?"
  —CBS president Bob Wood turning down the chance to broadcast "Monday Night Football" in 1970.

In 1973 NBC decided to make room in its warehouse by burning some worthless old negatives. At least 15 episodes of "You Bet Your Life" went into the fire before the show's producer John Guedel got wind of it and reclaimed the rest of the stock. As "The Best of Groucho," the show became a hit in syndication.

141

Bad Predictions

"Think about the future. Can you really visualize Barbara Walters at last having a national news program without a co-anchor man?"

> —advertising writer Jane Trahey,
> *Woman in the Year 2000*, 1974.

Hal Linden was so certain his new 1975 series "Barney Miller" would be canceled within a year that he didn't bother moving his family from New York to California, The program was not canceled until 1982.

"I'm fifty now, and I am sure I won't be doing the 'Tonight Show' in ten years. I doubt if I'll be doing it at fifty-five."

> —Johnny Carson, 1976. He retired from the
> "Tonight Show" at age 66.

"They all thought I'd be the first to go. I was one of the live-fast, die-young, leave-a-good-looking-corpse types, you know. But I guess they were wrong."

> —John Belushi in a 1978 segment of "Saturday
> Night Live" in which he played an elderly version
> of himself. He died of a drug overdose four years
> later.

"This woman will never drown."

> –comic Pat McCormick joking, on television, with
> actress Carol Wayne, who had a buxom figure.
> Wayne died January 11, 1985. She drowned.

"This is an adventure you and I will take together."

> —Geraldo Rivera, in a live 1986 broadcast in
> which Al Capone's "secret underground vault"
> was opened for the first time in 50 years to reveal... an empty bottle.

142

"A gaggle of talk hosts, from Joey Bishop to Alan Thicke, have emerged over the years to challenge [Johnny] Carson, only to slink away in failure. But [Pat] Sajak and [Arsenio] Hall have one potential advantage: they could simply outlast Carson."

> —Richard Zoglin, *Time*, 1989. This prediciton is half right. Although Arsenio Hall was still on the air, Carson's 1992 retirement did not turn out to be a boon to Hall's show. It was canceled due to falling ratings in 1994. The Pat Sajak Show, on the other hand, was canceled after a 14-month run.

"ABC is not the kind of network that will turn and run just because you're struggling in the ratings."

> —Producer Steven Bochco predicting a long life for his new show "Cop Rock" in 1990. The show, a musical police drama, cost an estimated $1.8 million per episode and failed to draw an audience. The network pulled it after three months.

"In the fifth season of 'Star Trek: The Next Generation,' viewers will see more of shipboard life in some episodes, which will, among other things, include gay crew members in day-to-day circumstances."

> —Executive producer Gene Roddenberry, 1991. This didn't happen.

"The plots of 'X-Files' can get pretty convoluted— even for the actors... [David] Duchovny doesn't know how his show will fare in its Friday-night, ABC-friendly time slot... We know— this show's a goner."

> -1993 Fall TV Preview, *Entertainment Weekly*. As of this writing, the program is still on the air in its 7th season.

"We never get sick of each other. That's how sick we are."

> —Rosanne Barr on her relationship with husband Tom Arnold, 1991. They divorced in 1995.

Bad Predictions

Movies

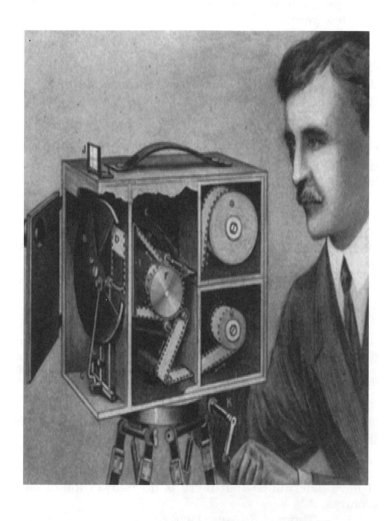

Bad Predictions

"Young man, you can be grateful that my invention is not for sale, for it would undoubtedly ruin you. It can be exploited for a certain time as a scientific curiosity, but apart from that it has no commercial value whatsoever."
　　　　—co-inventor of the Lumiere motion picture
　　　　camera, Auguste Lumiere, 1895.

"It is probable that the [cinema] fad will die out in the next few years."
　　　　—*The Independent*, March 17, 1910.

"The cinema is little more than a fad. It's a canned drama. What audiences really want to see is flesh and blood on the stage."
　　　　—Charlie Chaplin, 1916.

"Speaking movies are impossible. When a century has passed, all thought of so-called speaking movies will have been abandoned. It will never be possible to synchronize the voice with the picture."
　　　　—director D.W. Griffith, early 1920s.

"We do not want now and we shall never want the human voice with our films."
　　　　—director D. W. Griffith, *Saturday Evening Post*, 1924.

"Other inventions, such as the speaking film, bear within themselves certain weaknesses which may prevent them from attaining great popularity."
　　　　—E. E. Fournier d'Albe, *Quo Vadimus, Some Glimpses of the Future*, 1925.

"People will tire of talkers. Talking is no substitute for the good acting we had in silent pictures."
　　　　—Thomas Alva Edison, 1925

"I have determined that there is no market for talking pictures, "
　　　　—Thomas Edison, 1926.

"Americans require a restful quiet in the moving pic-

146

ture theater, and for them talking... on the picture screen destroys the illusion. Devices for projecting the film actor's speech can be prefaced, but the idea is not practical."
—Thomas Alva Edison, 1927.

"Who in blazes wants to hear actors talk?"
—Harry Warner, co-founder Warner Brothers Pictures in 1927.

"Novelty is always welcome, but talking pictures are just a fad."
—MGM producer Irving Thalberg, 1927.

"Moving pictures need sound as much as Beethoven symphonies need lyrics."
— Charlie Chaplin, 1928.

"Talking films are a very interesting invention, but I do not believe that they will remain long in fashion. First of all, perfect synchronization between sound and image is absolutely impossible, and secondly, cinema cannot and must not, become theater."
—Louis-Jean Lumiere, 1928.

"Canned drama, canned music, canned vaudeville. We think the public will tire of mechanical music and will want the real thing."
—Joseph N. Weber, president of the American Federation of Musicians, leader of a campaign to stem the advance of what they called "Robot Music" in film as opposed to having a live musician playing an organ in theaters, ca. 1931.

"Color and steroscopy will make the cinema into the greatest art in the world. Bad films will be impossible."
—John Betjeman, underestimating the ability of film makers in 1935.

"Get ready for the 'surround screen' and 'surround sound.'

Bad Predictions

The screen [in 1982] will be all about you— you will be in the picture, not in front of it. Movie theaters will be circular and simple."
—*Changing Times Magazine*, 1957.

"Cinemas will have disappeared [by 1984] because it requires less effort to view the same kind of programme on the television screen. But driven out by boredom and satiation the younger people will crowd into dives where they can expend their unused energies in dancing like dervishes to the jazz bands."
—Sir Herbert Read, *New Scientist*, 1964.

Specific Pictures

"Every woman is frightened of a mouse."
—MGM head Louis B. Mayer in 1926 rejecting the idea that a cartoon mouse would ever be popular.

"Anyone can moan and grunt. I will not be a babbling idiot for anybody. I need a part where I can act."
—Bela Lugosi turning down the role of the monster in the 1931 film "Frankenstein." The role made the formerly unknown Boris Karloff a household name.

"Forget bus pictures. People don't want 'em. MGM and Universal just made two bus operas and they both stink."
—Columbia Pictures' chief Harry Cohn in 1934 advising Frank Capra not to make a movie out of a story he'd read in *Cosmopolitan* magazine. Capra rejected the advice and made "It Happened One Night" anyway.

Myrna Loy turned down the role of Ellie Andrews in "It Happened One Night" because she was also aware of the recent films set in busses that had failed, and she didn't believe Capra's film could do any better.

"I've just finished the worst picture of the year."
>—Actress Claudette Colbert on "It Happened One Night," which went on to win five Oscars, including Best Picture and Best Actress.

"No Civil War picture ever made a nickel."
>— movie executive Irving Thalberg turning down "Gone With the Wind."

"'Gone With The Wind' is going to be the biggest flop in Hollywood history. I'm glad it'll be Clark Gable who's falling on his face and not Gary Cooper."
>—Gary Cooper on turning down the role of Rhett Butler, 1938.

"I offered Vivien Leigh the secondary role of Isabella in 'Wuthering Heights.' She turned it down. I was astounded. I told Vivien she was totally unknown in America and that she wouldn't get anything better than Isabella for her first Hollywood part."
>—Director William Wyler. Vivien Leigh decided to accept a part in "Gone with the Wind," instead. Her first Hollywood part was Scarlett O'Hara.

"It will be the biggest bust in town."
>—Moviemaker Jack Warner attempting to convince Olivia de Havilland not to take the role of Melanie Wilkes in "Gone with the Wind". She took it anyway and was nominated for a Best Supporting Actress Oscar for her performance.

"Don't be a damn fool, David. This picture is going to be one of the biggest white elephants of all time."
>— director Victor Fleming refusing David O. Selznick's offer of a percentage of the profits of "Gone with the Wind" instead of salary.

Walt Disney's first feature film was so expensive that Hollywood insiders dubbed it "Disney's Folly" and predicted it would be his last picture. The film: "Snow White and the Seven Dwarves."

Bad Predictions

"That the character Snow White is a failure in every way is undisputable. As a moving figure she is unreal, as a face and body she is absurd, and in terms of what she does she is ludicrous... Another Snow White will sound the Disney death-knell."
—V.F. Calverton, *Current History*, 1938.

"I feel strongly that 'The Maltese Falcon'... is not an important picture."
—Actor George Raft turning down the role of Sam Spade to appear in a movie called "Manpower." "The Maltese Falcon" was honored by the National Film Preservation Board. "Manpower" was not.

"This may fetch some susceptible ladies in the crowd, but I think it will be hard on everybody else."
—John McCarten, *New Yorker*, 1950, on "Father of the Bride," which became one of the top five box-office hits of 1950 and was nominated for Academy Awards for Best Picture, Screenplay and Actor.

In 1955 Michael Garrison and his partner Gregory Ratoff made a good prediction. After reading the novel *Casino Royale* by a then-obscure writer, Ian Fleming, the pair thought it and its main character James Bond would be a great movie. They bought the rights to the book and pitched it to 20ᵗʰ Century Fox. The studio, however, had less of a knack for prediction in this case. They passed on Bond. When Ratoff died, his widow, short of cash, sold her half of the film rights, and Garrison included his as part of the deal. Garrison, by the way, went on to produce the television series "Wild, Wild, West."

RKO Radio Pictures said it was a film of "magnificence" and "lasting importance." When "Underwater!," produced by Howard Hughes, was released in 1955, however, the entire crowd walked out of its premiere showing.

"Anyone with a nostalgic feeling for the De Mille badness of the past will be sorry that this film, which may be the last of its genre from the master, had to be such an utter catastrophe."
> —Robert Evett, *New Republic*, December 10, 1956 on "The Ten Commandments."

"How can so many critics have fallen for all this frenzied hokum?... I would guess that in a few decades the dances in 'West Side Story' will look as much like hilariously limited, dated period pieces as Busby Berkeley's 'Remember the Forgotten Man' number in Gold Diggers of 1933."
> —Pauline Kael, *Film Quarterly*, 1962.

"Sean Connery can't play the sophisticated James Bond. He looks like a bricklayer."
> —producers of "Dr. No," 1962. They wanted David Niven, Rex Harrison or Cary Grant for Bond. Author Ian Fleming's first choice was Roger Moore. "Dr. No," incidentally, was not the producers' first choice for the first Bond film, either. They wanted to make "Thunderball. Legal wrangles with its co-author led them to release "Dr. No" instead.

"[Dr. Zhivago is] the biggest disappointment of 1965."
> —Andrew Sarris, *Village Voice*, 1965.

"I was at Paramount all day yesterday, and they want me to direct this hunk of trash. I don't want to do it. I want to do art films."
> —Francis Ford Coppola to his father in 1970 about "The Godfather." His father talked him into it.

"Francis, as president of Paramount Pictures, I must tell you that under no circumstances will Marlon Brando appear in "The Godfather." And, as president, I no longer wish to waste the company's time even discussing it."
> —attributed to Paramount Pictures president Stanley Jaffe by Francis Ford Coppola.

151

Bad Predictions

"It's unreleasable! You boys let me down."

—Universal executive Ned Tanen to George Lucas and Francis Ford Coppola on "American Graffiti" in 1973. Despite the fact that "American Graffiti" was not only releasable, but also very popular and profitable, Universal turned down George Lucas' next project, "Star Wars."

"A supremely silly movie about nothing at all... For any one except the film buff, 'Carrie' is a waste of time."

—Vincent Canby, *New York Times*, December 5, 1976. "Carrie" earned Academy Award nominations for Best Actress and Best Supporting Actress and was successful enough to warrant the making of a sequel.

"I think 'The Swarm' is going to be the most terrifying movie ever made."

—producer Irwin Allen, on the 1978 bomb the *New York Times* called "the surprise comedy hit of the season."

"Up to a point, I'm willing to overlook egg on a guy's face, but really, there's such a thing as too much— especially when they're promoting this bloated, pseudo-epic as a low-budget Oscar-bound winner."

—*Washington Star*, December 21, 1976 on "Rocky," which did go on to win Oscars for Best Picture and Best Director.

"You can't use 'war' in the title," and "robots could turn off the mass majority of moviegoers."

—Initial market research for the 1976 film "Star Wars."

"'Annie Hall'... is a film so shapeless, sprawling, repetitious and aimless as to seem to beg for oblivion."

—John Simon, *New York*, May 2, 1977.

152

"In my humble opinion, the picture will be a colossal flop."
>—business reporter William Flanagan on
>"Annie Hall," 1977.

"I get really offended when people compare [Orca] with 'Jaws.' It's going to make that movie look like an anemic sprat alongside it. It's enormous in the true meaning of the word. Enormous and truly grand and majestic and beautiful."
>—Richard Harris, 1978. Critic Leonard Maltin, who did not star in the movie, described it as being "for undiscriminating action fans whose idea of entertainment is watching Bo [Derek] getting her leg bitten off."

"'Alien,' like 'Dawn of the Dead,' only scares you away from the movies."
>—Michael Sragow, *Los Angeles Herald Examiner*, 1979 on a film that would become one of the top five box-office hits of that year.

"'Apocalypse Now' stinks. After years of work and the expenditure of multiple millions of dollars, director Francis Ford Coppola has brought forth a very ugly, very minor work."
>—Scott Cain, *Atlanta Journal*,
>October 12, 1979.

"'Dustin and I are talking about another movie about the two characters we play in 'Ishtar.'"
>—Warren Beatty in *People Magazine* in 1987 while wrapping up production on the $50 million film that would become synonymous with film flops.

"We brought the [Batman] logo back to Warner Brothers and they said, 'You can't use that as a campaign. You can't have a movie logo without Nicholson, Keaton and Batman on it.'"
>—producer John Peters on a logo that became the hottest fashion item of 1989.

Bad Predictions

As James Cameron's epic "Titanic" was being made, its budget became bloated far beyond even the most extravagant original estimates. So the director went to studio president Bill Mechanic and said, "Look, I'm not happy this happened. A studio shouldn't be put into a situation where even in a success scenario, by everyone's standards, they don't make money. I feel responsible. I will not compromise the film, but I'll do what I can to make it easier for you to see a return on your investment by removing the only gross player— me. I'm reassigning my profit participation back to Fox." Mechanic turned down the offer because he said it didn't make any difference, since "Titanic" was not even going to break even, and profit sharing was, therefore, irrelevant.

"Director James Cameron's 'Titanic' is the latest of 17 [films about the ship], almost all of which have flopped. That may well be a foretaste of what is to come for the film."
—Victoria Harper, "The Curse of the Titanic," *Mail on Sunday*, November 23, 1997.

"The regretful verdict here is: Dead in the Water."
—*Time* movie critic Richard Corliss on "Titanic," December 8, 1997. "Titanic" became the first film to gross more than $1 billion worldwide and won 11 Academy Awards.

Movie Stars

"Try another profession. Any other."
—Head instructor of the John Murray Anderson Drama School to Lucille Ball, 1927.

"What can you do with a guy with ears like that?"
— movie producer Jack Warner on viewing Clark Gable's screen test for the movie "Little Caesar," 1930.

"Can't act. Slightly bald. Can dance a little."
> —1933 memo from MGM testing director regarding Fred Astaire. Astaire supposedly kept that memo over the fireplace in his Beverly Hills home. (Some sources doubt this story.)

"He's passe. Nobody cares about Mickey any more. There are whole batches of Mickeys we just can't give away. I think we should phase him out."
> —Roy Disney, 1937.

The lead role in "Casablanca" was originally offered to George Raft, but he didn't like the script and turned it down. Raft also declined the part of Sam Spade in "The Maltese Falcon" because he didn't want to work with a director as young as John Huston. He turned down the lead role in "High Sierra" because he thought it was bad luck to die on screen. All of those roles went to the same actor, Humphrey Bogart, who became a star by playing them.

"You'd better learn secretarial work or else get married."
> — Emmeline Snively, Director of the Blue Book Modelling Agency to an aspiring Marilyn Monroe, 1944.

"It is hard to work up enthusiasm for the Warners' new starlet, Doris Day."
> —Bosley Crowther, *New York Times*,
> June 26, 1948.

"She's too sexy."
> —Dore Schary, turning down Marilyn Monroe for a contract with MGM. Columbia Pictures then let Monroe's contract lapse in 1949 because producer Harry Cohn felt she lacked "star quality."

"Take it easy driving. The life you save may be mine."
> —public service announcement recorded by James Dean two weeks before he was killed speeding in his Porsche in 1955.

Bad Predictions

"We drew up a formula for a happy marriage and we're following it. Bet on us."
> —Janet Leigh on her marriage to Tony Curtis, May 3, 1953. They divorced in 1962.

"You're gonna make a little black and white film, no one's ever going to hear of it, you're gonna think you're a star and you're not gonna be a star."
> —Spencer Tracy telling actor Ernest Borgnine in 1954 not to take the lead in a small film by an unknown director. Borgnine did it anyway. He went on to beat out fellow nominee Spencer Tracy to win the 1955 Academy Award for Best Actor for his role in "Marty."

In 1959, a Universal Pictures executive dismissed Clint Eastwood and Burt Reynolds at the same meeting. Reynolds, the executive said, had "no talent." Eastwood was rejected for his looks: "You have a chip on your tooth, your Adam's apple sticks out too far, and you talk too slow."

Jean-Luc Godard's "directorial abilities seem to me to be rather flash-in-the-pan-ish."
> —*Films in Review*, March, 1961 on the multiple-award winning director whose career would go on to span four decaces.

"I am told Hollywood hopes to make [Warren Beatty] a star, but his face, at least in this picture, is on the weak side, and doesn't always photograph well."
> —*Films in Review* on Beatty's first film "Splendor in the Grass," November 1961.

"Reagan doesn't have the Presidential look."
> —A United Artists executive dismissing the suggestion that Ronald Reagan be offered the starring role in "The Best Man," 1964.

"I genuinely do not believe in divorce."
> —Elizabeth Taylor. She went on to marry and divorce 8 times.

156

"This marriage will last forever."
>—Elizabeth Taylor, 1964, on her marriage to fifth husband Richard Burton.

"A listless little chickadee from Laugh-In, who plays Matthau's mistress like an illustration for a bird seed commercial. Maybe those wide-eyed one-liners and pregnant pauses work on television, but if [Goldie] Hawn is to have any kind of future in movies, she needs to learn something about the rudimentary techniques necessary to sustain a comic scene without putting the audience to sleep."
>—Rex Reed, *Holiday*, November 1969.

"I have no intention of getting married."
>—Warren Beatty, *People Magazine*, April 14, 1975. He married actress Annette Bening in 1992.

"It remains to be seen what ["Saturday Night Fever"] will do to or for John Travolta. I have grave doubts about the romantic potential of a young actor whose most appealing expression is a kind of dumb vulnerability—Brian De Palma seemed to have the right idea when he cast Travolta as a stooge in 'Carrie.'"
>—Gary Arnold, *Washington Post*, December 16, 1977.

"This film doesn't need publicity. The people will go to see it because we're in it."
>—Sean Penn in 1986 on his film with then-wife Madonna, "Shanghai Surprise." The $15 million picture earned back only $2.3 million.

"NOW PLAYING: 'Perfect.' John Travolta's career— already in rickety shape after his 'Staying Alive' fiasco with author Sylvester Stallone—officially comes to an end with this fatuous celebration of health clubs as the new singles bars."
>—Paul Slansky, *The Clothes Have No Emperor*, 1989.

Bad Predictions

Robin Williams, in high school, was voted "Least likely to succeed."

"This is forever."
>—Elizabeth Taylor in 1991 to her marriage to Larry Fortensky. "Forever" was four years.

"It took a long time to come to the realization that I loathe acting. And, unless someone tempts me with a vast sum of money to secure my daughter's future, I'll never do it again."
>—actor Sean Penn, 1991. He has acted in more than a dozen films since, including "Dead Man Walking," "Carlito's Way" and "Thin Red Line."

Visual Arts

Visual Art, Cultural Institutions and Museums

Auguste Rodin was rejected three times for admission to the Ecole des Beaux-Arts in Paris.

"Rembrandt is not to be compared in the painting of character with our extraordinarily gifted English artist, Mr. Rippingille."
—19th Century art critic John Hunt.

In 1872, the Royal Academy received a painting from an artist named James MacNeil Whistler. The Academy deemed the painting, *Arrangement in Gray and Black, No. 1: The Artist's Mother*, "worthless." It was hidden away in the cellar until a powerful member took an interest in it and insisted it be put in the gallery. The other members of the Academy brought it up, but hung it in a dark corner. *Whistler's Mother*, as it is more commonly called, is now one of history's most famous works of art.

"I would like to know of what this Institution consists. I would like the gentleman from New York or the gentleman from Vermont to tell us how many of his constituents ever saw this Institution or ever will see it or ever want to see it? It is enough to make any man or woman sick to visit that Institution. No one can expect to get any benefit from it."
—Mr. Lewis Selye in the House of
   Representatives on the Smithsonian
   Institution, 1901.

"The next century will be yet more critical than this. Every one of the fine arts will be more generally and more subtly appreciated than now."
—T. Baron Russell, *A Hundred Years Hence*,
   1905.

"His prestige is rapidly waning, and the custodians of his fame—and his pictures— are fighting a losing battle to elevate him to a position among the immortals."
> —art critic Thomas Craven on Pablo Picasso,
> *Art Digest*, November 15, 1934.

When he was a struggling young artist, Walt Disney was told by a prospective employer to try another line of work. He said Disney didn't have any creative, original ideas.

Theater and Dance

"The American theater is on its last beloved legs... We are being mechanized out of the theater by the talkies and radio and by people who prefer convenience to beauty."
> —actress Jane Cowl, 1929.

"Talking pictures will [within 10 years] take the place of theater as we know it today."
> —Norman Bel Geddes, "Ten Years from Now,"
> *Ladies' Home Journal*, 1931.

"[Pygmalion] wouldn't be made any richer with music."
> –theatrical producer Robert Whitehead on George Bernard Shaw's modestly successful drama. Alan Jay Lerner and Frederick Loewe reluctantly agreed to write the music and the result was the hit musical *My Fair Lady*.

"Don't put a dime in it."
> —Robert Benchley to theatrical patron John Hay Whitney, who was considering investing in the play "Life With Father." Whitney rejected Benchley's advice. The play opened in 1939 and ran for seven and a half years.

Bad Predictions

Columbia Pictures and MGM were two of the biggest names among many potential investors who passed on the stage musical "Away We Go." The executives felt the play with the farm theme would not strike a chord with audiences. The authors rewrote the second act and the show opened on Broadway under the title "Oklahoma."

"No legs, no jokes, no chance."
> — Broadway producer Michael Todd on the musical "Oklahoma!" to columnist Walter Winchell after seeing the New Haven, Connecticut tryout, 1943.

"Who would want to see a play about an unhappy traveling salesman? Too depressing."
> — Broadway producer Cheryl Crawford passing up an offer from Elia Kazan to stage Arthur Miller's drama,"Death of a Salesman" in 1948.

"The Arts, in any historical meaning of the word, will have disappeared [by 1984]... Style, in any of the arts, will be regarded as an anachronism, like ornament in architecture. The stage may still exist as a training ground for actors, but no poets will write for it; plays will be produced by involving the actors in 'situations,' for which they must improvise 'solutions'."
> —Sir Herbert Read, *New Scientist*, 1964.

"It seems clear this is no smash hit, no blockbuster."
> — Review in *Variety* after the Detroit tryout opening of the musical "Fiddler on the Roof," July 28, 1964.

Music

Bad Predictions

"I am sorry that I must give you sad news but I cannot conceal the truth from you. 'La Traviata' was a failure. Let us not investigate the reasons. That is what happened. Farewell. Farewell."
> —Giusseppe Verdi to his publisher, 1853.

"Tchaikovsky's First Piano Concerto, like the first pancake, is a flop."
> —Nicolai Feopemplovich Soloviev,
> November 13, 1875.

"The overture will be very loud and noisy but I have written it without affection or enthusiasm, so it will probably have little artistic merit."
> —Peter Ilich Tchaikovsky on his 1812 Overture,
> 1882.

In 1912, Bernhard Samuels patented a device known as the Aerophor. The Aerophor consisted of a pair of bellows that supplied air to the corner of a player's mouth through a long tube. It was praised by a few top musicians and composers: "...a magnificent invention, not to say one of genius. Equipped with your apparatus, an orchestra becomes a living organ. I look forward even now to the pleasure of conducting such a long-breathed orchestra and hope that soon all orchestral wind-players will make music with your apparatus."
> —W. Mengelberg, September, 1911.

"My heartiest thanks to Herr Bernhard Samuels for his epoch-making invention. I hope that this will shortly be introduced into all orchestras. With it begins a new era in orchestral technique."
> —composer Richard Strauss, April 15, 1912
> Strauss and Mengelberg failed to recognize
> that getting air near the player's mouth is not
> really a problem— the challenge is getting that
> air into the lungs, something with which the
> Aerophor was little help. Strauss was,
> nevertheless, so certain it would catch on that
> he stipulated its use in two of his compositions.
> Modern conductors always ignore the reference.

164

"A passing fad."
>—*Musical America's* 1957 pronouncement on
>rock-and-roll.

"Rock N Roll seems to have run its course."
>—Bing Crosby, 1962.

"The lighter forms of opera will survive [into 1984] because they are entertaining but composers like Beethoven, Wagner, and Stravinsky will be forgotten."
>—Sir Herbert Read, *New Scientist*, 1964

"I think rock musicians are realizing they've reached a saturation point with their guitars."
>—jazz musician Moe Koffman, *Macleans*,
>December 1969.

"'Don't trust anyone over 30' was the motto of the '60's counter culture— but now Woodstock, the ultimate celebration of peace, love and rock-n-roll, is turning 30... 'Woodstock isn't just a concert— it's a rite of passage,' said Michael Lang, one of the producers of the original Woodstock Festival as well as the '94 event. 'Woodstock has become the 'Olympics' of live music— so that every five years we can step out of ourselves and celebrate diversity, great music and each other.'.. Daniel W. Flynn, who will serve as Director of Planning, [said], 'Security and safety are definitely our top priority.'"
>—press release announcing Woodstock '99, which ended in rioting, destruction of property and bonfires raging out of control. The fires were, ironically, started by candles provided by an organization called Pax, which intended the flames to be part of a vigil of peace.

Specific Musicians

Georg Friederich Handel was born in 1685, the son of a barber-surgeon. His father had high hopes for him, in the words of John Mainwaring: "From his very childhood, Handel had discovered such a strong propensity to Music that his father, who always intended him for the study of Civil Law, had reason to be alarmed... and strictly forbade him to meddle with any musical instrument."

Beethoven handled the violin awkwardly and preferred playing his own compositions instead of improving his technique. His teacher called him hopeless as a composer.

Giacomo Puccini's music teacher gave up on him because he had "no talent."

"I do not believe that a single one of Wagner's compositions will live after him."
—composer Moritz Hauptmann, 1871.

"You've got to call yourself 'Rock' or 'Jack' or something. Anything as long as it's not 'Elvis Presley.'"
—Canadian rock musician Ronnie Hawkins to the young Elvis Presley.

"You ain't goin' nowhere...son. You ought to go back to drivin' a truck."
—Grand Ole Opry manager Jim Denny to Elvis Presley after one performance, September 25, 1954.

"I tell you flatly, Elvis can't last."
—actor Jackie Gleason.

"The biggest no-talent I ever worked with."
—Decca Records Paul Cohen on dropping Buddy Holly in 1956.

John Lennon's aunt Mimi, who raised him, advised him, "The guitar is all very well, but you'll never make a living from it." Later, when the Beatle was a multi-millionaire, he had the words carved on a plaque and presented it to her.

When young Paul McCartney tried to join his local cathedral choir he was rejected on the basis that he was "tone deaf and couldn't sing."

"We don't like their sound, they sound too much like The Shadows, and guitar music is on the way out."
    —Decca Records rejecting the Beatles,
     1962.

"They [the Beatles] are a passing phase. All are symptoms of the uncertainty of the times and the confusion about us."
    —Billy Graham, 1963.

"We don't think they'll do anything in this market."
    —Capitol Records president Alan Livingston
     on The Beatles, 1964.

"They've got their own groups. What are we going to give them that they don't already have?"
    —Paul McCartney, 1964, before the band's
     first visit to the U.S.

New York Daily News critic Anthony Burton dismissed the Beatlemania in his February 11, 1964, column by saying that in another month, "America will have had its giggle and once more will be worrying about Castro and Kruschev."

"The Beatles? They're on the wane."
    —The Duke of Edinburgh, 1965.

Bad Predictions

"The Lennon-McCartney song writing partnership becomes more and more remarkable and unstoppable, its shades combining Paul's deep commitment to the suburbs and John's to a species of light anarchy. One suspects that it could flourish anywhere, even by post."

> —Phillip Norman, *Show: the Magazine of Films and the Arts*, January 1970 shortly before Paul McCartney announced the Beatles were splitting.

"No one in his right mind ever thought [Alice's Restaurant] would have gotten played on the radio. It was almost written in stone that you couldn't play anything over two and a half minutes."

> —musician Arlo Guthrie on the 20-minute song that continues to get radio airplay every Thanksgiving.

"We're going to make everybody forget the Beatles."

> —Barry Gibb of the Bee Gees on the band's 1976 movie "Sgt. Pepper's Lonely Heart's Club Band." Most music fans forgot about the film instead.

"Rod will stay with me forever."

> —Actress Britt Ekland, 1976 on rock-star husband Rod Stewart. They divorced a year later.

"They may be world famous, but four shrieking monkeys are not going to use a privileged family name without permission."

> —Frau Eva von Zeppelin on the band Led Zeppelin, which did not change its name.

"As I look out there tonight, I can't help but think that just about every company out there turned this song down. As a matter of fact, I think that about ten of you turned it down twice, so I must admit this tastes sweet."

> –Joe Brooks accepting a 1977 Grammy Award for Song of the Year for "You Light Up My Life."

"Don't worry. It's not loaded, see?"
  –last words of Terry Kath, lead singer of the
  rock group Chicago, 1978.

"The biggest prize of all is when you die. A really big one
when you die in public. That is not something we're
interested in doing."
  —John Lennon shortly before he was killed by
  an assassin in 1980.

"The worst advice I ever got was from someone who lived
locally who told us to give up because success didn't
happen to people like us."
  —Simon Le Bon, lead singer of Duran Duran,
  one of the most popular bands of the 1980s.

Literature

Bad Predictions

"His fame is gone out like a candle in a snuff and his memory will always stink."
—William Winstanley on John Milton, 1687.

"Shakespeare's name, you may depend on it, stands absurdly too high and will go down."
—Lord Byron, 1814.

"John Keats's friends, we understand, destined him to the career of medicine, and he was bound apprentice to a worthy apothecary in town... It is a better and wiser thing to be a starved apothecary than a starved poet, so back to the shop, Mr. John, back to plasters, pills and ointment boxes. But for heavens sake be a little more sparing of extenuatives and soporifics in your practice than you have been in your poetry."
—*Blackwood's Magazine*, 1818.

"We fear we shall seem to our children to have been pygmies, indeed, in intellect, since a man as [Samuel Taylor] Coleridge would appear great to us!"
—*London Weekly Review*, 1828.

"The school to which [Percy Bysshe Shelley] belonged, or rather which he established, can never become popular."
—*Philadelphia Monthly Magazine*, 1828.

"His versification is so destitute of sustained harmony, many of his thoughts are so strained, his sentiments so unamiable, his misanthropy so gloomy, his libertinism so shameless, his merriment such a grinning of a ghastly smile, that I have always believed his verses would soon rank with forgotten things."
—John Quincy Adams on Lord Byron, 1830.

"We do not think it would be at all suitable for the juvenile market in this country."
—British publisher rejecting *Moby Dick* by Herman Melville, 1851.

"We fancy that any real child might be more puzzled than enchanted by this stiff, overwrought story."
—*Children's Books* review of Lewis Caroll's *Alice in Wonderland*, 1865.

"I see no good reasons why the views given in this volume should shock the religious sensibilities of anyone."
—Charles Darwin, *The Origin Of Species*, 1869.

"It is becoming painfully evident that [Henry] James has written himself out as far as the international novel is concerned, and probably as far as any kind of novel-writing is concerned."
—William Morton Payne, *The Dial*, 1884, before James wrote *The Bostonians, The Turn of the Screw* and others.

"I'm sorry, Mr. Kipling, but you just don't know how to use the English language."
— Rejection letter from the *San Francisco Examiner* in 1889 to writer Rudyard Kipling.

"An eccentric, dreamy, half-educated recluse in an out-of-the-way New England village— or anywhere else— cannot with impunity set at defiance the laws of gravitation and grammar... Oblivion lingers in the immediate neighborhood."
—Thomas Bailey Aldrich on Emily Dickinson, *Atlantic Monthly*, 1892.

In 1899, The George M. Hill Company rejected L. Frank Baum's *The Emerald City*, which later evolved into *The Wonderful Wizard of Oz*, because children were happy with the fairy tales they already had and their parents wouldn't buy an American fairy tale. Another publisher said that if there were a need for such a book, someone would have produced something like it already.

Bad Predictions

"A hundred years from now it is very likely that [of all Mark Twain's works] The Jumping Frog alone will be remembered."
> —Harry Thurston Peck, *The Bookman*, 1901.

Beatrix Potter's *Peter Rabbit* was rejected by at least six publishers in 1900. Potter finally paid to publish what is now considered to be a children's classic.

"It would be useless to pretend that they can be very widely read."
> —*Manchester Guardian* on Joseph Conrad's
> *Youth* and *Heart of Darkness*, 1902.

"Only a minor writer of no large promise."
> –rejection of author H.G. Wells, 1903.

"It is not interesting enough for the general reader and not thorough enough for the scientific reader."
> –publisher rejecting H.G. Wells' *The Time Machine*.

Publisher Frederick Mac Millan rejected H.G. Wells' novel *Ann Veronica* in 1908 because the plot developed "on lines that would be exceedingly distasteful to the public which buys books published by our firm." The book was published in 1909 by another publisher and was a great success. It is still in print today.

"No, no, this kind of thing won't do... The good folks down below (I mean posterity) will have none of it."
> —James Russell Lowell on Walt Whitman's
> *Leaves of Grass*, quoted in *The Complete Works*,
> 1904.

Upton Sinclair's *The Jungle* was turned down by numerous publishers before it got into print in 1906. "It is fit only for the wastebasket," said one. "As to the possibilities of a large sale, I should think them not very good," said another.

"I've written a silly book, but I don't suppose any publisher will take it."
>—Dorothy L. Sayers, 1920 on *Whose Body?* which was published three years later. It became the first of a series of twelve highly successful mystery novels about the protagonist Lord Peter Wimsey.

"This is a book of the season only."
>—*New York Herald Tribune* on F. Scott Fitzgerald's *The Great Gatsby*, 1925.

"A little slack, a little soft, more than a little artificial. *The Great Gatsby* falls into the class of negligible novels."
>—*Springfield Republican*, 1925.

"For your own good do not publish this book"
>—Rejection letter to D. H. Lawrence in 1928 for the book, *Lady Chatterley's Lover*.

"We did find it of very great interest, but I regret to say that it does not appear to me possible as a publishing venture."
>—T.S. Eliot rejecting Eric Arthur Blair's *Down and Out in Paris and London* in 1930. Blair was so discouraged that he subsequently submitted the novel under a pseudonym because he was no longer "proud of it." He chose the pen name George Orwell. The book was a success and he was stuck with the pseudonym.

"Regret the American public is not interested in anything on China."
>—publisher rejecting Pearl Buck's *The Good Earth*. It was published in 1931. Considered a modern classic, the novel won Pearl Buck a Pulitzer Prize.

Bad Predictions

"I wouldn't touch this book with a barge-pole... The book is damned– and you wouldn't sell the book even on its title."

> —publisher rejecting Samuel Beckett's *Dream of Fair-To-Middling Women*, first published in 1932 and still in print.

"I think it is only a matter of time before you reach out into more substantial efforts that will be capable of making some real money as books."

> —publisher rejecting *The Postman Always Rings Twice* by James M. Cain. Cain later explained that he gave his 1934 novel that title because it was rejected dozens of times, and each time the postman brought a letter of rejection, he rang twice.

"There's no way to sell a book about an unknown Dutch painter."

> —Doubleday and Company rejecting Irving Stone's first book, *Lust for Life*. The book about Vincent Van Gogh was put out by another publisher and became a 1934 best-seller.

"The final blowup of what was once a remarkable, if minor, talent."

> —Clifton Fadiman on William Faulkner's *Absalom, Absalom*, 1936.

"Too different from other juveniles on the market to warrant its selling."

> —one of the 27 publishers to reject Dr. Seuss' first children's book *And To Think That I Saw it on Mulberry Street*. finally published in 1937 by Vanguard.

"I wish there were an audience for a book of this kind. But there isn't. It won't sell."

> —Little, Brown and Company rejecting Ayn Rand's *The Fountainhead* in 1940.

176

"It is impossible to sell animal stories in the U.S.A."
  —letter rejecting George Orwell's
  Animal Farm, 1945.

"A long, solemn, tedious Pacific voyage best suited, I would think, to some kind of drastic abridgement in a journal like *National Geographic*."
  —McGraw-Hill editor William Styron in 1947 rejecting *Kon-Tiki* by Thor Heyerdhal. The book, published by Rand McNally after being rejected by 20 publishers, went on to be a top-ten best-seller for two years and inspired an Oscar-winning documentary.

"The girl doesn't, it seems to me, have a special perception or feeling which would lift that book above the 'curiosity' level."
  –rejection letter for the book,
  The Diary of Anne Frank, published in 1952.

"A man would never get the notion of writing a book on the particular situation of the human male."
  —Simone de Beauvoir, author of the groundbreaking book *The Second Sex*, 1953.

"There will be no proof that I ever was a writer."
  —last words of author Franz Kafka, 1953.

"*1984* is a failure."
  —British literary critic Laurence Brander on George Orwell's classic, 1954.

"It will not sell, and it will do immeasurable harm to a growing reputation... I am most disturbed at the thought that the writer has asked that this be published. I can see no possible cause that could be served by its publication now. I recommend that it be buried under a stone for a thousand years."
  –publisher rejecting *Lolita* by Vladimir Nabokov. It was published elsewhere in 1955.

177

Bad Predictions

"Bill, please God, don't ask us to publish a book called *The Rise and Fall of the Third Reich*."

> —William L. Shirer's editor. Shirer took it to another publisher, Simon and Schuster, and it became one of the best selling books of all time.

"I feel rather hopeless about his having a future."

> —rejection of John Knowles' *A Separate Peace*. Published in 1959, the book is now considered a classic and is required reading in some school systems.

Author Giuseppe di Lampedusa sent a manuscript for *The Leopard*, the only book he'd ever written, to a publisher. The rejection letter seemed so reasonable to Lampedusa that he gave up writing and hid the manuscript. It was discovered and published posthumously in 1958 and became the third best-selling novel of 1960 in the United States.

"Does not have commercial value."

> — Simon and Schuster rejecting John Kennedy Toole's Novel *Confederacy of Dunces* in 1962. The young writer spent the next eight years accumulating rejection slips from publishers. Despondent, in 1969 Toole committed suicide. His mother continued to look for a publisher, enlisting the help of author Walker Percy. The novel became a worldwide best-seller and received the Pulitzer Prize in 1981. The title of the book was from Jonathan Swift, "When a true genius appears in the world, you may know him by this sign, that the dunces are all in confederacy against him."

"It ain't a kid's book and it ain't an adult one. I'm sorry, but I don't think you're going to find a publisher for it."

> —Simon and Schuster editor William Cole rejecting *The Giving Tree* by Shel Silverstein in 1963.

"Already in 1964, few people read books for pleasure; they 'use' them, or even 'view' them... Poetry, already an arcane activity, will have totally disappeared [by 1984]. Fiction, even now a dwindling form of entertainment, will fade out and the only writers will be script-writers for the television screen."
—Sir Herbert Read, *New Scientist*, 1964.

"I can foresee no commercial possibilities for such a book and consequently can offer no encouragement."
—editor at McGraw-Hill rejecting Laurence J. Peter's *The Peter Principle*, 1964. The book was rejected by 30 more publishers before being sold to William Morrow & Co. It sold out, it became an almost instant best-seller and remained on the best-seller list through 1970.

"I had fiddled with a hundred alternatives [for a title]. *Great White, The Shark, Leviathan Rising, The Jaws of Death*, a few Francoise Sagan rip-offs, like *A Silence in the Water*, and a few helpful suggestions from my father, to wit: *What's That Noshin' on My Laig?* At last, my editor and I agreed that we didn't like any of the suggested titles, and in fact, the only word we liked in any permutation was 'jaws.' I recall saying something to the effect of 'Screw it, then, let's call it *Jaws*,' and my editor saying something like 'Okay, what the hell...' My father didn't like it, my wife didn't like it, and I didn't much like it. But the bottom line was, who cares? Nobody reads first novels anyway."
—author Peter Benchley.

According to Danielle Steel, the first literary agent to read her first novel, *Going Home*, told her to go home and learn how to cook because her book would never sell.

Bad Predictions

"We are not interested in science fiction which deals with negative utopias. They do not sell."
> —rejection of Stephen King's first novel *Carrie*, early 1970s. King was so discouraged that he put the novel in a drawer and did not submit it to another publisher for almost 10 years.

"Jonathan Livingston Seagull will never make it as a paperback."
> —James Galton of the Popular Library turning down an opportunity to bid on the paperback rights to Richard Bach's book in 1972.

"And what about publishing and women's image in 2000? Well, let's be practical. Except in very special presentations, hardcover books will probably be gone forever. Perhaps paper will be so rare, so expensive, the publishers will have to find a new way to publish, or they will perish... Certainly, fewer books will come out."
> —advertising writer Jane Trahey, *Woman in the Year 2000*, 1974.

"Print and paper technology will appear as primitive as the pre-Caxtonian hand-copying of manuscripts seems to us. In sum, the 1980s will see the book as we know it, and as our ancestors created and cherished it, begin a slow but steady decline into oblivion."
> —computer scientist Christopher Evans, *The Micro Millennium*, 1979. There are now more than 1 million book titles in print, and in the United States alone about 65,000 new titles are produced a year.

"When I throw in the balance the book's unrelenting lack of commerciality, I am afraid I just have to pass."
> –publisher rejecting William Kennedy's *Ironweed*. Published in 1983, the novel won a Pulitzer Prize and was made into a movie starting Jack Nicholson and Meryl Streep.

"Never, never. You can't take a special relationship of trust and then do a kiss-and-tell book."
> —Michael Deaver, former aide to Ronald Reagan, in 1985 on whether he would write a White House memoir. In 1987 he published *Behind the Scenes: In which the author talks about Ronald and Nancy Reagan and himself.*

9/7

"The title is too long... Nobody cares what a bunch of old women have to say."
> —advice from colleagues to Sandra Haldeman Martz on her proposed book *When I am an Old Woman I Shall Wear Purple.* By 1994, Papier-Mache Publishers had sold more than one million copies of the book.

8/13

"Authors of self-help books will be required to provide proof that they have actually helped themselves."
> —Jane Wagner, *Ms. Magazine*, in a 1990 prediction for the year 2000.

6/27

"I thought [*The Crisis Years*] would take three years, since I was writing about a three-year period. Three years of history, three years of writing. I often say it was a good thing I wasn't writing about the Hundred Year's War."
> —Michael R. Beschloss in 1991.
> His book actually took six years to write.

Sports

Bad Predictions

"I make bold to say that I don't believe that in the future history of the world any such feat will be performed by anybody else."
> —Mayor of Dover to Matthew Webb
> after his English Channel swim, 1875.

"The baseball mania has run its course. It has no future as a professional endeavor."
> —*Cincinnati Gazette*, 1879

"The man who made the mile record is W.G. George.... His time was 4 minutes 12.75 seconds, and the probability is that this record will never be beaten."
> — Harry Andrews, 1903.

"The growing gentleness of mankind will abolish, as barbarous, games which take the form of modified assault, as football, boxing, wrestling, fencing and the like."
> —T. Baron Russell, *A Hundred Years Hence*, 1905.

"It seems safe enough to put it down that heavyweight prizefights have gone the way of the tournament and the duel... We have outgrown prizefights; that's all there is to it."
> —*Life*, July 21, 1910.

"Babe Ruth made a great mistake when he gave up pitching. Working once a week, he might have lasted a long time and become a great star."
> —Tris Speaker, manager of the Cleveland Indians on Babe Ruth's plans to change from a pitcher to an outfielder, spring 1921.

"Just a fad, a passing fancy."
> —Chicago Cubs owner Phil Wrigley on night baseball, 1935.

"You bought yourself a cripple."
—New York Giants manager Bill Terry in 1935 berating farm team director George Weiss, who had just signed a young rookie with an injured knee. His name was Joe DiMaggio.

"Kid, you're too small. You ought to go out and shine shoes."
—Brooklyn Dodgers manager Casey Stengel rejecting future Hall-of-Famer Phil Rizzuto, 1936.

"I don't believe this kid will ever hit half a singer midget's weight in a bathing suit."
—Boston sportswriter Bill Cunningham on Red Sox rookie Ted Williams, 1938.

"We don't believe Jackie Robinson, colored college star signed by the Dodgers for one of their farm teams, will ever play in the big leagues. We question Branch Rickey's pompous statements that he is another Abraham Lincoln and that he has a heart as big as a watermelon and he loves all mankind."
—Jimmy Powers, *New York Daily News*, 1945.

"Just so-so in center field."
—*New York Daily News* on Willie Mays, after his major league debut in 1951.

"That kid can't play baseball."
—Milwaukee Braves farm team manager Tommy Holmes on Hank Aaron in 1952.

"My roots are in Brooklyn, so why should I move?"
—Brooklyn Dodgers owner Walter O'Malley in the mid-1950s. The team moved to Los Angeles after the 1957 season.

Bad Predictions

"This team of ours is the worst I've ever seen in training."
> —Detroit Lions' coach Buddy Parker explaining why he was quitting before the 1957 season in which the Lions went on to win the NFL title.

"He's too skinny, too weak."
> — Bibb Falk, University of Texas baseball coach on why he didn't recruit the famed pitcher Nolan Ryan when he was at Alvin High School (Texas) in the early 1960s.

"In Britain the American N.A.T.O. bases have led to widening interests in basketball and baseball. The World Series (which is at present a U.S. monopoly) may more properly justify its name in 1984 through the competition of European communities and the Yankees or Dodgers."
> —Dr. H.M. Finniston, *New Scientist*, 1964.

At the end of the 1965 baseball season, Cincinnati Reds General Manager Bill DeWitt decided that Frank Robinson, at age 30, was too old to be valuable to the team. He traded the player for pitcher Milt Pappas of the Baltimore Orioles. In his first year with the Orioles, Frank Robinson went on to win the Triple Crown with a .316 batting average, 49 home runs and 122 Runs Batted In. Baltimore won the pennant that year, and Robinson was voted the league's Most Valuable Player— the first player ever to win that honor in both leagues. Milt Pappas, meanwhile, was a competent pitcher, but made no headlines. He won 30 and lost 29 of the games he pitched.

"He won't make it."
> —Chicago Cubs' scout Gordon Goldsberry on Hall of Fame pitcher Tom Seaver, 1966.

"The New York Jets would do well to trade Joe Namath."
> --*New York Times'* sportswriter William Wallace, 1968. Namath led the Jets to victory in the Super Bowl that year.

186

"Baseball is doomed."
    —Marshall McLuhan, 1969.

"He possesses minimal football knowledge. Lacks moti-
vation."
    —An expert appraising the future potential of
        football coach Vince Lombardi.

"Can't make a double-play, can't throw, can't hit left-
handed and can't run."
    — scouting report on Pete Rose by the
        Cincinatti Reds.

"We are confident that if the city acquires Yankee Stadium and completes its plans for modernization of the
stadium, the New York Giants will remain in New York
City."
    —Mayor John Lindsay, 1971. The Giants
        moved to New Jersey seven years later.

"Stanley Matthews lacks the big match temperament.
He will never hold down a regular first-team place in top
class soccer."
    —sports writer on Matthews' debut at the age of
        17. Considered by many to be one of the great-
        est players in the history of soccer, he was the
        first British soccer player to be knighted.

"We plan absentee ownership. I'll stick to building ships."
    —George Steinbrenner, quoted in *The New York*
        Times after purchasing the New York Yankees,
        1973.

"Baseball's sex barrier had fallen in 1983, when the
young girls who cut their teeth in Little League in the
1970s became good enough to break into the majors."
    —*Ms. Magazine* editor Letty Cottin Pogrebin,
        "Born Free: A Feminist Fable" in the 1974 book
        Woman in the Year 2000.

Bad Predictions

In 1974 the U.S. Forest Service published a study on "Future Leisure Environments." Thanks to the widespread use of artificial snow, it predicted, skiing would be a year-round sport by 1989.

"This time we're going to win the Super Bowl."
 —Minnesota Vikings quarterback Fran
  Tarkenton, 1976. They didn't.

"We expect within two or three years to have virtual parity with the NFL."
 —Donald Trump in 1983 on his team the New
  Jersey Generals and the U.S. Football League,
  which folded three years later.

"He'll never be any good."
 —Baltimore Colts' owner Robert Irsay on
  quarterback John Elway, 1983.

"The kid will never last more than two or three years."
 —Gino Marchetti, Baltimore Colts' defensive
  end on Fran Tarkenton.

Sports Illustrated in 1987 picked the Cleveland Indians to win the World Series and put them on their cover. They lost 100 games and finished last.

"Harding and her down-home All-American appeal and charm will knock the winter socks off many Americans. Add to this that she is a young woman and happily married and you have an excellent spokesperson for family-oriented products and services."
 —press release on skater Tonya Harding from
  Sports Marketing Group, October 1991.

188

7/6 "As long as I own the Cleveland Browns they will remain in Cleveland."

—owner Art Modell in 1993. Three years later he moved the team to Baltimore. Determined to keep the team in Cleveland, Browns fans demanded the team be returned to their city. The NFL worked with Cleveland City officials and provided for a new state-of-the-art stadium, and guaranteed the return of pro football to Cleveland by no later than 1999. Art Modell agreed to relinquish the "Browns" name to the new owner of the suspended fran chise.

"We've built a yellow brick road to the summit."

—advertisement for mountain climber Scott Fischer's organization before the 1996 climb to the top of Mt. Everest that resulted in eight deaths including his own.

Business

Less than a week after Lee Iacocca was named one of Korbel Champagne's Top Ten Romantic People of 1986, he filed for divorce from his wife, Peggy.

Products, New Businesses and Investments

"Drill for oil? You mean drill into the ground to try and find oil? You're crazy."
— workers whom Edwin L. Drake tried to enlist in his project to drill for oil in 1859.

In 1876, author Mark Twain turned down an opportunity to invest $5,000 in Alexander Graham Bell's new telephone company. Instead, he put $25,000 into a company that made a new typesetting machine. The machine, as it turned out, made typesetting more complicated. Twain was forced to declare bankruptcy when the company went out of business in 1894. Bell's invention, on the other hand, was doing quite well, indeed.

In 1886, prospector Sors Hariezon sold his gold claim in South Africa for $20. The mines on and near his former claim have since yielded about 70 percent of the world's gold.

Herbert Henry Dow earned himself the nickname "Crazy Dow" because of his plan to extract bromides from the prehistoric saltwater sea buried beneath Michigan's soil. Although the Midland Chemical Company initially agreed to invest, they balked at Dow's idea to mass produce the byproduct of his chlorine and bromide removing process— bleach. After they pulled the plug on the improbable scheme Dow moved to Ohio. There he perfected his bleach and bromide production technique and created his own company— the Dow Chemical Company. In 1900 he returned to Michigan and bought out Midland Chemical.

"Who ever heard of a green giant?"
— Minnesota Valley Canning Company Vice
President Bill Dietrich, 1929.

"I had the idea of a new kind of pen that used a ball
instead of a nib. But I decided it wouldn't work, so I
dropped the project."
—Chester Carlson (1906-1968), inventor
of the Xerox copier.

George Parker never liked the game Monopoly. When
Charles B. Darrow brought his game to the manufac-
turer, Parker turned it down, saying no one would buy a
game that took more than 45 minutes to play. Darrow
released the game on his own and sold so many copies
that Parker was forced to reconsider. Despite its popularity, George Parker was sure it was a fad. In December 1936 he sent out the following memo: "Cease absolutely to make any more boards or utensil boxes. We
will stop making Monopoly against the possibility of a
very early slump." The fad did not end, and Parker was
again forced to reconsider.

Adam Smith, author of *The Money Game* and *Super
Money*, reported that he was talked out of buying Tampax
stock at $5 a share. "I feel dumb every time I think
about it," he said with 20/20 hindsight when the
tampon's stock was selling at $120.

"Let them eat burgers, like everyone else!"
—Ray Kroc's response to a suggestion by a Cincinnati McDonald's manager that the company
add a fish sandwich to the menu so Catholics
could eat there on Friday.

"Now look at 1975. You will ride into a cylindrical building on a covered moving sidewalk. An attendant will
give you a special marker bearing a code number. You
step onto a continuous moving elevator, ride to the top
of the building, step onto another moving sidewalk. As
you ride past shelves of groceries, you spot what you
want, step off the sidewalk, stamp it with your marker,

and deposit it in a receiving station. The moving sidewalk takes you down a spiral ramp of the supermarket past every item on display, until you finally reach an automated checkout counter. Every item you selected is ready on the counter before you."

> —Arnold B. Barach and the *Kiplinger* Washington Editors, *1975: and the Changes to Come*, 1962.

"The more dramatic changes in products [in the next 20 years] will include such innovations as plastic houses, ultrasonic dishwashers, disposable clothing for factory workers and home handymen, electronic highways, and automatic trains."

> —Harvard professor George P. Baker, *New Scientist*, 1964.

In 1968 the Crocker Bank in California decided to target its advertisements to attract members of the huge baby boom generation who were then in their teens and early 20s. The ad executive they hired decided to play on the theme of just starting out in life and hired Paul Williams to pen a theme song. The song, "We've Only Just Begun" was not only used for the commercial, it was also sold to the Carpenters and became a hit for them. The bank discovered, however, that attracting young customers had not been such a great idea. When young people without established credit or collateral flocked to Crocker Bank seeking loans, they ended the campaign.

In 1974 the U.S. Forest Service published a study on "Future Leisure Environments." By 1995, it said, all commercial products in the U.S. would be packaged in non-polluting containers.

"The most significant soft drink development in the company's history...The surest move ever made"

> —Coca-Cola chairman Roberto Goizueta, 1985, on New Coke, which was phased out after three months of poor sales and customer complaints.

194

"He gave me some brilliant financial advice, I must say. Only my opinion, of course— but I think ten percent of Jeans West would be worth a few bob by now, don't you? I was offered that deal for only $10,000 when they were just starting up, but the Inspector didn't like the sound of it. 'Jeans? No way— they'll never sell,' he said. Same again with Fuji Film and Mattel Toys."

> —former Monkee Davy Jones on his financial advisor in the 1960s from his 1987 book *They Made A Monkee Out of Me.*

"The concept is interesting and well-formed, but in order to earn better than a 'C', the idea must be feasible."

> — A Yale University management professor in response to student Fred Smith's paper proposing reliable overnight delivery service. Smith went on to found Federal Express.

"A cookie store is a bad idea. Besides, the market research reports say America likes crispy cookies, not soft and chewy cookies like you make."

> —Response to Debbi Fields' idea of starting Mrs. Fields' Cookies.

Office Life

A June 30, 1975, article in *Business Week* magazine touted "the office of the future," saying word-processing equipment would allow workers to work on and transfer files electronically. "For them," it said, "it will be the start of the paperless office."

"I don't know how much hard copy I'll want in this world."

> — George E. Pake, head of Xerox Corp.'s Research Center in Palo Alto, California, in 1975, predicting that the use of printed paper would decline as offices became digital.

Bad Predictions

"By the turn of this century, we will live in a paperless society."
> —Roger Smith, Chairman of
> General Motors, 1986.

Around 1980, Reliance Insurance launched an office-automation project with the slogan "Paper Free in 1983." Although they spent money to print up coffee cups, posters and stationery with the slogan, the company has more paper in its office than ever before. "It was not a realistic goal in 1983," senior vice president Ronald Sammons told *Time Magazine* in 1991, "and it isn't a realistic goal in 1993. Maybe in the year 2003."

The Average Work Week and Length of Employment

"Daily toil [in the next century] will be shortened to four or five hours."
> —U.S. Senator Willizm Alfred Peffer of Kansas to
> the American Press Association, 1893.

"Three hours will constitute a long day's work by the end of the next century. And this work will liberally furnish infinitely more of the benefits of civilization and the comforts of life than 16 hours' slavish toil will to-day."
> —reformer Mary E. Lease, 1893.

"They [the people of the next century] will have more leisure to think. The present rate of headlong material activity cannot be kept up for another 100 years."
> —author Andrew Carpenter Wheeler, 1893.

"There will be work for all [by 1950]."
> —a National Education Association spokesperson in *The Literary Digest*, January 10, 1931.

196

"It would be a rash prophet who denies the possibility that this generation may live to see a two-hour day"
—Arthur Pack, *The Challenge of Leisure*, 1932.

"By 1960 work will be limited to three hours a day."
—John Langdon-Davies, *A Short History of the Future*, 1936.

"Men will [by 1984] be working shorter and shorter hours in their paid employment. It follows that the housewife will also expect to be able to have more leisure in her life without lowering her standard of living. It also follows that human domestic servants will have completely ceased to exist."
—Professor M. W. Thring, *New Scientist*, 1964.

"The highly productive employee of 2000 will work a week that his 1966 counterpart would envy... It will be only 31 hours long, on the average, barely three-quarters the length of today's average workweek."
—Alfred L. Malabre, Jr., *Wall Street Journal*, 1966.

"By the year 2000, people will work no more than four days a week and less than eight hours a day. With legal holidays and long vacations, this could result in an annual working period of 147 days and 218 days off."
—*New York Times*, 1967.

"By A.D. 2000 one can retire with a comfortable income at the age of 50; and retirement will be compulsory at 60, except for those with skills in scant supply."
—R.G. Ruste, *American Heritage*, 1967.

"Within the coming 30 years, the report assumes, technology will provide far more leisure and everyone, whether he works or not, will receive a guaranteed annual income."
--*The Honolulu Advertiser*, July 31, 1970, reporting on the Hawaiian Education Task Force's report on the Year 2000.

197

Bad Predictions

"With the galloping pace of automation even now in the 1960s and 1970s and the rapidly narrowing gap between automation and cybernation (not to mention the state of affairs following the end of the Vietnam War) it would seem that the burden of 30 hours of work in the 1990s would unnecessarily press down the autonomy, esteem and freedom of the population."
—Merrill Jacks n, *Motive Magazine*, 1971.

"By 1984, we should see a much more fluid labor market, where... part-time workers have the same rights as full-time workers."
—Richard N. Farmer, *The Real World of 1984*, 1973.

According to a 1975 issue of *Futuremics*, in 2000, the average retirement age for American workers would be 47.

"By 1990, for example, most people will be retiring at the age of 40 or thereabouts."
—computer scientist Dr. Christopher Evans, "Computers and Artificial Intelligence" in *Science Fact*, 1978.

"There will be 32-hour work weeks by 1990 and 25-hour flexible work weeks by 2000."
—Marvin Cetron and Thomas O'Toole, *Encounters with the Future*, 1982.

It's The Economy, Stupid

"One ton of aluminum, if it could be produced, would supply the world's demand for a full year."
—Report of a famous English engineering firm when asked for its opinion by a bank in 1889.

"There will be no very rich or very poor [by 1993]."
—labor leader T.V. Powderly, 1893.

"All forests in the United States will be gone (in the 1990s). Lumber will be so scarce that stone, iron, brick, slag, etc. will be largely used in the construction of houses. As a result, fires will be almost unheard of, and insurance companies will go out of business."
—author John Habberton, 1893.

"By the end of the next century, great corporations and business interests will be conducted harmoniously— on the principle of the employees and workers sharing the profits."
—journalist Junius Henri Browne, 1893.

"A social revolution is certain to be accomplished within less than 50 years, and that will end the accumulation of wealth in the hands of the few."
—minister and lecturer Thomas Dixon, Jr., 1893.

"Capitalism is dying, and its extremities are already decomposing. The blotches upon the surface show that the blood no longer circulates. The time is near when the cadaver will have to be removed and the atmosphere purified."
—labor organizer and socialist, Eugene V. Debs, 1904.

"A hand from Washington will be stretched out and placed upon every man's business; the eye of the federal inspector will be in every man's counting house...The law will of necessity have inquisitorial features, it will provide penalties, it will create complicated machinery. Under it men will be hauled into courts distant from their homes. Heavy fines imposed by distant and unfamiliar tribunals will constantly menace the tax payer. An army of federal inspectors, spies, and detectives will descend upon the state."
— House Speaker Richard E. Byrd in 1910 on what would happen if a federal income tax became law.

Bad Predictions

A cartoon in 1913 entitled "The Future of the Ticker" showed a stock ticker in a museum and the 1925 museum attendant saying: "These instruments, known as stock tickers, were in use in Wall Street up to the year 1914. They were abandoned when the public got out of the market, and they are now very rare."

"We may look with confidence to the progress of business in 1929."
　　　—IBM founder Thomas Watson, 1928.

"A chicken in every pot and two cars in every garage."
　　　—Republican campaign slogan of 1928. The reporter who coined the phrase was driven out of work by the depression two years later and by 1933 was forced to beg on the streets to keep his wife and children from starving.

"We in America today are nearer to the final triumph over poverty than ever before in the history of any land. The poorhouse is vanishing among us. We have not yet reached the goal but, given a chance to go forward with the policies of the last eight years, we shall soon with the help of God be in sight of the day when poverty will be banished from this nation."
　　　—President Herbert Hoover, August 11, 1928.

"Hoover and Happiness or [Alfred E.] Smith and Soup Houses- Which Shall it Be?"
　　　—Republican campaign slogan, 1928.

"There may be a recession in stock prices, but not anything in the nature of a crash."
　　　— economist Irving Fisher, 6 weeks before the October 1929 stock market crash that started the Great Depression. On October 17, 1929, he added, "Stocks have reached what looks like a permanently high plateau."

"1930 will be a splendid employment year."
> —U.S. Department of Labor, *New Year's Forecast* in 1929, just before the market crash October 29.

"This crash is not going to have much effect on business."
> —Arthur Reynolds, Chairman of Continental Illinois Bank of Chicago, October 24, 1929.

"In most of the cities and towns of this country, this Wall Street panic will have no effect."
> —Paul Block, editorial November 15, 1929.

During the 1930s, Bernard E. Smith made a fortune in the stock market by following the rule of thumb that the market would decline every time Hoover issued an optomistic statement about the economy.

"This nation has entered an era of vast industrial expansion."
> —Samuel P. Arnot, president of the Chicago Board of Free Trade, January 1, 1930.

"With the underlying conditions sound, we believe that the recession in general business will be checked shortly and that improvement will set in during the spring months."
> —Harvard Economic Society's *Weekly Letter*, January 18, 1930. The newsletter folded in 1931 due to the financial restrictions of the Great Depression.

"In thirty years the United States will see the end of dire poverty, distress, and unnecessary suffering. Proper housing will solve our pproblems— proper housing for the families of the poor."
> —journalist August Heckscher, *New York Herald Tribune*, August 27, 1930.

201

Bad Predictions

"Branch banking... will mean, I suggest in all humility, the beginning of the end of the capitalist system."
> —John T. Flynn, "The Dangers of Branch Banking," *The Forum*, April 1933.

"We must expect another world-wide depression when the next war is over."
> —Malcolm Logan, *What Will Happen and What to Do When War Comes*, 1939.

"This [economic] collapse may probably come around in 1953, not later than 1956. It may be very servere with much unemployment, accompanied by foreclosures on hundreds of thousands of homes, stores and factories. Upon these the governments is now lending money. This depression may bring a labor government into power if such has not already seized control. National planning will be attempted and many socialistic experiments will be tried."
> —economist Roger W. Babson, *Looking Ahead Fifty Years*, 1950.

"The American habit of letting customers collect their own groceries from the shelves of the store is said to lead to increased sales, so temptingly are the tins displayed. It is likely to spread to other countries and other goods. There are limits of course. Some people enjoy or need personal contacts in shopping. I cannot see it applying to hats for example. Men would get discouraged, ladies would miss their fun."
> —Nobel Laureate Sir George Thomson, *The Foreseeable Future*, 1955.

"The Japanese don't make anything the people in the U.S. would want."
> — Secretary of State John Foster Dulles, 1954, on why we ought to give Japan most favored trade terms.

"In all likelihood, world inflation is over."
> —Managing Director of the International Monetary Fund, 1959.

"By 2000, the machines will be producing so much that everyone in the U.S. will, in effect, be independently wealthy. With government benefits, even non-working families will have, by one estimate, an annual income of $30,000-$40,000 (in 1966 dollars). How to use leisure meaningfully will be a major problem."
—*Time*, 1966.

"In reaching a saturation point in the demand for possessions, we are already facing unemployment. This could rise to 50 percent of the population by the year 2000. Fifty percent of all people could then feel degraded, discontented and anxious— and be, therefore, easily roused to find a solution in war."
—M.W. Thring, *Man Machines and Tomorrow*, 1973.

A 1973 study "Florida 10 Million" by the Florida Division of State Planning predicted that by 1982 the pay for such work as garbage collection, domestic service and dishwashing would be equivalent to that of white-collar employment.

"By 1980 losses on credit cards will overwhelm the industry and they will become extinct."
— economist Ray Zablocki, Stanford Research Institute in *Forbes* magazine, 1977.

"The New York Stock Exchange will move to New Jersey, but enough corporations will stay behind to ensure the city's viability... By 1995, the city will be diminished in size and influence..."
—Marvin Cetron and Thomas O'Toole, *Encounters with the Future*, 1982.

"America will enter an age of financial disaster [in 1995] that will dwarf the Great Depression and hail the end of the United States as we know it."
—Harry Figgie and Gerald Swanson, *Bankruptcy 1995: The Coming Collapse of America and How to Stop It*, 1992.

Bad Predictions

"Hundreds of companies will go bankrupt [in the 1990s]. Real estate markets, already down by 30% in some areas, will go into free fall. Unemployment will reach 15%, putting many middle-class families out on the streets. Retirees will find their investments and pensions turning to dust."
> —futurist Barry Minkin, *Econoquake*, 1993.

"We must issue a strong warning about mutual funds. By the end of 1995, mutual funds will be the most despised investments."
> —talk show hosts Ken and Daria Dolan,
> February, 1995.

"The newly elected Congress has not yet convened, but it is already time for the Republicans to think seriously about how they are going to handle the recession of 1996."
> —economist John M. Mueller, December 1994.
> They apparently handled the recession by not having one.

"The October 1999 crash could see prices smash through all the controls currently in place to prevent a catastrophic onetime loss. The Dow Jones Industrial Average could lose a total of 2,000 or 3,000 points sometime during this month alone and perhaps drop 5,000 or 6,000 points during the entire 1999-2001 bear market."
> —Russ Ray, professor of finance at the University of Louisville, *The Futurist*, August 1, 1998.

Business

U.S. History
And Politics

History

If the American colonists ever broke away from England, said British economist Josiah Tucker in 1766, they would "heartily wish and petition to be again united to the mother country."

"Many thinking people believe America has seen its best days."
> — Revolutionary patriot James Allen in his diary for July 26, 1775.

"Suppose the colonies do abound in men, what does that signify? They are raw undisciplined cowardly men... Believe me, my Lords, the very sound of a cannon would carry them off... as fast as their feet could carry them."
> –John Montagu, Lord Sandwich on the American rebellion, 1775.

"We cannot in this country conceive that there are men in England so infatuated as seriously to suspect the Congress, or people here, of a wish to erect ourselves into an independent state. If such an idea really obtains among those at the helm of affairs, one hour's residence in America would eradicate it. I never met one individual so inclined."
> —John Adams, 1775.

"This will be the commencement of the decline of my reputation."
> —George Washington on being elected as Commander-in-Chief of the Continental Army, 1775.

"The second day of July 1776 will be the most memorable Epocha in the History of America. I am apt to believe that it will be celebrated by succeeding generations as a great anniversary festival."
> —John Adams, July 2, 1776. It was on this day that the Continental Congress voted to separate from England. The Declaration of Independence was posted two days later.

"Nothing of importance happened today."
     —July 4, 1776, diary entry of King George III.

"If the Congress had in America twice the force both by
sea and by land which they have at present, there would
be little chance even then of their succeeding."
     —Henry Bate, Editor of the *London
     Morning Post*, 1776.

"The power of the rebellion is pretty well broken, and
thus 'tis probable the colonies may make some further
efforts, those efforts will only be feeble and ineffectual."
     —Speaker of the Pennsylvania Assembly Joseph
     Galloway in a letter to British Admiral Richard
     Howe, January 21, 1777.

"The merit of this gentleman is certainly great, and I
heartily wish that fortune may distinguish him as one
of her favorites. I am convinced that he will do everything that his prudence and valor shall suggest to add
success to our arms."
     —George Washington on Benedict Arnold.

"As to the Louisiana, this new, immense unbounded
world, if it should ever be incorporated into this Union,
which I have no idea can be done but by altering the
Constitution, I believe it will be the greatest curse that
could at present befall us; it may be productive of innumerable evils, and especially of one that I fear even to
look upon. Gentlemen on all sides, with very few exceptions, agree that the settlement of this country will be
highly injurious and dangerous to the Unites States...
Louisiana must and will become settled if we hold it,
and with the very population that would otherwise occupy part of our present territory. Thus our citizens
will be removed to the immense distance of two or three
thousand miles from the capital of the Union, where they
will scarcely ever feel the rays of the General Government; their affections will become alienated; they will
gradually begin to view us as strangers...When I con-

template the evils that may arise to these states, from this intended incorporation of Louisiana into the Union, I would rather see it given to France, to Spain or to any other nation of the earth, upon the mere condition that no citizen of the United States should ever settle within its limits."
—Senator Samuel White, 1803.

"What do we want with this vast, useless area? This region of savages and wild beasts, of deserts, of shifting sands and whirlwinds of dust, of cactus and prairie dogs? To what use could we ever hope to put these great deserts, or those endless mountain ranges, impenetrable and covered to their very base with eternal snow? What can we ever hope to do with the Western coast?"
—Daniel Webster, speaking against a bill that would establish a mail route from Missouri to the West Coast, 1829.

"I have never heard of anything, and I cannot conceive of anything more ridiculous, more absurd, and more affrontive to all sober judgement than the cry that we are profiting by the acquisition of New Mexico and California. I hold that they are not worth a dollar."
—Daniel Webster, 1848.

"[The South] has too much common sense and good temper to break up [the Union]."
—Abraham Lincoln, Presidential campaign of 1860.

"The Grand Canyon is, of course, altogether valueless. It can be approached only from the south, and after entering it there is nothing to do but leave. Ours has been the first, and will doubtless be the last, to visit this profitless locality. It seems intended by nature that the Colorado River, along the greater portion of its lonely and majestic way, shall be forever unvisited and undisturbed."
— Lieutenant Joseph C. Ives, U.S. Corps of Engineers report to Congress on the Colorado River, 1861.

"The world will little note nor long remember what we say here,"
>—Abraham Lincoln in the Gettysburg Address,
>   November 19, 1863.

"The cheek of every American must tingle with shame as he reads the silly, flat, and dish-watery utterances of the man who has to be pointed out to intelligent foreigners as President of the United States."
>—*Chicago Times* reviewing the Gettysburg Address, 1863. (Do you know who Everett M. Dirksen was? He was the man who delivered the *other* speech at Gettysburg. Everett's speech was detailed, long... and forgotten.)

"From now until God's judgment day, the minds of men will not cease to thrill at the killing of Abraham Lincoln."
>—The Houston *Tri-Weekly Telegraph*,
>   championing John Wilkes Booth in 1865.

"Emboldened by his success in this Russian purchase [Alaska], report has it that, having exhausted regions of perpetual snow and ice, the Secretary of State has turned his attention to the tropics and has negotiated another treaty proposing to pay a still larger sum, also in gold, to purchase if possible a more worthless possession than Russian America.... If it should ever come to the point when we are asked to make an appropriation to pay for it I will attempt to demonstrate the utter worthlessness of an acquisition made to meet the pretended wants of our navy in a region where tornadoes and earthquakes are the constant fear of the inhabitants, and where the yellow fever prevails all the year around."
>—Representative Cadwalader C. Washburn,
>   on the acquisition of the Virgin Islands, 1867.

"Alaska, with the Aleutian islands, is an inhospitable, wretched, and God-forsaken region, worth nothing, but a positive injury and incumbrance as a colony of the United States... No country on this earth has yet been found of the least possible worth or importance unless

211

Bad Predictions

it was capable of profitable agricultural improvement.
Alaska is not, nor are the Aleutian Islands... That it will
never be populated by an enterprising people is equally
certain... with a population of seventy-five thousand,
about ten thousand of whom are Siberian malefactors,
half-breeds, Kodiaks, Aleoots and a very few Russians,
not one of whom can speak our language, who by the
terms of this treaty are made citizens of the United States,
and the balance composed entirely of Indians."
—Representative Orange Ferriss, 1868.

"A civilized population will never be attracted to that
country (Alaska). There can be expected speculators,
but no permanent settlers; there can be expected no
civilized population, no permanent industry, but rather
spiliators of the natives, and depredatory working out of
the riches as well on the surface as in the womb of the
earth. Such system can devastate, but not organize the
country."
—Extract from Memorandum Descriptive of the
Russian Imperial System of Russian America as
quoted by Representative Orange Ferriss in the
Congressional Globe, 1868.

"A hundred years hence... my eye detects on the dim
horizon an American republic which shall embrace not
only the present United States and Alaska, but all the
remainder of the North American continent now under
British, Mexican or minor domination.... It will be a government of perhaps 60 states of the Union."
—George Westinghouse, 1893.

"Nicaragua and Mexico will be the next two states admitted to the Union."
—*Ladies' Home Journal*, 1900

"I don't see much future for the Americans. Everything
about the behavior of American society reveals that it's
half judaized and the other half negrified. How can one
expect a state like that to hold together."
—Adolf Hitler.

"There will be no cars, radios, washing machines or re-frigerators after [World War II]... The post-war world will be so poor that women will have to return to their grand-mother's spinning wheel and men will have to build their own cottages."

—Dr. Hans Elias, *New York Herald Tribune*, 1942.

"The war will abolish mass unemployment in America... After the war no American will be allowed to receive more than $25,000 a year."

—Quincy Howe, "Twelve Things the War Will Do to America," *Harper's Magazine*, November, 1942.

"Few predictions seem more certain that this: Russia is going to surpass us in mathematics and the social sci-ences... In short, unless we depart utterly from our present behavior, it is reasonable to expect that by no later than 1975 the United States will be a member of the Union of Soviet Socialist Republics."

—physicist George R. Price, *Life*, 1957.

"As future historians look back on our times [the 1960s], what will they conclude to have been the most signifi-cant event of the present decade in terms of its impact on the future? The riots in the cities? The Vietnam War? The Great Society programs? The hippie move-ment? Student protest? Technological and scientific advances? Man to the moon? None of these, I would make bold to guess."

—Willis Harman, "The New Copernican Revolu-tion," *Stanford Today*, 1969. The author sug-gested the exploration of "transpersonal experi-ence" as presented at the April, 1969, Council Grove conference on "voluntary control of inner states" would stand out as the most important legacy of the 60s.

Presidents and Politics

"A shilly shally thing of milk and water, which could not last... A weak and worthless fabric."
> — Alexander Hamilton on the newly-finished U.S. Constitution, 1787.

"You see that an elective government will not do."
> —John Adams, 1792.

"Can serious and reflecting men look about them and doubt that if Jefferson is elected... that those morals which protect our lives from the knife of the assassin— which guard the chastity of our wives and daughters from seduction and violence— defend our property from plunder and devastation, and shield our religion from contempt and profanation, will not be trampled upon and exploded?"
> —A Short Address to the Voters of Delaware, signed "A Christian Federalist," Sept 21, 1800.

The Connecticut Courant warned in 1800 that if Jefferson were elected: "Murder, robbery, rape, adultery, and incest will be openly taught and practiced, the air will be rent with the cries of the distressed, the soil will be soaked with blood, and the nation black with crimes." The paper added several days later: "Look at your houses, your parents, your wives and your children. Are you prepared to see your dwellings in flames, hoary hairs bathed in blood, female chastity violated, or children writhing on the pike and the halberd?...GREAT GOD OF COMPASSION AND JUSTICE, SHIELD MY COUNTRY FROM DESTRUCTION."

"The idea that I should become President seems to me too visionary to require a serious answer. It has never entered my head, nor is it likely to enter the head of any other person."
> —Zachary Taylor, 1847, two years before becoming the 12th President of the United States.

214

"Your constitution is all sail and no anchor. As I said before, when a society has entered on this downward progress, either civilization or liberty must perish. Either some Caesar or Napoleon will seize the reins of government with a strong hand; or your republic will be as fearfully plundered and laid waste by barbarians in the Twentieth Century as the Roman Empire was in the fifth; — with this difference, that the Huns and Vandals who ravaged the Roman Empire came from without, and that your Huns and Vandals will have been engendered within your own country by your own institutions."
—Thomas Babington Macaulay letter to
Henry Stephens Randall, May 23, 1857.

"Mr. Lincoln is already beaten. He cannot be re-elected and we must have another ticket to save us [the Republicans] from utter overthrow."
— journalist Horace Greeley, August 14, 1864.

"It seems exceedingly probable that this administration will not be re-elected. Then it will be my duty to so cooperate with the President-elect as to save the Union between the election and the inauguration, as he will have secured his election on such ground that he cannot possibly save it afterward."
—Abraham Lincoln, in a note that he had the members of his Cabinet sign without reading then put aside before the 1864 election.

"The Negro will disappear from the field of national politics. Henceforth the nation, as a nation, will have nothing more to do with him."
—The Nation, 1876.

"I think we are defeated in spite of recent good news. I am of the opinion that the Democrats have carried the country and elected [Samuel J.] Tilden."
—Rutherford B. Hayes, three days after the election of 1876.

215

Bad Predictions

"The American President will be elected for 6 to 8 years. He will not be eligible for a second term. Near the close of the next century, some rare, noble woman will be elected President of the United States."
>—theologian David Swing, 1893.

"All of North America will be under one government [in 1993] managed by a council consisting of a few men."
>—Kansas Senator William Alfred Peffer, 1893.

In 1893, columnist Bill Nye predicted that in 1993 "politically, there will be far less money expended in electing officials."

"My little man, I am making a strange wish for you— it is that you may never be president of the United States."
>—President Grover Cleveland to a five-year-old visitor to the White House. The young man was named Franklin Delano Roosevelt.

"I have no enemies. Why should I fear?"
>—President William McKinley, who was shot in the back on September 6, 1901, and died eight days later.

When William McKinley was inaugurated for the second time in 1897, his new vice president, Theodore Roosevelt, told friends he "now expected to be a dignified nonentity for four years."

"There will be more strict suffrage qualifications [in the 20th Century]... Some kind of property qualification or substitute in the form of knowledge of a trade and the civic qualifications of industry and abstention from crime will of necessity be adopted in states whose urban population exceeds 50 percent. These arrangements will make an end of the influence of the slum on our republic."
>—U.S. Commissioner of Education William T. Harris, *Brooklyn Daily Eagle*, December, 1900.

"I shall never be elected to [the presidency]. They don't want me."

> —Teddy Roosevelt in 1904, complaining to a friend about the impression that he was only president by accident and would never be elected in his own right. He won a decisive victory in the polls that year.

That same year Roosevelt announced he would not be a candidate for a third term. He did not, in fact, run in the following election, but came back to run again in four years. In 1912 he tried to explain away this apparent contradiction by saying, "My position on the third term is perfectly simple. I said I would not accept a nomination for a third term under any circumstances, meaning, of course, a third consecutive term."

On election night, 1916, Woodrow Wilson was so convinced he had lost that he wanted to issue a concession statement before the final count was in, but his secretary Joseph Tumulty prevented him from doing so. Wilson was not defeated in the election.

"I am very happy in the Senate and much prefer to remain there. I do not believe I could be happy as president. I don't want it."

> —Warren G. Harding, 1920.

"In 1999/ in 1999/ Although today we ride in style/ They'll look back on us and smile/ In 1999, it surely will be fine/ We'll have a lady president in 1999."

> —lyrics to the 1924 song "1999" by vaudevillian Al Bernard.

Bad Predictions

In 1924, H.L. Mencken was covering the Democratic Convention for the *Baltimore Sun*. He sent in a report reading: "Everything is still uncertain in this convention but one thing. John W. Davis will never be nominated." Only minutes later the convention indeed picked Davis as its candidate. When he heard the news, Mencken was said to have responded: "Why that's incredible! I've already sent off a story that it's impossible. I wonder if those idiots in Baltimore will have sense enough to drop the negative."

"In 1932 the chimneys will be smoking, the farmers will be getting good crops that will bring good prices, and so Mr. Hoover will be re-elected."
>—*New York Herald Tribune*, 1930. The economy did not improve and Hoover was no re-elected.

"FDR will be a one-term president."
>—columnist Mark Sullivan, 1935.

"The race will not be close at all. Landon will be overwhelmingly elected and I'll stake my reputation as a prophet on it."
>—William Randolph Hearst, on the political race of Franklin Delano Roosevelt vs. Alfred "Alf" Landon, 1936.

"I have never felt more certain of anything in my life than the defeat of President Roosevelt. My mid-October people will wonder why they ever had any doubt about it."
>—newspaper publisher Paul Block, September, 1936.

"Franklin Delano Roosevelt will lose the election by a landslide."

> — *Literary Digest* in 1936. This prediction had serious consequences for the *Digest*. That year, rival George Gallup spent $250,000 on a new technique in which he queried a small representative sampling of individuals and forecast the results. Gallup's polls showed that Roosevelt would be the winner. FDR won 523 electoral votes to Landon's 8. This is why the name Gallup, and not *Literary Digest*, is now synonymous with polling.

"Democracy will be dead by 1950."

> —John Langdon-Davies, *A Short History of the Future*, 1936.

"Although the answer to the question, Does Mr. Roosevelt want a third term? is definitely Yes, to the other question, If he does, can he get it? the answer is emphatically No."

> —Frank R. Kent, *The American Mercury*, 1938.

"I believe that we are going to get along very well with him [Joseph Stalin] and the Russian people— very well indeed."

> —Franklin Delano Roosevelt, December 24, 1943.

"Look, son, I cannot conceive of any circumstances that could draw out of me permission to consider me for any political post from dog catcher to Grand High Supreme King of the Universe."

> —Dwight D. Eisenhower, at a Pentagon press conference, 1948.

"I am not available for and could not accept nomination for high public office. My decision is definite and positive."

> —Dwight D. Eisenhower, 1948.

Bad Predictions

In September, 1948, Elmo Roper reported that Thomas Dewey was leading Harry Truman in the pre-election polls by a margin of 41 to 31 percent and that "no amount of electioneering" could change the outcome.

"Dewey-Warren will be unbeatable... So, it's to be Thomas Edmund Dewey in the White House on January 20, with Earl Warren as a backstop in event of any accident during years just ahead."
—*U.S. News and World Report*, July 1948.

"Thomas E. Dewey's election as President is a foregone conclusion."
—Leo Egan, *New York Times*, 1948.

"Dewey will be in for eight years— until '57."
—*Kiplinger News Letter*, 1948.

"Dewey is going to be President, and you might as well get used to him."
—columnist Richard Stroudt, *New Republic*, October, 1948.

"The main question is whether Governor Dewey will win by a fair margin or a landslide."
—*New York Sun*, October 4, 1948.

"President Truman appears to be the only American who doesn't think Thomas E. Dewey will be our next President."
—*New York Daily News*, October 15, 1948.

"The next President of the United States."
—caption of a photo of Thomas Dewey in *Life Magazine*, 1948.

"The Party might as well immediately concede the election to Dewey and save the wear and tear of campaigning."
—*New York Post*, 1948.

"Truman put up a courageous fight... [but] he cannot possibly win"
> —columnist Drew Pearson, *Washington Post*,
> November 1, 1948.

"Mr. Truman in a cocky speech the other day said: 'The polltakers and wrong-guesser faces will be red!' The gamblers are betting Mr. Truman's will be white."
> –columnist Walter Winchel, November 2, 1948.

"DEWEY DEFEATS TRUMAN"
> —famous premature *Chicago Daily Tribune* headline, November 3, 1948. Dewey did not defeat Harry S. Truman.

"Hence the importance of some means of prohibiting the unworthy from voting. This latter idea appeals to many Republicans and Democrats...Most people feel that the voting franchise should be restricted to those who are worthy of it; but they believe it will be impossible to bring about such change without a severe economic collapse or a revolution. As to how it will be brought about, I do not know; but I am certain that the change will be made somehow and sometime during the next fifty years. People are not created 'free and equal,' and it is a travesty on both democracy and common honesty for us to say so."
> —economist Roger W. Babson,
> *Looking Ahead Fifty Years*, 1950.

"Within fifty years Washington will receive a rude awakening. The masses then will be in no mood to 'play with politics' any longer. We will at last vote for what is right, rather than for what is expedient. Politicians who continue to preach untruths in order to get votes will wind up in concentration camps."
> —economist Roger W. Babson, *Looking Ahead Fifty Years*, 1950.

Bad Predictions

"Someday the American people will erect a monument to his memory."
> —Eddie Rickenbacker on Senator Joseph McCarthy.

When Dwight and Edgar Eisenhower graduated from high school, their yearbook predicted one of the brothers would grow up to be president of the United States—Edgar. Dwight, the students forecast, would one day be a history teacher.

"Actors are citizens and should exert those rights by speaking their minds, but the actor's first duty is to his profession. Hence, you can rest assured that I will never again run for mayor or anything but head man in my own household."
> — Ronald Reagan, *The Hollywood Reporter*, November, 1955.

"You won't have Nixon to kick around anymore, because, gentlemen, this is my last press conference."
> —Richard Nixon, 1962.

"By 2000, politics will simply fade away. We will not see any political parties."
> — architect and futurist R. Buckminster Fuller, 1966.

"I'll never run again. Politics is a filthy business."
> —Edward Koch in 1962 before being elected in 1968 to the House of Representatives and his three terms as Mayor of New York City.

"We can tell you with comparative assurance that Aristotle Onassis is not likely to be marrying Jackie Kennedy or anyone else."
> —columnist Earl Wilson, September, 1968, two weeks before the couple announced their engagement.

"All political systems are on the way out. We're finally gonna get to the point where there's no more bigotry or greed or war. Peace is the way... In 20 years all that stuff will be over. People are simply gonna learn that they can get more from being groovy than being greedy."
—musician Arlo Guthrie, *Newsweek*, 1969.

"I have no political ambitions for myself or my children."
—Joseph P. Kennedy.

"Let us begin by committing ourselves to the truth, to see it like it is and to tell it like it is, to find the truth, to speak the truth and live with the truth. That's what we'll do."
—Richard Nixon, nomination acceptance speech, 1968.

"It's just like communism. We'll push for small doses of socialism until one day everyone will wake up to find their grandchildren living under communism."
—an unnamed citizen quoted in *The Berkley Tribe*, a counter-cultural newspaper, 1970. And what was this individual commenting on? A meeting of the Telegraph Avenue Concerns Committee on the subject of whether or not to widen the sidewalks.

"If I do nothing else as President, I'm going to restore respect for the American flag."
—Richard Nixon, 1970.

The 1972 book *Futures Conditional* by Robert Theobald cites a forthcoming book by Arthur Waskow, which creates a new constitution for the United States of 1990. Waskow wrote: "By 1990 there are autonomous Black, Chicano, Jewish, Indian, Quebecois, Puertoriqueno and Italian commonwealths in North America; there are Autonomous Regions in the Bay Area, the Northwest, New England and about six other areas; there are Workers Control Alliances in all major industries on the continent; there is democratic and socialist planning, initiated by a Congressional Congress of recallable delegates,

223

the White House is a museum and the Pentagon a vast Department of the History of the American Empire, wherein all the people are busy publishing and evaluating all the documents they formerly kept secret. The USA in any recognizable sense is, in short, gone. The American peoples and workers are free."

The book also featured an article on "Headlines of the Near Future" by Billy Rojas. He predicted that in November, 1972, the "team of [Edmund] Muskie and Adalai Stevenson III defeats Republicans for Presidency."

"If I had to put money on it, I'd say that on January 20, 1973, the guy with his hand on the Bible will be John V. Lindsay."
> —Jerry Bruno and Jeff Greenfield, from *The Advance Man*, 1972, losing money on who would be sworn in as the next President of the United States.

"I will not resign if indicted. Our Constitution says that every man is entitled to a fair trial and a presumption of innocence. I intend to rely on the spirit as well as the letter of the guarantee. I would forsake the principles of the Founding Fathers if I abandoned this fight. And I do not intend to abandon it."
> —Spiro Agnew, 1973. He resigned a few days later.

"I don't think you're going to see a great, great uproar in this country about the Republican Committee trying to bug the Democratic headquarters."
> —Richard Nixon, four days after the Watergate break in.

"Watergate is water under the bridge."
> —Richard Nixon, September, 1973.

"I have no intention whatever of walking away from the job I was elected to do."
> —Richard Nixon nine months before his resignation.

"He is our President, and I feel that if Richard Nixon is impeached, there will be mass suicides, mass nervous breakdowns, and total demoralization of the country."
    —Helen Buffington, branch vice-chairperson
       of the Committee to Reelect the President.

4/19/02

"The country had changed to the parliamentary system of government after the second administration of Gerald Ford."
    —*Ms. Magazine* editor Letty Cottin Pogrebin,
       "Born Free: A Feminist Fable" in the 1974 book
       Woman in the Year 2000.

In the 1976 *Playboy* article "The Democratic Handicap: Who'll Be Our Next President?" Dick Tuck predicted that it would definitely not be Jimmy Carter. "Jimmy Carter will get a little run for his money, but I can't help but think that to most people he looks more like a kid in a bus station with his name pinned on his sweater on his way to summer camp than a President on his way to the White House."

"I got a mama who joined the Peace Corps and went to India when she was 68. I got one sister who's a Holy Roller preacher. I got another sister who wears a helmet and rides a motorcycle. And I got a brother who thinks he's going to be President. So that makes me the only sane person in the family."
    —Billy Carter, 1976.

"When elected, Newt will keep his family together."
    —Ad for Congressman Newt Gingrich, 1978. He
       filed for divorce less than two years later.

In 1980 Catholic priest Andrew M. Greeley told the editors of *The Book of Predictions* that by 1990 The Republican party would be replaced as one of the nation's two major political parties.

Bad Predictions

"By 1993, the U.S. will have ceased to be a great power and will be struggling to hold itself together as a viable nation. The Soviet Union will be approaching hegemony over most of the world."
> —David S. Sullivan, Soviet foreign policy
> analyst for the CIA, 1980.

"I would like to suggest that Ronald Reagan is politically dead."
> —NBC political correspondent Tom Pettit,
> "The Today Show," January 22, 1980.

Two days after Ronald Reagan was shot in 1981, CNN aired a videotape of psychic Tamara Rand predicting the shooting. The film reportedly came from a Las Vegas talk show and had been filmed three months earlier. Rand said she felt Reagan was in danger "at the end of March" from a "thud" in the "chest area." She said the shots would be fired by a fair-haired young man with a name resembling "Jack Humley." In fact, Ronald Reagan was shot March 30th by John Hinckley, Jr. The prediction would have been startling in its accuracy, were it not for one thing. It was filmed March 31st.

In 1981, Washington D.C. Mayor Marion Barry predicted that by 2000 his city would have gained both population and voting rights. Instead, the District lost more than 210,000 residents, and the ones who remain still aren't represented fully in Congress.

"Anyone who suggests I run for governor is no friend of mine. It's a terrible position, and besides, it requires living in Albany, which is small-town life at its worst. I wouldn't even consider it."
> —New Yor Mayor Edward Koch, *Playboy*, 1982, a
> few months before accepting the gubernatorial
> bid.

In 1982 Richard Nixon predicted the 1984 Democratic presidential nominee would be "[Ted] Kennedy, of course," not Mondale. "No way... Mondale— blah!— he just doesn't come over... No, Kennedy is going to be the

226

nominee." Mondale went on to run against Ronald Reagan. The only correct part of Nixon's prediction, therefore, was that Mondale didn't "come over." Reagan won by a sizable margin.

"Follow me around. I don't care. I'm serious. If anybody wants to put a tail on me, go ahead. They'd be very bored."

>—Presidential candidate Gary Hart in 1987 dismissing charges of womanizing and making the very bad prediction that the press would not take him up on his challenge. The Miami Herald staked out his home and discovered that the candidate had spent two days in the company of an attractive woman, Donna Rice, who was not his wife.

"Read my lips— no new taxes!"

>—1988 campaign pledge by presidential hopeful George Bush, who went on to add $21.7 billion in new "receipts proposals" and "user fees" in his 1991 budget as president.

"The fire of an election no longer burns in me."
—Governor Bill Clinton, 1990.

"The days of blacks being politically aligned to the liberal [Democratic] party are about to be ended."
—Claudia A. Butts, 1991.

"I am today proposing a Middle East arms control initiative... halting the proliferation of conventional and unconventional weapons in the Middle East."

>—President George Bush, March 1991. Less than 24 hours later, Bush announced plans to sell more than $5 billion in new weapons to Egypt, Israel, Baharain, Oman, Saudi Arabia, Turkey and the United Arab Emirates.

"Today's the end of the Clinton campaign."
—U.S. Representative Vin Weber, Feb 6, 1992.

The *New Republic's* Senior Editor Fred Barnes was so certain Bill Clinton had no political future after 1992 that he wrote a book entitled *Loser: Why Clinton Can't Win.* Explaining his thesis in *The American Spectator* he said, "Allegations of cheating on Hillary and dodging the draft... [have] all but wiped out Clinton's chance to win a Southern state outside Arkansas— and made Arkansas iffy. And since a Democrat has to win some Southern states to capture the presidency, Clinton is practically a goner."

"By the end of the year or early in the next year, Bill Clinton will announce that he is not going to run again for the presidency, and Al Gore will take up the standard for the Democrats."
> —Sam Donaldson, January 1, 1995.

"We happen to believe, despite the polls, that Bill Clinton will lose to any Republican who doesn't drool on stage."
> —*Wall Street Journal*, October, 1995.

"Mr. [Bob] Dole will win. Go down to William Hill and bet on it."
> —*American Spectator* editor R. Emmett Tyrell, Jr., *Sunday Telegraph*, 1996.

"He insists he won't resign, but how can he continue to govern if he stands in disgrace? It's hard to see how even Clinton could brazen this one out... Trouble is, despite all his charm, and he is a very charming individual, he has seemingly made one move too many on the chessboard of life."
> —editorial on the Monica Lewinsky scandal, *Calgary Sun*, 1998.

"If he's lying, he's gone. This is not complicated anymore."
> — Democrat Bob Beckel on Clinton's assertion that he "did not have sex with that woman," *The Washington Post*, February 2, 1998.

The same article, written by Charles Krauthammer, asserted: "Clinton's fate does not rest on any obstruction of justice. It rests with the denial, issued not only on national TV but also, apparently, under oath in his Paula Jones deposition. That lie alone will do it... If it can be shown that he did, nothing else matters. His presidency is over."

"I am confident that [in 2000] the Republican Party will pick a nominee that will beat Bill Clinton."
> —Dan Quayle, 1998. While the Republicans may well have nominees that would be able to beat Bill Clinton in 2000, Quayle was incorrect in predicting Clinton would run for a third term in office.

Bad Predictions

World History

"What God hath joined together, let no man put asunder."
>—Henry VIII in a book on the subject of marriage he sent to Pope Leo before divorcing the first of his six wives.

"No question about it. This officer will reach one of the highest posts in the royal artillery corps."
>—General Jean-Pierre du Teil on Napoleon Bonaparte.

"For the last quarter of a century there has not been recollected a month so favourable for all purposes of agriculture as the one just closed, or one which has given most promise of an early and abundant harvest."
>—From the *London Times* correspondent in Dublin, Ireland, June 3, 1846. Two months later a blight wiped out the potato crop, causing the Irish Potato Famine.

"The British dominions have [by 2000] been consolidated into the empire of United Britain; and not only is it the most powerful empire on the globe, but at present no sign is shown of any tendency to weakness or decay."
>—former New Zealand Prime Minister Sir Julius Vogel, *Anno Domini 2000*, 1889.

"At the close of the nineteenth century... resistance to the thought and mechanical inventions of the West was rapidly giving way, and doubtless one of the triumphs of the twentieth century will be the rejuvenation of China, which we may look to see rivaling Japan on the path of progress. Of the other great centre of intellectual activity in Asia, the populous Hindoostan [India], its progress is likely to depend far more on its British overlords than on the people themselves. While as mentally active as the Chinese, the Hindoos are far less practical... The Hindoo is a dreamer, remarkably lacking the business instinct, and is so deeply imbued with the ancient religious culture of his land that it will not be easy to rouse him from the fatalistic theories in which his whole nature is steeped. National progress in that land must be the work of British energy. The future of the remainder of the world is less assured. The slow thinking peoples of the remainder of Asia, the fanatical populations of Mohammedan lands, the Negroes of Africa, the natives of Brazil and Patagonia, the inhabitants of the islands of the Pacific, the peoples of the tropics in general, all are likely to act as brakes upon the wheels of progress, and the 'white man's burden' with these tribes and races during the twentieth century is certain to prove an arduous one."

> —Charles Morris, *The Marvelous Record of the Closing Century*, 1899.

"Of all the nations, [Germany] is probably the least corrupted by the lust of conquest, the accumulation of fabulous colonial wealth and the demoralizing influence of great cities... That she will leave a powerful impress upon the century now opening is assured."

> --*Boston Daily Globe*, January 1, 1901. Correct about the "impress" if not the nature of the impress.

"England is at last ripe for revolution."

> —Leon Trotsky, 1925.

"Australia will [by 1982] be abandoned to the Japanese by its white inhabitants, who will return to an England capable of supporting by agriculture almost double its present population."

> —Lewis Mumford, "The World Fifty Years from Now," *The Forum*, December, 1932.

"Many of you may think [the pressures of war] would soon 'drive you to drink.' Don't be so sure. There might be nothing to drink. Prohibition came to America once as the result of war. It can come again."

> —W. W. Chaplin, *What Will Happen and What to Do When War Comes*, 1939.

Bad Predictions

"One can only smile at the thought of England and the United States planning for the year 2000. They will be lucky if they survive until 1950."
—Joseph Goebbels, 1941.

"The Japanese are occupying all the islands, one after another. They will get hold of Australia, too. The White Race will disappear from those regions."
—Adolf Hitler, *Table Talk*, 1941.

"Among the really difficult problems of the world, [the Arab-Israeli conflict is] one of the simplest and most manageable."
— journalist Walter Lippmann, April 1948.

"I give Castro a year. No longer."
—exiled Cuban dictator Fulgencio Batista, 1959.

"I give [Castro] no more than six months. He will be overthrown by next June."
—Justo Carillo Hernandez, *U.S. News and World Report*, January 16, 1961.

"The quantitative balance of the world's population but also its economic potential are going to shift in favor of the East... By 2000 A.D. the East will have left the West far behind... It is, moreover, inevitable for the number of industrial workers in the Communist countries to exceed those in the capitalist world two to one... No visas, not even passports will be required [in 2000], because the world of tomorrow is conceivable only if governments surrender a large part of their national sovereignty."
—Fritz Beade, *The Race to the Year 2000*, 1962.

"By 1984 a solution will have been found, I think, to Canada's serious problem of supporting two cultures and using two languages."
—Dr. K. F. Tupper, Vice-President, National Re-

search Council, Canada, *New Scientist*, 1964.

"We are now witnessing the start of the disintegration of the Castro regime."

—U.S. analyst in *U.S. News and World Report*, April 25, 1966.

"Using our three indices, then, we suggest that the international hierarchy of 2018 is likely to show ten major powers, with the U.S. and the U.S.S.R. still the superpowers."

—Herman Kahn and Anthony J. Wiener of the Hudson Institute, *Toward the Year 2018*, 1968.

"No woman in my time will be Prime Minister or Chancellor or Foreign Secretary— not the top jobs. Anyway, I wouldn't want to be Prime Minister; you have to give yourself 100 percent."

8/15

—Margaret Thatcher interview with the *London Sunday Telegraph*, October 26, 1969.

"I don't want to be Prime Minister again. It's pretty tough going."

—Indira Gandhi, 1974. She ran again, and won.

"Capitalism [is] a museum piece... [We] will demonstrate conclusively to 'all and everyone' how right Marx, Lenin and their followers were in history's eyes."

—Comrade V. Kosolapov, *Mankind and the Year 2000*, 1976.

"It is too early for a Polish Pope."

—Karol Cardinal Wojtyia shortly becoming Pope John Paul II, 1978.

"After a series of local wars around the world in which the U.S.S.R continues to suppress rebellion against Soviet hegemony, the U.S.A. will finally begin to revive itself and fight back against Soviet repression."

—David S. Sullivan, strategic and Soviet Foreign Policy Analyst for the CIA, 1980.

Bad Predictions

"Any realistic sense of the world today leaves it clear that there isn't going to be any German reunification this century, nor probably in the lifetime of anyone who can read this."

> —foreign affairs columnist Flora Lewis,
> *The New York Times*, September 7, 1984.

"The socialist German Democratic Republic and the capitalist Federal German Republic cannot be merged, let alone reunited. It is as impossible as bringing together fire and water."

> —East German Foreign Minister Oskar
> Fischer, 1984.

"Historically [the Soviet Union] benefits from the instinctive feeling among the Russian people that this is the regime that they've always had, as it were, and it oughtn't to be changed."

> —British author Paul Johnson,
> *Christian Science Monitor*, 1987.

"The cheer with which Western commentators greeted Mikhail Gorbachev's tease that the Berlin Wall might come down when the conditions that generated the need for it disappear is another sign of how credulous we have become in receiving blandishments from Moscow."

> —Martin Pertez, Editor-in-Chief,
> *The New Republic*, July, 1989.

"It is a good strong marriage. It works very well. They are fond of each other. That marriage will last forever."

> —reporter Penny Junor on Prince Charles and
> Princess Diana, *McCall's*, 1991.

"I am never going to get divorced and that's that."

> —Princess Diana, *Good Housekeeping*, 1991,
> five years before the royal couple split.

In his end-of-year wrap-up for 1998, Steve Wilson of the *Arizona Republic* predicted that Saddam Hussein would be "knocked off" in 1999.

Military

Weapons of War

"I will ignore all ideas for new works and engines of war, the invention of which has reached its limits and for whose improvement I see not further hope."

> —Sextus Julius Frontius Chief Military Engineer during height of Roman Empire rule under Emperor Trajan, 98-110 AD.

"The bow is a simple weapon, firearms are very complicated things which get out of order in many ways... a very heavy weapon and tires out soldiers on the march. Whereas also a bowman can let off six aimed shots a minute, a musketeer can discharge but one in two minutes."

> —Colonel Sir John Smyth, opposing a change from bows to muskets, 1591.

"The weapons used [in the Franco-Prussian War] have reached such a stage of perfection that further progress which would have any revolutionizing influence is no longer possible. Once armies have guns which can hit a battalion at any range at which it can be distinguished, and rifles which are equally effective for hitting individual men, while loading them takes less time than aiming, then all further improvements are more or less unimportant for field warfare. The era of evolution is therefore, in essentials, closed in this direction."

> —German social philosopher and revolutionary Friedrich Engles, 1878.

"I prophesy that in the year 2000 we shall have reverted almost to the methods of savage warfare: shock weapons, undisciplined hordes and pedestrianism. The most powerful nation will be that which musters the largest number of 'toughs.' I mean men who are tough in nerve as well as body, that is to say, men as near the beasts as may be."

> —C.W. Macoy, *Brooklyn Daily Eagle*, December, 1900.

"War is to be robbed of its ghastliness... machines will do the fighting... and sustain all the hard knocks."
    —Syndicated columnist George L. Kilmer's prediction for the 20th Century, December 28, 1900.

"A popular fallacy is to suppose that... flying machines could be used to drop dynamite on an enemy in time of war."
    —astronomer William H. Pickering, 1908.

"Wilbur Wright has made the statement that in his opinion the use of the aeroplane for dropping bombs or explosives into a hostile army is impracticable, as the machine must rise 1,000 or 1,500 feet above the ground to escape shell fire. At that height accuracy would be impossible in dropping explosives when moving at 40 to 50 miles an hour."
    —*Popular Mechanics*, July, 1909.

"To affirm that the aeroplane is going to revolutionize naval warfare of the future is to be guilty of the wildest exaggeration."
    —*Scientific American*, July 16, 1910.

"Make no mistake, this weapon will change absolutely nothing."
    —French Director-General of Infantry on the machine gun, 1910.

"Airplanes are interesting toys, but have no military value."
    —French military leader Marechal Ferdinand Foch, 1911.

"Most improbable and more like one of Jules Verne's stories."
    —British Admiral Sir Compton Dombile in 1914 on submarine warfare, which was suggested in a recent story by Sir Arthur Conan Doyle.

Bad Predictions

"The idea that cavalry will be replaced by these iron coaches is absurd. It is little short of treasonous."
> —Aide-de-Camp to Field Marshal Douglas Haig, at tank demonstration, 1916. Haig also proclaimed the machine gun "a grossly overrated weapon."

"I cannot conceive of any use that the fleet will ever have for aircraft... Aviation is just a lot of noise."
> —Admiral Charles Benson, Chief of Naval Operations after WWI.

"Cavalry will never be scrapped to make room for the tanks; in the course of time cavalry may be reduced as the supply of horses in this country diminishes. This depends greatly on the life of fox-hunting."
> —*Journal of the Royal United Services Institution*, 1921.

"The day of the battleship has not passed, and it is highly unlikely that an airplane, or fleet of them, could ever successfully sink a fleet of Navy vessels under battle conditions."
> —Franklin Delano Roosevelt, then Assistant Secretary of the Navy, 1922.

"Nobody now fears that a Japanese fleet could deal an unexpected blow on our Pacific possessions... Radio makes surprise impossible."
> —Josephus Daniels, former U.S. Secretary of the Navy, October 16, 1922.

"It is highly improbable that there is any appreciable amount of available sub-atomic energy for man to tap... [Those] who are living in fear lest some bad boy among the scientists may some day touch off the fuse and blow this comfortable world of ours to star dust, may go home and henceforth sleep in peace with the consciousness that the Creator has put some foolproof elements into His handiwork, and that man is powerless to do it any titanic physical damage."
> —physicist Robert Millikan, 1929.

"The most revolutionary war invention since the discovery of gunpowder."
> —*Modern Mechanics*, July, 1932,
> on a proposed flying tank.

"I do not believe in the probability of anything much worse than mustard gas being produced."
> —British scientist J.B.S. Haldane, 1937.

"It is not possible... to concentrate enough military planes with military loads over a modern city to destroy that city."
> —Colonel John W. Thomason, Jr., 1937.

"As far as sinking a ship with a bomb is concerned, it just can't be done."
> —Clark Woodward, Rear Admiral,
> U.S. Navy, 1939.

"Atomic energy might be as good as our present-day explosives, but it is unlikely to produce anything very much more dangerous."
> —Winston Churchill, 1939.

"As for tanks, which are supposed by some to bring us a shortening of wars, their incapacity is striking."
> —French Marshal Henri Philippe Petain,
> *Is an Invasion Still Possible?*, 1939.

"It is significant that despite the claims of air enthusiasts no battleship has yet been sunk by bombs."
> —Caption for a photograph of the USS Arizona in the program for the Army-Navy game, November 29, 1941. The Arizona sank at Pearl Harbor eight days later.

"There has been a great deal said about a 3,000-mile high-angle rocket. In my opinion such a thing is impossible for many years. The people who have been writing these things that annoy me, have been talking about a 3,000-mile high-angle rocket shot from one continent to another, carrying an atomic bomb and so directed as

to be a precise weapon which would land exactly on a certain target, such as a city... I feel confident that it will not be done for a very long period of time to come... I think we can leave that out of our thinking. I wish the American public would leave that out of their thinking."
— scientist Vannevar Bush in a report
to a Senate committee, 1945.

"This is the biggest fool thing we have ever done... The atomic bomb will never go off, and I speak as an expert in explosives."
—U.S. Navy Admiral William D. Leahy to President Truman on the U.S. atomic bomb project in 1945.

"The dangers of atomic war are overrated. It would be hard on little, concentrated countries like England. In the United States we have lots of space."
—Colonel Robert Rutherford McCormick, 1950.

"Afraid of A-Bomb contamination? In the event of an A-Bomb attack wash contamination away with Flobar... It can be carried about for immediate use."
—advertisement, early 1950s.

"Mankind also faces the ominous possibilities of armies of asexually produced identical soldiers, the potential of controlling thoughts of individuals by electrodes and the behavior of societies by drugs, gross invasions of privacy, and other dangers."
—William Helton, *Honolulu Advertiser*, July 27, 1970.

War and Peace

"Everything announces an age in which that madness of nations, war, will come to an end."
>—Jean-Paul Rabaut Saint-Etienne, 1792.

"They couldn't hit an elephant at this dist..."
>—reportedly the last words of Gerneral John B. Sedgwick of the Union Army at the Battle of Spotsylvania, 1864.

"War is a relic of barbarism probably destined to become as obsolete as dueling."
>—physicist William Thompson, Lord Kelvin.

"I could whip all the Indians on the continent with the Seventh Cavalry."
>—General George Armstrong Custer turning down an offer of extra men and Gatling guns, 1876.

"Beyond a doubt all stories about large bodies of Indians being here are the merest bosh."
>—General George Armstrong Custer, 1876.

"On to Little Big Horn for glory. We've caught them napping."
>—George A. Custer before the charge on the Sioux in the Battle of Little Big Horn, 1876.

"The presence of standing armies in Europe of to-day is the maddest of all insanities; the demarcations of kingdoms have long since been mapped out; and excepting on the Eastern frontier of Germany and along the Danubian frontier— where the danger exists of an inroad by the hordes of ravening savages who people that earthly hell ruled by devils incarnate and called Russia— there should not be a soldier in Europe."
>—"A Free Lance," *Towards Utopia*, 1894.

Bad Predictions

The Chicago Tribune editorialized on Jan. 1, 1901, that the 20th century would be "a century of humanity [bringing] a keener realization of the brotherhood of man."

"What shall we say of the Great War of Europe, ever threatening, ever impending, and which never comes? We shall say that it never will come.   Humanly speaking, it is impossible."
> —David Starr Jordan, *The Independent*,
> February 27, 1913.

"Has there ever been danger of war between Germany and ourselves, members of the same Teutonic race? Never has it even been imagined."
> —Andrew Carnegie, "The Baseless Fear of
> War," *The Independent*, 1913.

"Though there is a cultural affinity between the United States and England which precludes war between them, it is still true that war between this nation and any other of the leading powers of Europe is almost equally inconceivable."
> —*The Nation*, 1913.

"It seems pretty clear that no civilized people will ever again permit its government to enter into a competitive armament race."
> —Nicholas Murray Butler, *Literary Digest*,
> 1914.

"This, the greatest of all wars, is not just another war—it is the last war!"
> —H.G. Wells in 1914 on World War I.

"In three months from now the war fever will have spent itself."
> —Harold Begbie, *The London Chronicle*,
> August 5, 1914.

"The War in Europe will last from nine to eighteen months."
> —*The New York World*, September 1914.

"I agree with the American people in thanking God we have a President who has kept—who will keep— us out of war."
—William Jennings Bryant on
Woodrow Wilson, 1916.

"I am not expecting this country to get into war. I know that the way in which we have preserved the peace is objected to, and that certain gentlemen say they would have taken some other way that would inevitably have resulted in war, but I am not expecting this country to get into war, partly because I am not expecting these gentlemen to have a chance to make a mess of it."
—Woodrow Wilson, October 21, 1916.

"The Lesson is Plain: If You Want WAR, Vote for HUGHES! If You Want Peace with Honor VOTE FOR WILSON! And Continued Prosperity."
—campaign slogan in the 1916 election.

"I would rather see Woodrow Wilson elected than Charles Evans Hughes because Wilson aggressively believes not only in keeping out of war, but in organizing the nations of the world to prevent war."
—Max Eastman, *The Masses*, 1916.

"There will be no war."
—President Woodrow Wilson, 1916. The U.S. entered World War I in April, 1917.

"I hope we may say that thus, this fateful morning, came to an end all wars."
—British Primer Minister David Lloyd George, November, 1918.

"Upon completion of his term [in prison], Hitler, who is not a citizen, will be expelled from the country. Further nationalist activity on his part, for the present at least, appears to be excluded."
—Robert Murphy, U.S. Foreign Service Officer in Munich, March 10, 1924.

247

Bad Predictions

"There is no doubt that he has become a much more quiet, more mature and thoughtful individual during his imprisonment than he was before and does not contemplate acting against existing authority."

> —Landsberg Prison Warden Otto Leybold in a letter about prisoner Adolph Hitler to the Bavarian Minister of Justice, September, 1924.

"People are becoming too intelligent ever to have another big war. Statesmen have not anything like the prestige they had years ago, and what is educating the ordinary people against war is that they are mixing so much. The motor-car, radio and such things are the great 'mixers.' I believe the last war was too much an educator for there ever to be another on a large scale."

> —Henry Ford, 1928.

"Hitler is a queer fellow who will never become Chancellor; the best he can hope for is to head the Postal Department."

> —Paul von Hindenburg, German Field Marshal and President of Germany, 1931.

"It is not unlikely that Hitler will end his career as an old man in some Bavarian village who, in the biergarten in the evening, tells his intimates how he nearly overturned the German Reich. Strange battle cries will struggle to his lips, and he will mention names that trembled at his name. But his neighbors will have heard the tale so often that they will shrug their shoulders and bury their faces deeper in their mugs of Pilsner to hide their smiles. The old man, they will think, is entitled to his pipe dreams. It is comforting to live on the memory of an illusion."

> —Harold Laski, *London Daily Herald*, November 21, 1932.

"Hitler's influence is waning so fast that the government is no longer afraid of the growth of the Nazi movement."

> —American diplomat William C. Bullit, 1932.

"Mistreatment of Jews in Germany may be considered virtually eliminated."
    —Secretary of State Cordell Hull, 1933.

In 1933, Field Marshal Paul von Hindenburg, President of the Republic of Germany, said he had "no intention whatever of making that Austrian corporal [Hitler] either Minister of Defense or Chancellor of the Reich."

"We are winning international respect."
    —Adolf Hitler, 1934.

"Believe me, Germany is unable to wage war."
    —British Prime Minister David Lloyd George, 1934.

"By this revolution the German way of life is definitely settled for the next thousand years."
    —Adolf Hitler, 1934.

"Germany has no desire to attack any country in Europe."
    —David Lloyd George, 1936.

"Democracy will never survive another world war."
    —former British Prime Minister David Lloyd George, September 21, 1936.

"Germany has no desire to attack Czechoslovakia."
    —Adolf Hitler, May 7, 1936. Germany annexed parts of that nation in 1939.

"Before 1940 has completed its first quarter it is thought that Hitler will have given place to another— probably General Goering."
    —*Raphael's Almanac*, 1939.

"Millions of people the world over tremble at what tomorrow may bring. They feel that, at any moment, a major disaster may unloose itself. It is as certain as anything can be that, before this book has been published a month, the majority of people will believe that the disaster of a world war is inevitable. Be reassured: there will be no war."

> —British astrologer Leonardo Blake, *Hitler's Last Year of Power*, 1939. The book, which, as the title suggests, claimed 1939 would be the last year of power for both Hitler and the Nazi party, also forecast, "Hitler's policy to drag the Far East into European conflicts will fail. England has nothing to fear from Japan, and a peace that will be made between China and Japan will bring home to the Japanese the futility of their present warlike policy."

"We shall not capitulate— no, never!"
> —Adolf Hitler, 1939.

"Britain will not be involved in a war. There will be no major war in Europe this year or next year. The Germans will not seize Czechoslovakia. So go about your own business with confidence in the future and fear not."
> —*London Daily Express*, September 30, 1938.

"A Japanese attack on Pearl Harbor is a strategic impossibility."
> —military expert George Fielding Eliot, 1938.

"In this column for years, I have constantly labored these points: Hitler's horoscope is not a war-horoscope... If and when war comes, not he but others will strike the first blow."
> —British astrologer R.H. Naylor, 1939.

"The Sudetenland is the last territorial claim which I have to make in Europe."
> —Adolf Hitler, September 26, 1938.

"Germany and Poland are two nations, and these nations will live, and neither of them will be able to do away with the other."
> —Adolf Hitler, May 1, 1938, before the September, 1939, invasion of Poland that started World War II.

"This is the second time in our history that there has come back from Germany to Downing Street peace with honour: I believe it is peace for our time."
—Prime Minister Neville Chamberlain, September 30, 1938.

"War between Japan and the United States is not within the realm of reasonable possibility."
—Major George Fielding Eliot, "The Impossible War with Japan," *American Mercury*, September, 1938.

"Only warmongers think there will be war. I think there will be a long period of peace."
—Adolf Hitler, January 30, 1939.

"In three weeks England will have her neck wrung like a chicken."
—General Maxime Weygand Commander-in-Chief of French Military Forces, June 16, 1940.

"Japan will never join the Axis."
—General Douglas MacArthur, September, 1940, one day before Japan announced it had joined the Axis.

"The United States will not be a threat to us for decades."
—Adolf Hitler, November, 1940.

"I've said this before, but I shall say it again and again and again: Your boys are not going to be sent into any foreign wars."
—Franklin Delano Roosevelt, campaign pledge, October, 1940.

"Defeat of Germany means the defeat of Japan, probably without firing a shot or losing a life."
—Franklin Delano Roosevelt.

Bad Predictions

"The Hawaiian Islands are over-protected; the entire Japanese fleet and air force could not seriously threaten Oahu."
> —Captain William T. Pulleston,
> *Atlantic Monthly*, August, 1941.

"No matter what happens, the U.S.Navy is not going to be caught napping."
> —U.S. Secretary of the Navy Frank Knox,
> December 5, 1941.

The Associated Press in 1950 published its predictions on life in the year 2000. "The earth," it said, "will still be reeking from the Third World War."

"Unless my observations are in error, I find the 1960s a time when constructive steps away from war are first being taken."
> —James Bryant Conant, "Predictions: Century in the Balance," American Chemical Society's Diamond Jubilee Meeting, 1951.

"The American aid program in Vietnam has proved an enormous success, one of the major victories of American policy."
> —General John O'Daniel, Official Military Aide to South Vietnam, September 7, 1959.

"Castro in Cuba will be overthrown within months."
> —*The Kiplinger Washington Letter*,
> February 18, 1961.

"U.S. aid to South Vietnam may be stepped up. But no U.S. combat troops are going into the jungle to engage in shooting war with Communist guerrillas."
> —*U.S. News and World Report*,
> November 13, 1961.

In the *Modern Almanac* published in 1962, author Harry Golden presents his plan for world peace. "STOP MAKING CARBON PAPER!" Golden suggested that "no general can order an attack without the message being carbon-copied sixteen ways from Sunday... With no carbon copies Washington would become a ghost town." It took another thirty years or so, but we finally did away with carbon paper. World peace, however, did not immediately follow.

"I'm not going to lose Vietnam."
  —Lyndon B. Johnson, 1963.

"We are not about to send American boys nine or ten thousand miles away from home to do what Asian boys ought to be doing for themselves."
  —Lyndon Johnson, campaign pledge,
    October, 1964.

"Whatever happens in Vietnam, I can conceive of nothing except military victory."
  —Lyndon B. Johnson,
    speech at West Point, 1967.

"Truth will become the hallmark of the Nixon administration... We feel that we will be able to eliminate any possibility of a credibility gap in this administration."
  —Herbert G. Klein, communications
    director for Nixon, November, 1968.

"The indices in Vietnam are good."
  —William F. Buckley, 1970.

"So far the 'balance of terror' has retained its equilibrium, but with every year that passes the chance of toppling over into war moves nearer to certainty. The number of nations with atomic weapons has so far increased at a rate of about one every five years, from 1945 onwards... The logical conclusion is that the weapons are likely to be let loose, probably before the end of the twentieth century."
  —Desmond King-Hele, *The End of the
    Twentieth Century?*, 1970.

Bad Predictions

"They're asking women to do impossible things. I don't believe women can carry a pack, live in a foxhole, or go a week without a bath."

> —U.S. Commander in Vietnam General
> William Westmoreland.

"I seriously doubt if we will have another war. This is probably the last."

> —Richard Nixon on Vietnam, 1971.

"I told you I would take you three centuries into the future... I do not offer what follows as a prediction. Perhaps... just bad dreams... In the last third of the 20th century the rage to demolish succeeded beyond the fondest dreams of the dismantlers. They brought everything tumbling down. Since the hostility to institutions was a product of modern minds, the demolition was most thorough in the most advanced nations. You will be pleased to know that unlike the fall of Rome, this decline was not followed by hundreds of years of darkness. In fact, there followed less than a century of chaos and disorder. In the latter part of the 21st century the rebuilding began."

> —John W. Gardner, "Uncritical Lovers, Unloving Critics," a speech given at the University of North Carolina, Greensboro, February 15, 1971.

A group of arms control experts was interviewed for a 1975 issue of *Harvard Magazine*. By the year 2000, they agreed, some nuclear wars were likely to have occurred.

"The Soviets don't pose the only threat to world peace in the next decade. There is a real possibility of an all-out black African offensive against South Africa, which is sure to defend itself with nuclear weapons."

> —Marvin Cetron and Thomas O'Toole,
> *Encounters with the Future*, 1982.

"When history is written on this, they will look back and say this was one of the United States' finest hours."
—Republican Congressman William S. Broomfield on the attack on Grenada, *Washington Post*, October 28, 1983.

Egyptian President Hosni Mubarak on July 25, 1990, said Saddam Hussein had "no intention to attack Kuwait or any other party." 6/29

"I'm plenty fed up with Saddam [Hussein] but there are no threats, just determination. I'm confident he doesn't want to fight. I don't think it will come to that."
—President George Bush, January, 1991.

The End of the
World and Other
Visions of Doom

Bad Predictions

Unlike other sections, I have arranged this chapter by the dates at which the world was expected to end, or when another spiritual sign was meant to occur, rather than by the date on which the prediction was made.

General Predictions of Doom

"When pictures look alive with movements free,
When ships like fishes swim below the sea,
When men outstripping birds can scan the sky,
Then half the world sore drenched in blood shall lie."
    –A tombstone in Essex, England ca. 1400.

Early Predictions

Early in Rome's history, there was a myth that 12 eagles had revealed to Romulus a mystical number representing the lifetime of Rome. Many Romans took each eagle to represent 10 years, thus the end of the world would have been around 634 B.C. on the modern calendar.

"There is no doubt that the Antichrist has already been born. Firmly established already in his early years, he will, after reaching maturity, achieve supreme power."
    —St. Martin of Tours (ca. 316-397).

Roman theologians Sextus Julius Africanus, Hippolytus and Irenaeus each believed the end of the world would occur 6000 years after the Creation. They assumed there were about 5531 years between the Creation and the Resurrection, which would have put the end at about 469 A.D.

Lotharingian prophets calculated the end of the world to Friday, March 25, 970, when the Annunciation and Good Friday fell on the same day.

Bernard of Thuringia said that the end would come when the Annunciation of the Virgin coincided with Good Friday in 992.

John of Toledo wrote what came to be known as the "Letter of Toledo" in 1179. The letter announced that a planetary alignment would occur in Libra on September 23, 1186. The result would be the end of the world as anyone had previously known it. Only a few would survive. People believed his forecast. In Germany they dug shelters. In Mesopotamia and Persia they prepared their cellars in much the same way people readied bomb shelters in the 1950s. The Byzantine emperor had the windows of his palace boarded over. While the planets did unite under the sign of Libra, the earthquakes and storms failed to appear. John was not daunted. He announced that his prophecy was meant to be symbolic of the Hunnish invasion and that he had actually been right.

Joachim of Fiore predicted the world would come to an end in 1260. When this failed to happen, his followers, known as Joachites, were undeterred. They recalculated the end 1335.

Gerard of Poehlde, in 1147 expressed his view that Christ's Millennium began when the emperor Constantine came to power. Constantine rose to power in 306, which would place the end of the Millennium at 1306.

Back in the 1360s, the Archdeacon of Prague, John Milic, spoke against the official doctrine of the Roman Catholic Church, insisting that corruption in the church proved the Antichrist had returned and the end was imminent. After his death in 1374, Matthew of Janov took up the cause, proclaiming Pope Clement VII "an antichrist." Matthew's beliefs were taken up and expanded by Hus, who spoke against the papacy and was excommunicated in 1411. Four years later he was found guilty of heresy and burned at the stake, becoming a martyr. His post-humous followers were known as Hussites, and they soon spawned a radical wing known as the Taborites. This group believed everyone in the world, except the Taborites, would be the victim of God's wrath in 1420. Although the world failed to end, the various factions of Hus' believers found themselves in a

259

civil war, which endured until the mid-1400s.

1500s

In June, 1523, a group of astrologers in London predicted a flood would destroy their city on February 1, 1524. So many astrologers concurred that 20,000 people took to the hills. The Prior of St. Bartholomew built a fortress and stocked it with a two-month supply of food. When the world failed to end, the astrologers discovered an error in their calculations. The flood would come in 1624, not 1524.

"The world will end by a giant flood on February 20, 1524."

> —German mathematician and astrologer Johannes Stoeffler, 1499. Stoeffler was certain that a planetary alignment in Pisces was a sure sign that the end would come. Since Pisces is a water sign, he reasonably predicted the world would be ended by a flood. This became something of a self-fulfilling prophecy. Although the world did not end, part of Germany was gripped by panic when it rained on the fateful day. One of those who believed Stoeffler was Count von Iggleheim, who ordered a three-story ark built in preparation for the day. In his case, February 20th was the end of the world. The count was trampled to death by a stampeding mob trying to board his vessel.

After the world failed to end in 1524, Johannes Stoeffler revised his prediction. The world would actually end in 1528. This time around no one paid much attention.

Reformer Hans Hut predicted it would all be over May 27, 1528.

Anabaptist leader Melchior Hofmann, a "peaceful activist," told his followers that Christ would return to earth in 1533. Many of his followers sold their possessions. When the year was over and Christ had not returned, Jan Matthys took control of the movement with one slight revision in doctrine— he believed violence was necessary to clear the path for Jesus' return on Easter, 1534. When Easter came and went, the victims of his followers' violence rose up and killed Matthys. Another follower, John Beukels declared himself head, not only of the religious group but also "ruler of the world." He added a few new doctrines, including polygamy to the religion. The world ended, for the group at least, in January, 1536, when they were captured and tortured to death by an army of Catholics and Protestants.

A German monk named Michael Stifel also believed doomsday would come in 1533. The date he chose was October 18. Stifel was assaulted by the townspeople of Lochau on October 19.

Easter, 1534, which was April 5 that year, was chosen as the fateful day by Jan Matthys, who believed only the city of Münster would be spared.

April 28, 1583, at noon should have marked the Second Coming of Christ, according to astrologer Richard Harvey. He was among many London astrologers who cited the conjunction of Jupiter and Saturn on that day as signaling the end.

Cyprian Leowitz, an astrologer, predicted the end would occur in 1584.

1600s

Dominican monk Tomasso Campanella wrote that the sun would collide with the Earth in 1603.

Numerologist Eustachius Poyssel preferred the year 1623.

Christopher Columbus even tried his hand at prophecy. He believed human history would climax in a Christian crusade in 1656.

In 1665 a Quaker named Solomon Eccles entered St. Mary's Church, London, wearing only a goatskin loincloth and balancing a chafing dish filled with burning coals on his head. He shouted to the assembled parishioners that the end was nigh. The city was in the middle of the last great outbreak of the Black Plague, and many of the frightened residents found this easy enough to believe. Eccles was eventually arrested for creating a panic.

"No later than 1673."
—New England Deacon William Aspinwall's doomsday.

John Napier, better known as the mathematician who discovered logarithms, also calculated that the world would end in 1688.

German prophet Johann Jacob Zimmerman convinced many followers that the second coming would occur in the fall of 1694 and that Jesus was coming to America. In February, Zimmerman and his cult, known as Woman in the Wilderness, made plans to cross the Atlantic, but Zimmerman died on the day they were set to sail. The group decided to continue under the leadership of member Johannes Kelpius. They arrived safely in America but did not meet Jesus there.

Fervent witch hunter Cotton Mather announced 1697 would be the last year for the world. When it didn't end, he revised his forecast. The world would end, he said, in 1716. When it failed to end a second time, Mather moved the date forward again. The world would definitely be finished in 1736.

1700s

On April 5, 1719, a comet would destroy the planet, according to Jacques Bernoulli. In his *Treatise upon the Comet*, Bernoulli said the tail of the comet "would be an infallible sign of the wrath of heaven."

According to the 15th-century Cardinal Nicolas of Cusa, the last years would fall between 1700 and 1734.

William Whitson predicted that London would be consumed by flood on October 13, 1736, prompting many Londoners to gather in boats on the Thames.

A giant earthquake failed to destroy London on April 5, 1761, much to the disappointment of William Bell, who had convinced many other people that it would happen. He based his prediction on two previous earthquakes, one on February 8 and another on March 8. They proved, in his mind, that the world must end in another 28 days. The believers gathered in boats on the Thames or headed for the hills. Following the day the earth stood still, Bell was thrown into Bedlam, London's notorious insane asylum.

Methodist George Bell chose February 28, 1763, as the date of Armageddon.

Retired English sailor Richard Brothers, who called himself "God's Almighty Nephew," said the Millennium would begin between 1793 and 1795. He was prepared to lead the ten lost tribes of Israel, because, he said, God told him he would become King of England. He was eventually committed to an insane asylum, but his followers protested. Nathaniel Brassey Halhead, arguing for Brothers' release, announced that the world was going to end November 19, 1795.

1800s

17th-century Presbyterian minister Christopher Love forecasted the destruction of the old world by an earthquake in 1805, followed by an age of everlasting peace.

In 1806 a hen belonging to Mary Bateman of Leeds, England, laid an egg inscribed with the words "Christ is Coming." Bateman showed this egg to the people of the town and invited them to her poultry shed, where she explained that God had told her that the hen would lay 14 such eggs, and then the world would come to an end in a blaze of fire. As she spoke, the hen laid another inscribed egg. Bateman told the people that God had also revealed to her a way that they could save themselves, and she would reveal it to anyone who gave her a penny. After everyone had paid, she revealed that God would allow anyone carrying a sealed piece of paper with the inscription "J.C." on it entry into Heaven. She just happened to have such pieces of paper, which she would sell for a shilling. Each time another inscribed egg was laid, another crowd of people came to buy the sealed papers. On the day the last egg was to be laid, town officials burst in on Mary Bateman and caught her in the act of inserting an inscribed egg into the egg duct of a hen. She was arrested. After her release she continued to make predictions about the end of the world, but few people believed her. She met her end in the gallows, convicted of performing an abortion.

A 64-year-old virgin, Joanna Southcott, claimed that she was pregnant with Christ's child, who would be born December 25, 1814. Instead, she died on Christmas day. An autopsy revealed she was not with child. This did not deter her believers. One of them, John Turner, went on to predict the end of the world was coming October 14, 1820. After this prophecy failed, John Wroe took over leadership of the cult. Wroe calculated his own doomsday date— 1863. Before its arrival, in 1823, he underwent a public circumcision and tried unsuccessfully to walk on water.

Astrologer Dr. John Dee predicted that St. Patrick's Day, 1842, would mark the end of Europe.

"I am fully convinced that sometime between March 21, 1843, and March 21, 1844, according to the Jewish mode of computation of time, Christ will come and bring all His Saints with Him; and then He will reward every man as his work shall be," said William Miller, one of the most famous millennialists. He wrote about his calculations in a book called *Evidence From Scripture and History of the Second Coming of Christ About the Year A.D. 1843.* His views attracted as many as 100,000 followers called "Millerites" and later "Adventists." When March 21, 1843, rolled around, the Millerites waited... and waited.... A few became disenchanted, but others became more determined than ever that Christ would arrive within the year. When March 21, 1844, arrived, some of the most fanatic jumped from roofs in the belief that Christ would catch them before they landed. He did not. Surprisingly, the Millerites did not disband. One of them, Samuel Snow, was certain that there had to be a simple explanation. He reworked the dates based on Jewish chronology and found that Miller should have said the end would come on October 22, 1844. Snow managed to convince Miller his math was correct, and the faithful waited once again. Obviously the world did not end, but Miller's ministry did. In a deep depression he disappeared from public view. Although the Millerites officially disbanded, some of the devotees continued on with a new religion that borrowed many of his teachings.

According to Paul F. Boller's book *Presidential Campaigns*, during the campaign of 1860 (which Abraham Lincoln won) several men were on a train in New England discussing the upcoming election. One of the men, a devout follower of William Miller, said, "Before the election of 1860, the world will have come to an end and Jesus Christ will be President of the Universe." After a brief silence one of the passengers replied, "Sire, I'll bet you ten dollars New Hampshire won't go for him."

Ellen G. White, once a follower of William Miller, took the leadership of a new religion, The Seventh Day Adventists. White explained that Miller's teachings had not been incorrect at all. Miller had spoken of the "cleansing of the sanctuary." White argued that the sanctuary had, in fact, been cleansed. The sanctuary, however, was not earth but a spiritual realm. White, further, refused to make the same mistake as Miller had and set no deadline for life on earth. A splinter group, the Second Adventists, was not as cautious. They prophesied that Christ would return between 1873 and 1874. One of the notable Second Adventists was Charles Taze Russell, who would live beyond 1874 to form his own religion.

Father George Rapp, leader of a sect known as the Harmonists, established a utopian commune in Economy, Pennsylvania. He was certain that Jesus would appear before his death. On August 7, 1847, as he lay in bed dying, he told his followers, "If I did not know that the dear Lord meant I should present you all to him, I should think my last moment's come." His last moment had, in fact, come. He died before Jesus could appear.

In 1857 a South African tribe, the Gealeke Xhosa, were awed by the skills of a 14-year-old prophetess, who reported she had seen a vision in the river of the faces of dead tribal elders. She reported that they could be brought back to life if all of their livestock were slaughtered before February 18, 1857. The tribe did as instructed, but the elders remained deceased. The rest of the tribe soon joined them. Without their livestock, they starved to death.

From the "I have one year to live and I'm going to spend it reading one title" file: In 1868 Anglican minister Michael Paget Baxter published a book that said the world would end within the year. It was called: *Louis Napoleon, the Infidel Antichrist Predicted in Prophecy to*

Confirm a Seven Years Covenant With the Jews, About the Year 1861, and Nearly to Succeed in Gaining A Universal Empire; and Then to be Deified, and Idolatrously Worshiped, and Also to Institute A 3 ½ Years Sanguinary Persecution Against the Christian Church, From 1864-1865 to 1868, During Which Time Wars, Famine, Pestilences & Earthquakes, If Not Religious Persecution, Will Prevail in England and America Until the Slaughter of the Witnesses, Elias and Another Prophet; After Which Napoleon, Their Destroyer, Together with the Pope Are Foreshown to Be Cast Alive Into the Lake of Fire At the Descent of Christ At Armageddon About the Year 1868.
Baxter was another prophet who continuously rescheduled his dates of doom. He had first predicted the end would come between 1861-1867. He later revised it to 1868. Then 1869. He then announced it would arrive between 1871-72. Then he published a book entitled *The End of This Age About the End of This Century* in which predicted the Rapture would come in 1896 and it would all be over in 1901. This, of course, did not come to pass. While a lesser man might have felt his credibility was strained, Baxter did not give up. His next book, *Future Wonders of Prophecy*, announced the Rapture was to take place on March 12, 1903 between 2pm and 3pm, and Armageddon would take place on April 23, 1908.

According to Irvin Moore's book *The Final Destiny of Man*, on June 28, 1870, France would fall, and Jerusalem would become the capital of the world.

Thomas Rawson Birk's book *First Elements of Sacred Prophecy* set the end of the world at 1880.

"Mother Shipton's Prophecy" was supposedly first published in England in 1485 before the discovery of America:

Carriages without horses shall go
And accidents fill the world with woe
Around the world thoughts shall fly
In the twinkling of an eye.
Waters shall yet more wonders do,

Bad Predictions

Now strange, yet shall be true.
The world upside down shall be,
And gold found at root of tree.
Through hills man shall ride,
And no horse or ass be by his side.
Under water man shall walk,
Shall ride, shall sleep, shall talk.
In the air men shall be seen
In white, in black, in green.
Iron in the water shall float
As easy as a wooden boat.
Gold shall be found 'mid stone,
In a land that's now unknown.
Fire and water shall wonders do,
England shall at last admit a Jew.
And this world to an end shall come
In eighteen hundred and eighty-one.

In 1873 Charles Hindley, who had published "Mother Shipton's Prophecy" in 1862, revealed it was a forgery, but it had already gained wide circulation. It even appeared in later books with the last line changed to "eighteen hundred and ninety-one" and "nineteen hundred and ninety-one" as proof that the world would end in those years.

Hundreds of people believed that Europe would be destroyed on St. Patrick's Day, 1842. They based their belief on a poem by Dr. John Dee, an Elizabethan astrologer who lived from 1527-1608. The poem, it was said, was in the Harleian Museum. It was later revealed that there was no such manuscript.

Reverend Ethan Smith of Poultney, Vermont's, 1811 *Dissertation on the Prophecies Related to Antichrist and the Last Times* revealed that the "last days" would occur in 1866.

A number of experts, after measuring the Great Pyramid of Cheops, concluded that Judgement Day would come in 1881. When it didn't, other experts used the Great Pyramid's measurements to prove the end would come in 1936. When it didn't end then, the pyramid revealed that 1953 would be the last year for mankind. Northern Paiute leader Wovoka, after a long trance during a solar eclipse in 1889, predicted the end would come the following year. Wovoka was a practitioner of the Ghost Dance cult, a hybrid of apocalyptic Christianity and Native American mysticism.

Nineteenth-century Scottish astronomer Charles Piazzi Smyth studied the dimensions of the Great Pyramid of Giza and concluded the Second Coming would occur between 1892 and 1911.

"In about 1897-8 the heat of the sun will be so enormously increased by the impact of a comet as to destroy life upon this earth."
　　　　—Sir Richard Proctor, quoted in
　　　　The Berkshire Courier, February 4, 1897.

"We know that the end of the age is within this generation, but whether the present generation began in 1870 or in 1871 we do not know... What is to become of the present United States when the end of the world comes? It will be carried over to England. McKinley is to be the last President of the United States. Before the end of his term there will be a terrible European war... What will become of Wall Street? That I can positively answer. Wall Street three years from now will be in Jerusalem. But the work will be over. Its usefulness will have been accomplished. Wall Street is not a bad institution and it will be saved if the men individually are right. And our politicians? Now you get down to personalities. I could pick out twenty good politicians and twenty bad ones. The bad ones will be cast into outer darkness and the good ones transported to Jerusalem where they can mix for a thousand years in the delights of the perfect reign of Christ.. Now when it comes to locating the day for this...All signs say that the world will come to an end March 29, 1899, but it may be September, 1901."
　　　　—Dr. Beverly O Kinnear, quoted in
　　　　The Berkshire Courier, February 4, 1897.

1900

A sect called the Brothers and Sisters of Red Death lived in the Russian district of Kargopol. The group forbid marriage and suffocated with a large red cushion those who engaged in sexual intercourse. The members believed the world would end on November 13, 1900. They planned to sacrifice themselves by burning on the fateful day. On hearing of the plan, troops rushed to Kargopol in an attempt to stop them. When they got there, 100 people had already burned to death. When the world did not end, the sect disbanded.

A sect called the Catholic Apostolic Church claimed that Jesus would return by the time the last of its 12 founding members died. The last member died in 1901.

A grocery store owner from York, Pennsylvania, Lee T. Spangler, announced that when he was 12, he had received a vision that the world would end by fire in October, 1908. He managed to convince a number of people, but October passed without so much as a storm.

"The deliverance of the saints must take place some time before 1914."
> —Charles Taze Russell, *Studies in Scripture*, 1910. The revised edition of the book, published in 1923, contained the line "The deliverance of the saints must take place some time after 1914." Russell, a former Second Adventist, was the founder, in 1884, of the Watch Tower Tract Society, the forerunner of the modern day Jehovah's Witnesses.

Albert Porta, a meteorologist and seismographer, announced that on December 17, 1919, a conjunction of six planets would cause a magnetic current to "pierce the sun, cause great explosions of flaming gas, an eventually engulf the Earth." Since Porta had been accurate in his predictions of earthquakes in the past, many people took his dire prediction seriously. There were small panics in various world cities, but otherwise the world kept going as before.

There is an old adage in Italy that Rome is safe as long as the Coliseum stands. In May, 1924, engineers discovered huge cracks in the amphitheater. There were those who believed it was a "sign" and that Rome would topple on May 24 of that year. Thousands of people headed to the Vatican and St. Peter's Square only to observe Rome still standing as before. Repairmen were sent to fix the cracks in the Coliseum.

"If Christ does not appear to meet his 144,000 faithful shortly after midnight on February 6th or 7th, it means that my calculations, based on the Bible, must be revised."

> — Margaret Rowan of Los Angeles, leader of the Church of Advanced Adventists, said in 1925. She got her information from the angel Gabriel. A New York house painter named Robert Reidt was convinced. He took out ads in a number of newspapers and attracted many believers, who followed him to a hilltop dressed in white robes. At midnight, they raised their arms and chanted "Gabriel! Gabriel! Gabriel!" When nothing happened, Reidt realized that, since Rowan lived in Los Angeles, the end of the world would probably come on Pacific time. The group waited three hours, but still no vast destruction. Reidt blamed news photographers, who came to cover the story. Their flashbulbs, he said, kept Gabriel away. Later Reidt consulted the *Book of Revelation* and came up with his own doomsday date— October 10, 1932. When the world failed to end, Reidt retired from the prophecy business.

The Prophetical Society of Dallas believed the world would end in 1931. It didn't.

271

"The world is going to go 'puff' and disappear in September, 1935."
     —Wilbur Glen Voliva.

"The present prevailing unrest will ultimately lead, in the abnormally disturbed period between May 29, 1928, and September 16, 1936, as to cause and effect the war of Armageddon... The Symbolism of the Great Pyramid clearly reveals that the 'time of trouble' is within the period of eight years ending in September, 1936."
     —Basil Stewart, based on studies of the
     Great Pyramid.

Chilean astronomer Munoz Ferradas predicted a comet would collide with Earth in August, 1944, and destroy all life on earth. Many people in Chile believed him. Some committed suicide, others drank heavily, some hid in the mountains and didn't come back for a month.

In 1938 Reverend Charles Long was wakened from a deep sleep. At the foot of his bed he saw a blackboard and a ghostly hand, which wrote "1945." Then a voice whispered that the world would end that year at 5:33 PM, September 21. Long wrote a 70,000-word text on his experience and sent it to the leaders of the world. A week before the end was to come, Long and his followers gave up food, drink and sleep. They sang, prayed and waited. When September 22nd arrived, they disbanded and went home to sleep.

He was known as "America's Greatest Prophet." John Ballou Newbrough, in 1889, predicted all nations would be destroyed, and anarchy would overtake the land in 1947.

1950s

"My figures coincide in fixing 1950 as the year when the world must go smash."
     —writer Henry Brooks Adams,
     March, 22, 1903.

Pyramidologist David Davidson wrote in *The Great Pyramid, Its Divine Message* that the Millennium would begin in August, 1953.

Relatives became worried when 44-year-old Charles Laughead, a respected physician at Michigan State College, announced that the end of the world was coming December 20, 1954. He got the information from his psychic Dorothy Martin who, he said, had taught him to communicate with an extra-terrestrial civilization. While much of Europe and the United States perished in a flood, those who believed would be whisked away in a spaceship. Laughead did not lose his faith when December 20th came and went. He simply explained that "God had stopped it all." Loughead's relatives tried to have him committed, but the judge ruled that his unusual ideas did not constitute mental illness. The story of the doomsday cult inspired Leon Festinger to write *When Prophecy Fails*.

January 9, 1954, was to be the last day for humans on earth according to Agnes Grace Carlson, the leader of the Children of Light, a Canadian religious sect. She and 35 of the faithful spent what they believed would be their last 17 days alternately singing hymns and sitting in silence. The group was disbanded when a sheriff served them with summonses under the School Attendance Act.

London speaker Hector Cox was well known for his colorful talks on the *Egyptian Book of the Dead*. On Sunday, June 27, 1954, Cox announced that the world would end within 24 hours. This proved accurate only in his own case. He was found dead the next morning with a knife in his heart. Police ruled it a suicide.

"Sometime between April 16 and 23, 1957, Armageddon will sweep the world! Millions of persons will perish in its flames and the land will be scorched."
—California pastor Mihran Ask.

Victor Houteff was the founder of the Davidians. Not to be confused with David Koresh's Branch-Davidians, the Davidians were an offshoot of another millenialist religion, the Seventh Day Adventists. Although he told his followers the end was nigh, he never set a date. After his death, however, his widow Florence announced that the Rapture would take place on April 22, 1959. The faithful gathered at Mount Carmel outside Waco on that day, but the world kept right on going.

1960s

At exactly 1:45 PM on July 14, 1960, an accidental thermonuclear explosion of a secret "E" bomb was going to destroy the world. That was what Elio Bianco's sister Wilma told him. Wilma had passed away since making this 1958 prophecy, but Elio, a 46-year old Italian pediatrician, was a believer. He convinced 40 others to build a 15 room ark 7,000 feet up Mont Blanc. Elio told the press about the impending disaster and waited. At 1:58 PM, in the absence of mushroom clouds, Dr. Bianco told the press: "Anyone can make a mistake. Be happy that I have. Our faith has not collapsed because of that." The police were not amused. They arrested the doctor for spreading false reports.

Celebrity psychic Jeane Dixon predicted the world would end February 4, 1962 and that the Anti-Christ would be born the next day.

In 1965 a Columbian man named Nelson Olmeido sued a preacher in Bogota. The minister had warned his congregation that the world would explode April 18, 1965. Olmeido did what anyone would do if they knew the world was going to end. He spent his entire life savings on one last spree.

When asked why the publisher of *Time*, *Life* and *Fortune* would produce a magazine on a subject as light-weight as sports, *Sports Illustrated* publisher Henry Luce replied, "I think the world is going to blow up in seven years. The public is entitled to a good time during those seven years."

Anders Jensen, the Danish leader of the Disciples of Orthon, told viewers of "The David Frost Show" that Christmas, 1967, would be the start of the Apocalypse. The faithful built a huge underground nuclear shelter and spent their Christmas there. When the members of the sect finally ventured out of the bunker, they "expected to see ash covering the ground, a red glow in the sky, and everything destroyed." Instead, they were met by applause from sightseers who had come to watch their emergence. How did they feel to know the nations of the world had averted a full-scale thermonuclear war? "It's all a bit disappointing," said Jensen.

Jim Jones believed a nuclear holocaust would happen in 1967. Although it did not, Jones' career was only beginning. He gained a reputation as a charismatic preacher and founded "The People's Temple" in San Francisco in 1971. His influence was such that hundreds of devotees followed him to Guyana and set up an agricultural commune called Jonestown in 1977. Once there, Jones confiscated their passports. The group made numerous practice runs at a mass suicide ritual up to 1978 when 913 members finally completed the ritual by drinking cyanide-laced Kool-Aid.

Maria Staffler, who gave herself the title "Popess," told her followers that a great disaster would befall the planet on February 20, 1969. She urged them to follow her to a mountain top, but only a few showed up. She rescheduled the catastrophe to March 17. A few more people showed up for the second great disaster. After a few hours, they got bored and went home.

UFO prophet George Van Tassel received messages from an alien named Ashtar. Ashtar told him that on August 20, 1967, the southeastern US would be destroyed by a Soviet nuclear attack.

Bad Predictions

Robin McPherson channeled a message from another alien, this one named Ox Ho. Ox-Ho believed the end of the world was coming November 22, 1969.

1970s

Members of the True Light Church of Christ in Charlotte, North Carolina, were shocked when the world did not end in 1970. The leaders of the church had calculated that the world would end 6,000 years from the time of the creation, which they believed occurred in 4,000 B.C. Figuring 30 years had been lost from the first century of the Christian calendar, they were sure their time was up.

"For the first time ever, everything is in place for the battle of Armageddon and the Second Coming of Christ... It can't be too long now. Ezekiel says that fire and brimstone will be rained upon the enemies of God's people. That must mean that they will be destroyed by nuclear weapons."
—Ronald Reagan at a 1971 political banquet.

In September, 1975, a 67-year-old Arkansas woman, Viola Walker, received a message from God. She told her relatives that the Second Coming was about to happen and the end of the world would follow. She and 21 family members joined her in a vigil in her three-bedroom home. The children were taken out of school, the bills were left unpaid, and the Walkers waited. They stayed in the house, praying and waiting until July 16, 1976. That was when they were evicted for not making mortgage payments on the house.

Fundamentalist cult leader William Branham predicted Los Angeles would fall into the sea after an earthquake, the Vatican would achieve dictatorial powers over the world, and all of Christianity would become unified. Then the Rapture, he said, would come no later than 1977.

Using parts of the Bible and measurements of the Great Pyramid, Australian businessman John Strong concluded that the Soviet Union would launch a nuclear attack in October, 1978. He published his prophecy in the 1973 book *The Doomsday Globe*. Strong believed the last day would be either October 2, October 15 or October 31. If the world did not end, then he was positive the attack would begin before September 23, 1979.

1980s

The 1980s were to be the "decade of shock," according to The Southwest Radio Church of Oklahoma City's 1978 pamphlet, "God's Timetable for the 1980s." In 1981, they predicted the Great Synagogue would be completed, and Jews would resume sacrifices. There would be peace between Arabs and Jews. In 1986 the armies of the world would join forces to fight off alien invaders. In 1987 two prophets would arise in Jerusalem. There would be storms and earthquakes. In 1989 more aliens would invade, and Christ would appear again.

Stephen D. Swihart wrote a book called *Armageddon 198?*, which predicted it would all be over sometime in the 1980s.

"They laughed at Noah," said Charles Gaines. Charles Gaines and Leleand Jensen, leaders of Bahá'ís Under the Provisions of the Covenant, a splinter group of the Bahá'ís (who disavow them), concluded that the final war would start April 29, 1980 at 5:55 PM. When it didn't, they recalculated and prepared for the worst on May 7.

"I'm convinced that the Lord is coming for His Church before the end of 1981."
    —Chuck Smith, founder of Calvary Chapel,
    in his book *Future Survival*.

Bad Predictions

Emil Gaverluk of the Southwest Radio Church, using *The Jupiter Effect*, by John Gribbin and Stephen Plagemann as research material, claimed that when the planets came into alignment on May 10, 1982, Jupiter would pull Mars out of orbit, and it would smash into Earth.

The Jupiter Effect also inspired Hal Lindsey, author of the 1970 book *The La e Great Planet Earth*. "If these scientists are right," he wrote, "then what we can expect in 1982— we'll have the largest outbreak of killer quakes ever seen in the history of planet earth along with radical changes in climate and most climatologists believe that the shift is already taking place." In 1981 he followed up with the book *Countdown to Armageddon*, which declared: "The decade of the 1980s could very well be the last decade of history as we know it... WE ARE THE GENERATION THAT WILL SEE THE END TIMES...AND THE RETURN OF JESUS." Lindsey postulated that the end of the world would come in or near 1988. When it did not, he published another book in 1994, *Planet Earth: 2000 A.D.* He revised his calculations and determined that the end would come in 2007.

Canadian Doug Clark was another believer in the *Jupiter Effect*. The massive earthquakes in 1982, he prophesied, would bring about the return of Christ, and "by 1985 we are going to have a food war." Using Hal Lindey's calculations, he determined the Rapture would come in 1988. When the Jupiter Effect failed to cause the expected tremors, Clark recanted and admitted he had made a mistake. Within a year, however, he was appearing on the television program "Praise the Lord" announcing World War III would begin before the year 2000.

"I am Jesus Christ. I am omnipotent. I am here to announce the end of the world."
—Mehmet Ali Agca, while on trial for shooting
Pope John Paul II in 1985.

In 1983, Nigel Calder, a British science writer, contributed an article on his predictions for the future to a book called *The Future of A Troubled World*, a project begun and edited by his father Ritchie Calder. The forecasts in the book were primarily made with a view to 2000. Nigel Calder, however, was not convinced that the year would come. "Discussions of the future usually take for granted that we shall avoid nuclear war," he wrote, "but to do so in the 1980s is a form of genteel irresponsibility. Of all my 'extremes' the Doomsday machine is the nearest to realization and more technological skill is going into Doomsday-like projects than any other area of human activity. Extinction, at least of northern civilization, is not probable enough for one to suppose, actually, that an individual is more likely to die from the effects of an H-bomb than of heart failure, or in a road accident... If we hastily switch to negotiated comprehensive disarmament, we might expect to scrape through with both lives and liberties intact. The improbability of such a profound change of heart on all sides, least of all among those who might expect to rule the world, suggests that our creative, freedom-loving civilization is doomed, one way or the other."

"Materialism is dead. It has been composted by today's youth to fertilize the seed of love and spirituality... Do not be troubled by unhappy events predicted. They will all come to pass. We are not evolved enough to circumvent the tragedies induced by cosmic cycles... This is a most exciting time to live, a time of cosmic high. Cataclysms of global scope have been foretold for the near future by many prophets and seers. Powerful astrological forces will soon come into play: a planetary alignment is forecast for 1984; it will be preceded by the Jupiter/Uranus alignment of March, 1983. Such alignments have historically coincided with widespread cataclysmic activities, and in this specific age, could lead to great earthquake and volcanic activity, which are likely, in turn, to trigger a nuclear holocaust of N-power plants and stored weapons, as well as fires and explosions from stored chemicals, gases and other toxic substances."
—Viktoras Kulvinskas, *Survival into the 21st Century*, 1975.

279

The Book of Predictions, a 1980 book by the authors of *The People's Almanac*, quoted gasoline expert Dan Lundberg as saying that by 1987 "Nature's remedy for the destruction of the planetary environment will have been applied in terms of a whole bewildering array of degenerating sickness and epidemics. We will find among the survivors only the most naturally healthy peoples of the worlds. Greatly reduced in numbers, they are discovering at long last that the only way to survive is to respect ecology in toto."

August 17, 1987 could be seen as either the date of a failed prophecy or a successful prayer vigil. Author José Argüelles claimed that to avert Armageddon on this day, 144,000 people would have to gather in various locations throughout the world to "resonate in harmony." Whether through the power of harmonic resonance or the lack of a real threat, the world did not end.

Another author predicting the second coming in 1988 was Edgar C. Whisenant, author of the book *88 Reasons Why The Rapture Will Be in 1988*. The Rapture would take place during Rosh Hashanah, he wrote, "Only if the Bible is in error am I wrong, and I say that unequivocally." When it did not, the author was undaunted. He revised his prediction and waited for the end to come by 10:55 AM September 15. By the end of the month of September with no end to life on Earth in sight, Whisenant did not lose his faith. "The evidence is all over the place that it is going to be in a few weeks," he said. When the world kept going, he released a new book, *The Final Shout: Rapture Report1989*. In this book he claimed Rosh Hashannah, 1989, was the big day. Other books by Whisenant include *The Final Shout: Rapture Report 1990, The Final Shout: Rapture Report 1991, The Final Shout: Rapture Report 1992...*

And from the "just because the end is nigh doesn't mean I can't make a buck" file: To coincide with Whisenant's prediction of the Rapture in 1988, a man named Charles Taylor announced a speacial $1,850 tour package to the Holy Land. "We stay at the Intercontinental Hotel right on the Mount of Olives where you can get the beautiful view of the Eastern Gate and the Temple Mount," the advertisement read. "And if this is the year of our Lord's return, as we anticipate, you may even ascend to Glory from within a few feet of His ascension." Taylor, however, hedged his bets. All travel packages included return airfare "if necessary."

1990s

Chen Heng-Ming, known to his followers as "Teacher Chen," predicted that God would appear world-wide on television channel 18 at 12:01 AM CST March 25, 1998. He also said that God would appear to his 150 followers in person on a flying saucer on March 31 of that year. Chen had said he would offer himself for stoning or crucifixion if his prophecies did not come to pass. When the time came, however, the television showed nothing but static. "Because we did not see God's message on television tonight," Chen said, "my predictions of March 31 can be considered nonsense."

Nostradamus is heralded as one of the most successful visionaries of the past. He is certainly the most famous. He owes his reputation to a set of 940 quatrains, four line verses of poetry, arranged in "centuries"— ten centuries in all. The wording of the verses is vague and open to wide interpretation, hence the continuing interest in his prophecy. Believers can, in hindsight, easily attribute the verses to happenings in particular centuries. By generously translating the Latinized French into English, Nostradomites have been able to give some of the quatrains a better "fit." Professional skeptic James Randi believes Nostradamus is the worst prognosticator in history. Nonetheless, his fame grows.

Bad Predictions

The only specific year mentioned in the prophecies of
Nostradamus is 1999. "The year 1999, seven months,
From the sky will come a great King of Terror
To bring back to life the great King of the Mongols,
Before and after Mars to reign by good luck."

In July, 1999, however, no one was aware of a great
King of Terror descending from the sky. True believers
in Nostradamus were not dissuaded. Convinced the
quatrain was correct and they were interpreting it
incorrectly, they devised a number of theories. There
is an Internet newsgroup devoted to Nostradamus—
alt.prophecies.nostradamus. The people who use it
first tried using the Julian calendar of Nostradamus'
time and came up with August 13.

When no King of Terror descended, they decided "sept
mois" must have referred to "September." Next they
turned to the Hebrew calendar, which put the 7th
month in October. Still no King of Terror. Some
Nostradamus fans are still waiting. They are now
convinced he was referring to the seventh month
AFTER 1999, or July 2000. Meanwhile, a Seattle-
based student of Nostradamus, John Hogue, claims
other Nostradamus references that seem to indicate
the world will end in 3797.

2000

"A study of all the prophets— Nostradamus, St. Odile, Mother Shipton, the Bible— indicates that we will cease to exist before the year 2000! Not one of these prophets even took the trouble to predict beyond the year 2000! And if you and I meet each other on the street that fateful day, August 18, 1999, and we chat about what we will do on the morrow, we will open our mouths to speak and no words will come out, for we have no future... you and I will suddenly run out of time! Who knows but what future generation from some other planet will dig down through seven layers of rubble and find us some 2,000 years hence, and crowd around a museum glass containing a broken fragment of a Coca Cola bottle, a bent hairpin and a parched copy of our Bible which managed to escape the terrifying destruction of civilization! They will wonder what on earth was meant by the words 'Henry Ford' or 'Hollywood'... and what in heaven's name was a Criswell!"
> —psychic Jeron Criswell, *Criswell Predicts*, 1968.

Jeanne Le Royer, a lay sister in a convent in Brittany, lived from 1732-1798. She predicted the papacy would fall and the world would end in 2000.

"I'll be astounded if this planet is still going fifty years from now. I don't think we'll reach 2000. It would be miraculous."
> —Alistair Cooke, 1950.

One of the more interesting 1994 doomsday books is Michael D. Evans' *Seven Years of Shaking: A Vision,* which claimed that Bill Clinton's 1993 inauguration was the beginning of a new age of depravity and destruction. "He will drag American down the dead-end road to complete and moral decay. America will no longer be a Christian nation in any shape or form by the end of the seventh year [2000]."

283

Bad Predictions

"Between 1999 and 2003, a nuclear war is sure to break out."

> —Shoko Asahara, author of *Day of Annihila tion*, 1987. The book explained that in 1999 Japan would sink into the ocean and that Russia, China, America and Europe would collapse, causing a nuclear war between October 30 and November 29, 2003. A race of super humans, made up of his followers, would then take over the world. Under the theory, perhaps, that God could not do it on his own, Asahara's message was, in the words of author Richard Abanes, "salvation through terrorism." He and his followers would help the end along with nerve gas. To bring on World War III, Asahara encouraged followers to attack government buildings and to research germ warfare. The group was responsible in 1995 for releasing nerve gas in the Tokyo subway system, resulting in 12 deaths and 5,500 stricken with symptoms ranging from nausea to permanent blindness.

According to Richard Keininger's 1962 *The Ultimate Frontier*, a planetary alignment will occur on May 5, 2000, which will cause the poles to shift. This will cause seismic activity, volcanic eruptions with poisonous gas that will blot out the sun, hurricanes and tsunami. Those who have "the strength of their convictions" will survive to see the formation on the Kingdom of God after October, 2001.

"On May 5th in the year 2000, our Moon, the planets Mercury, Venus, our Sun, Mars, Jupiter and Saturn will be aligned with the Earth, significantly increasing the centrifugal momentum exerted on the Earth's crust. On that day, the ever growing ice buildup at the South Pole will upset the earth's axis sending trillions of tons of ice and water sweeping over the surface of our planet."

> —Richard Noone, *5/5/2000— Ice: The Ultimate Disaster.*

Jeffrey Goodman, PhD, consulted a number of psychics and compared their forecasts for similarities. He then took their predictions about earthquakes, California falling into the sea, and so on and compared them to scientific research on the study of earthquakes. He published his findings in the 1978 book *We are the Earthquake Generation*. Goodman predicted the planetary alignment in May, 2000, would bring about catastrophic earthquakes. "By 2000 the ice buildup at the poles should be much greater and the earth's rotational balance more tenuous. If 2000 brings more and greater earthquakes, which lead to even greater wobble, perhaps the earth's balance will be disturbed enough so that it flips over in space just as the psychics have predicted. This would also bring the long-overdue magnetic reversal."

The ancient Mayan calendar begins with 13.0.0.0.0 and counts backwards (in the way that we count dates Before Christ) towards the fourth creation of the cosmos. The end date on this system will be, by our calendar, between December 21 and 23, 2012. Mayan watchers believe that on that date all that has been created or subjugated by man will rear up and attack him thus bringing about a reinforcement of the universal order.

You will note that I have included a few doomsday predictions that are set in the near future as of this writing. I feel safe in doing so because if these predictions prove accurate, no one will be around to notice I goofed. If, on the other hand, you are the only person left on earth, you have taken shelter in the basement of an old book store and you have opened this book to get you through your lonely post-apocalyptic existence, feel free to say, "They told you so."

We Predict....

That this will not be the last edition of *Bad Predictions*. Did we miss your favorite? Has your local newspaper or magazine printed a bad prediction we should know about? Tell us. Send the prediction and its source to:

Laura Lee c/o
Elsewhere Press
1326 Gettysburg
Rochester, MI
48306.

If you are the first to send in a quote, and we use it, you will receive a free copy of Bad Predictions version 2.0.

Want to order additional copies of *Bad Predictions*?
Visit our Web page: www.elsewherepress.com or write to the above address.

The author would like to thank the following individuals for their support: Christopher and Jennifer Lee who compiled an exceptionally thorough index (it would have been more thorough if space permitted). Tammy Pethtel for enthusiastic promotional help and Larry Flanigan because great minds think alike.

Author (predictor) Index

20th Century Fox 150
ABC 141
Adams, Douglas 89
Adams, Henry Brooks 102, 272
Adams, John 209, 214
Adams, John Quincy 172
Africanus, Sextus Julius 258
Agassiz, Louis 97, 114
Agate, James 40
Agca, Mehmet Ali 278
Agnew, Spiro 92, 224
Airy, George Bidell 105
Albe, E. E. Fournier d' 146
Aldrich, Thomas Bailey 173
Allen, Irwin 152
Allen, James 208
American Advertising Federation 11
American Federation of Musicians 147
American Forest and Paper Association 12
American Institute of Electrical Engineers 39, 67, 132
American Motors Corporation 74
Anabaptists 261
Andrews, Harry 184
Anti-Saloon League of America 40
Apple Computer 108
Archdeacon of Prague 259
Argüelles, José 280
Armstrong, James W. 36
Arnold, Gary 157
Arnot, Samuel P. 201
Arthritis Foundation 125
Ashara, Shoko 284
Asimov, Isaac 105
Ask, Mihran 273
Aspinwall, William 262
Associated Press 252
AT&T 135
Aubrey, John 123
Auston, Diane 111
Babbage, Charles 105
Babson, Roger W. 23, 27-8, 48, 202, 221
Bacon, Josephine Daskam 47
Baker, George P. 194
Baltimore Colts 188
Bank of Japan 71
Banks, Joseph 60
Barach, Arnold B. 24, 34, 66, 90, 125, 139, 193-4
Barnes, Fred 228
Barr, Roseanne 143
Barrow, John 133
Barry, Gerald 133
Barry, Marion 227
Bate, Henry 209
Bateman, Mary 264
Batista, Fulgencio 234
Baxter, Michael Paget 266-7
Bayer Company 124
Bateman, Mary 264
Batista, Fulgencio 234
Baxter, Michael Paget 266-7
Bayer Company 124
BBC 29
Beade, Fritz 234
Beatty, Warren 153, 157

Beauvoir, Simone de 177
Beck, Simone 29
Beckel, Bob 228
Begbie, Harold 246
Bell Labs 136
Bell, George 263
Bell, Thomas 114
Bell, William 263
Belushi, John 142
Benchley, Peter 179
Benchley, Robert 161
Benson, Charles 242
Bergier, Jaques 72, 99, 121, 125
Berlin University 46
Bernard of Thuringia 258
Bernard, Al 217
Bernoulli, Jacques 263
Bertholle, Louisette 29
Beschloss, Michael R. 181
Betjeman, John 147
Beukels, John 261
Bianco, Elio 274
Bianco, Wilma 274
Bibby, Cyril 43
Bickerton, William 87, 88
Bird, Arthur 19
Birk, Thomas Rawson 267
Blair, Eric Arthur 175
Blair, Tony 109
Blake, Leonardo 249-50
Block, Paul 201, 218
Bloomingdale, L. M. 70
Blue Book Modelling Agency 155
Bochco, Steven 143
Boeing Corporation 82
Bohr, Neils 9
Boller, Paul F. 265
Bonaparte, Napoleon 60
Borah, William E. 40
Born, Max 115
Bouillaud, Jean 97
Brander, Laurence 177
Branham, William 276
British Association for the Advancement of Science 26
British Film Institute 23
British Interplanetary Society 89
British Navy 60
British Parliament 96
British Post Office 135
British Royal Society 60
Brock, Sidney G. 54
Brooklyn Dodgers 185
Brooks, Joe 168
Broomfield, William S. 255
Brothers and Sisters of Red Death 270
Brothers, Richard 263
Brougham, Henry Peter 113
Browne, Junius Henri 39, 199
Bruno, Harry 70
Bruno, Jerry 224
Bryan, William Jennings 247
Buckley, William F. 253
Buffington, Helen 225
Buick Motor Company 74
Bullitt, William C. 248
Burke, James 99

Bad Predictions

Burnet, Frank MacFarlane 124
Burns, Eleanor 13
Burton, Anthony 167
Bush, George 227, 255
Bush, Vannevar 243-244
Butler, Nicholas Murray 246
Butts, Claudia A. 227
Byrd, Eldon 126-127
Byrd, Richard E. 199
Byron, William 49
Cain, James M. 176
Cain, Scott 153
Calder, Nigel 278-279
Calder, Ritchie 103, 278-279
Callenbach, Ernest 52, 75
Calverton, V. F. 150
Cameron, James 154
Campanella, Tomasso 261
Canby, Vincent 152
Capitol Records 167
Caputo, Vincent F. 72
Carlisle, Norman V. 27
Carlson, Agnes Grace 273
Carlson, Chester 193
Carnegie, Andrew 246
Carr, W. P. 128
Carson, Johnny 142
Carter, Billy 225
Catholic Apostolic Church 270
CBS 140, 141
Centers for Disease Control
    and Prevention 122
Central Intelligence Agency 226
Cetron, Marvin 31-32, 47, 52,
    198, 203, 254
Century 21 83
Chamberlain, Neville 251
Chanel, CoCo 24
Chanute, Octave 79
Chaplin, Charlie 146, 147
Chaplin, W. W. 48, 233
Chen, Heng-Ming 281
Chesterton, G. K. 133
Chicago Board of Free Trade
    201
Chicago Cubs 184, 186
Chief of Naval Operations 242
Child, Julia 29
Chow, Gin 55
A Christian Federalist 214
Church of Advanced Adventists
    271
Churchill, Winston 27, 243
Cincinnati Reds 186, 187
Clark, Doug 278
Clark, John Bates 54
Clark, William 125
Clarke, Arthur C. 20, 35, 74,
    83, 92, 93
Clemens, Samuel Langhorne
    (see Twain, Mark)
Clementine College 86
Cleveland Clinic 125
Cleveland Indians 184
Cleveland, Grover 46, 216
Clinton, Bill 109, 227, 228
Club of Rome 43
CNN 226
Cobbett, William 123
Cochran, Johnnie 42
Cohen, Paul 166
Cohn, Harry 148, 155
    162

Cohn, Victor 13, 23, 28, 33,
    36, 40, 71, 89, 98
Culbert, Claudette 149
Cole, William 178
Coleman, R. R. 45
Collins, Patrick S. 50
Colorado State University 28
Columbia Pictures 148, 155,
Columbus, Christopher 262
Committee to Reelect the
    President 225
Committee on the Year 2000
    57
Conant, James Bryant 252
Continental Army 208
Continental Congress 208
Continental Illinois Bank 201
Cooke, Alistair 283
Cooper, Gary 149
Coppola, Francis Ford 151
Corliss, Richard 154
Cowl, Jane 161
Cox, Hector 273
Craven, Thomas 161
Crawford, Cheryl 162
Criswell, Jeron 283
Crocker Bank 194
Crookes, William 26
Crosby, Bing 165
Crowther, Bosley 155
Cunningham, Bill 185
Custer, George Armstrong 245
Daimler-Benz 68
Dalton, John 100
Daniels, George H. 66
Daniels, Josephius 242
Darwin, Charles 173
Darwin, Robert 114
Davidians 274
Davidson, David 273
Davy, Humphrey 113
De Angelis, Augustion 86
De Forest, Lee 89, 138
De Lana-Terzi, Francesco 75
Dean Telephone Company 137
Dean, James 155
Dean, W. W. 137
Debs, Eugene V. 199
Decca Records
    166, 167
Dee, John 265, 268
DeFord, Charles S. 116
Denny, Jim 166
Department of Highways of
    Brooklyn 67
Depew, Chauncey 54, 68
Detroit Lions 186
DeWitt, Bill 186
Dickson, Paul 8
Dietrich, Bill 193
Digital Equipment 107
Disciples of Orthon 275
Disney, Roy 155
Disney, Walt 149
Disraeli, Benjamin 61
Dixon, Jeane 274
Dixon, Thomas, Jr. 39, 199
Dolan, Daria 204
Dolan, Ken 204
Dombile, Compton 241
Donaldson, Sam 228
Doubleday and Company 176

Douglas, Paul F. 99
Dover, Mayor of 184
Dow, Herbert Henry 192
Dreser, Heinrich 124
Du Tell, Jean-Pierre 232
Duke of Edinburgh 167
Duke of Wellington 63
Dulles, John Foster 202
Durant, William C. 74
Dusenberg, Peter 127
Eastman, Max 247
Eccles, Solomon 262
Ecole des Beaux-Arts 160
Edison, Thomas Alva 48, 69,
    77, 101, 102, 146, 147
Edler, Henry G. 83
Edman, Irwin 55
Egan, Leo 220
Ehrlich, Paul 31
Eisenhower, Dwight D. 219
Ekland, Britt 168
Elias, Hans 213
Eliot, George Fielding 250, 251
Eliot, T. S. 175
Ellsworth, Henry L. 96
Engels, Friedrich 240
Englehardt, Vladimir 125-126
Ericksen, John Eric 128
Ernst, Morris L. 40, 45
Evans, Christopher 21, 41, 51,
    75, 107, 180, 198
Evans, Michael D. 283
Evett, Robert 151
Fadiman, Clifton 176
Falk, Bibb 186
Falwell, Jerry 111
Farmer, Richard N. 22, 38, 74,
    121, 139, 198
Federal Communications
    Commission 140
Federal Trade Commission 69
Feinberg, Gerald 93
Ferradas, Muñoz 272
Ferriss, Hugh 44
Ferriss, Orange 211-212
Festinger, Leon 273
Figgie, Harry 203
Finck, Henry T. 46
Finniston, H. M. 186
Fischer, Oskar 236
Fischer, Scott 189
Fisher, Irving 200
Fitzroy, Robert 114
Flanagan, William 153
Fleming, Victor 149
Florida Division of State Planning 136, 203
Flynn, Daniel W. 165
Flynn, John T. 202
Foch, Marechal Ferdinand 241
Forbes, J. Murray 102
Ford Motor Company 13, 25, 30, 37, 106
Ford, Henry 69, 248
Ford, Henry (II) 71
Foster, Richard J. 259
Francis, P. H. 117
Franklin, P. A. S. 62
Frantzen, Ulrich 72
Freeman, Orville 31
French Academy 75
French Academy of Sciences
    97
French Director-General of Infantry 241
French Laboratories 121
Friedenthal, Hans 46
Frontius, Sextus Julius 96,
    240
Fuller, R. Buckminster 222
Gaines, Charles 277
Galloway, B. T. 26
Galloway, Joseph 209
Gallup, George 219
Galton, James 180
Galvin, Jan 108
Gandelot, Howard 71
Gandhi, Indira 235
Gardner, John W. 254
Garratt, Arthur 136, 140
Garrison, Michael 150
Gates, Bill 108
Gaverluk, Emil 278
Gealeke Xhosa 266
Geddes, Norman Bel 82, 98,
    103, 124, 161
General Motors 55, 70, 71, 72,
    196
George M. Hill Company 173
George, David Lloyd 247, 249
George, Don 53
Gerard of Poehlde 259
Gernreich, Rudi 25
Gibb, Barry 168
Gibbs, Philip 70
Giga Information Group 12-13
Gillette, George Francis 116
Gingrich, Newt 225
Girtanner, Christoph 114
Gleason, Jackie 166
Goebbels, Joseph 234
Goethals, George Washington
    62
Goizueta, Roberto 194
Golden, Harry 252-253
Goldsberry, Gordon 186
Goldsmith, Teddy 104
Goodman, Jeffrey 285
Gordon, Theodore 125
Governor's Conference on the
    Year 2000 50
Graham, Billy 167
Grant, George E. 112-113
Greeley, Andrew M. 225
Greeley, Horace 215
Greenfield, Jeff 224
Greenleaf, William 68
Gribbin, John 278
Griffith, D. W. 146
Guedel, John 141
Guggenheim, Harry 81
Gunnison, Walter B. 47
Guthrie, Arlo 168, 223
H. M. S. Beagle 114
Habberton, John 53, 199
Haig, Douglas 242
Haldane, J. B. S. 102, 243
Halhead, Nathaniel Brassey
    263
Hamasaki, Cory 110, 112
Hamilton, Alexander 214
Harbord, James J. 138
Harding, Warren G. 217
Hardy, Alister 29
Hariezon, Sors 192
Harman, Willis 213
Harper, Victoria 154

Bad Predictions

Harris, Richard 153
Harris, William T. 216
Hart, Gary 15-16, 227
Hartford Woman's Friday Club 100
Harvard Economic Society 201
Harvard University 97
Harvard University Center for Population Studies 56
Harvey, Richard 261
Hauptmann, Moritz 166
Hawaiian Education Task Force 50, 197
Hawkins, Ronnie 166
Hayes, Rutherford B. 135, 215
Hearst, William Randolph 44, 218
Heckscher, August 201
Hedge, Frank S. 74
Helton, William 73, 244
Henderson, Paul 81
Heritage West 2000 111
Hernandez, Justo Carillo 234
Herr, John K. 67
Hertz, Heinrich Rudolf 136
Hetzel, Pierre-Jules 19, 96
Hewitt, Don 140
Hill, L. Erskine 115
Hindenburg, Paul von 248, 249
Hindley, Charles 268
Hippolytus 258
Hirschorn, Robert 42
Hite Research International 57
Hite, Shere 57
Hitler, Adolf 14, 212, 234, 249, 250, 251
Hoffa, Jimmy 41
Hofmann, Melchior 261
Hogue, John 282
Holmes, Tommy 185
Hooker, Michael K. 32
Hoover, Herbert 137, 200, 201
Hörbiger, Hans 116
House of Commons 61, 101
Houteff, Victor 274
Hess, Karl 51
Howard, L. O. 26
Howe, Quincy 213
Hubbard, Gardiner Green 135
Hudson Institute 235
Hugo, Victor 76
Hull, Cordell 249
Hunt, John 160
Hussites 259-260
Hut, Hans 260
Huxley, T. H. 53
Huygens, Christiaan 86
Hyatt, Michael S. 112-113
IBM 106, 107, 200
Ichimada, Hisato 71
Iggleheim, Count von 260
Ingalls, John J. 77
Institute for the Future 108, 122
International Mercantile Marine Company 62
International Monetary Fund 202
Irenaeus 258
Irsay, Robert 188
Ives, Joseph C. 210
Jackman, W. J. 80

Jackson, Merrill 198
Jaffe, Stanley 151
James, Thomas L. 22
Jenner, Edward 123
Jennings, William 44
Jensen, Anders 275
Jensen, Leleand 277
Jewell, James 139
Joachim of Fiore 259
Joachites 259
Jobs, Steve 108
John Murray Anderson Drama School 154
John of Toledo 259
Johnson, Lyndon B. 253
Johnson, Paul 236
Johnson, Samuel 76
Jones, Davy 195
Jones, Jim 275
Jones, T. K. 104
Jordan, David Starr 246
Junor, Penny 237
Kael, Pauline 151
Kaempfert, Waldemar 35, 81, 83
Kafka, Franz 177
Kahn, Herman 20, 57, 235
Karman, Theodore von 82
Kath, Terry 169
Kauffman, Felix 127
Keininger, Richard 284
Kellogg Corporation 57
Kelpius, Johannes 262
Kemble, E. W. 68
Kennedy, Joseph P. 223
Kent, Frank R. 219
Kilmer, George L. 241
King George III 209
Lord Byron 172
Lord Kelvin 77, 113, 135, 245
Lord, Jim 110
Lord Sandwich 208
Lotharingian prophets 258
Love, Christopher 264
Lowell, James Russell 174
Loy, Myrna 148
Loyola College 49
Luce, Henry 274-275
Lugosi, Bela 148
Lumiere, Auguste 146
Lumiere, Louis-Jean 147
Lundberg, Dan 280
Luther, Martin 86
MacArthur, Douglas 251
McCarten, John 150
McCartney, Paul 167
McClimans, Fred 112
McCormick, Pat 142
McCormick, Robert Rutherford 244
McDuffie, George 134
McGraw-Hill 177, 179
McKinley, William 216
McLuhan, Marshall 187
McPherson, Robin 276
Macaulay, Thomas Babington 215
Macmillan, Frederick 174
Macoy, C.W. 240
Mainardi, Pat 13-14
Mainwaring, John 166
Malabre, Alfred L. 197

Maltin, Leonard 153
Marchetti, Gino 188
Marles, M. de 76
Martin, Dorothy 273
Maruyama, Magoroh 45
Mason, Gregory 47
Massey, Harrie 90
Mather, Cotton 262
Matthew of Janov 259
Matthys, Jan 261
Mauldin, John 111
Maxwell, Arthur S. 91
Mayer, Louis B. 148
Mechanic, Bill 154
Melville, George W. 77-78
Mencken, H. L. 218
Menen, Aubrey 7
Mengelberg, W. 164
Metcalfe, Bob 108
MGM 147, 148, 155, 162
Michelson, Albert A. 115
Michigan Savings Bank 68
Midland Chemical Company 192
Milic, John 259
Milikan, Robert 242
Miller, William 265, 266
Millikan, Robert Andrews 102
Milwaukee Braves 185
Minkin, Barry 204
Minnesota Valley Canning Company 193
Minnesota Vikings 188
Modell, Art 189
Montagu, John 208
Montesquieu 42
Moore, Irvin 267
Morris, Charles 54, 97-98, 232-233
Morton, Henry 97
Mother Shipton 283, 267-268
Moulton, F. R. 87
Ms. Magazine 21, 50-51, 122, 187, 225
Mubarak, Hosni 255
Mueller, John M. 204
Muir, Bill 111
Mulady, Kathy 110
Mullins, Eustace 125
Mumford, Lewis 233
Murphy, Robert 247
Napier, John 262
NASA 92
National Academy of Science 82
National Advisory Committee on the Recruitment... 99
National Aviation and Space Council 83
National Education Association 40, 196
The National Film Preservation Board 150
National Geographic Society 135
National Hemophilia Foundation 127
Naylor, R. H. 250
NBC 140, 141
Neumann, John von 106
New York Giants 185
Newbrough, John Ballou 272
Newcomb, Simon 78, 78-79, 80

Nicolas of Cusa 263
Nixon, Richard 222, 223, 224, 226-227, 254
Nkoloso, Edward Mukaka 90
Noel, F. J. B. 66
Noone, Richard 284
Norman, Phillip 168
North, Gary 109
Nostradamus 282, 283
Nye, Bill 46, 216
O'Daniel, John 252
O'Kinnear, Beverly 269
Olimeido, Nelson 274
Olive, John R. 28
Olsen, Ken 107
O'Malley, Walter 185
O'Neill, Gerard 93
O'Toole, Thomas 31-32, 47, 52, 127, 198, 203, 254
Pachet, Pierre 123
Pack, Arthur 197
Page, Irvine 125
Pake, George E. 195
Pan Am 91-92
Paramount Pictures 141, 151
Parker, Buddy 186
Parker, George 193
Parsons, Floyd W. 103
Payne, William Morton 173
Pearson, Drew 220
Peck, Harry Thurston 174
Peffer, William Alfred. 196, 216
Penn, Sean 157, 158
Pennsylvania Assembly 209
The People's Almanac 93
Pepper, Robert 140
Pertez, Martin 236
Petain, Henri Philippe 243
Peters, John 153
Pettit, Tom 227
Phillip Morris 140
Pickering, William H. 80, 241
Plagemann, Stephen 278
Pogregin, Letty Cottin 21, 50-51, 122, 187, 225
Polaroid 98
Pope John Paul II 235
Pope, Ralph W. 39, 67, 132
Popular Library 180
Porta, Albert 270-271
Postmaster General 22, 23
Powderly, T.V. 39, 42, 198
Powers, Jimmy 185
Poyssel, Eustachius 262
Preece, William 135
Prentice Hall 106
Prep 2000 109
Price, George R. 213
Princess Diana 237
Prior of St. Bartholomew 260
Proctor, Richard 269
Producer's Council of Delphi 31
Prophetical Society of Dallas 271
Pulleston, William T. 252
Pyssel, Eustachius 262
Raft, George 150, 155
Rand Corporation 29
Rand, Tamara 227
Randi, James 281
Rapp, George 266

Bad Predictions

Quad, M. 23
Ratoff, Gregory 150
Ray, Russ 204
RCA 104, 107, 139
Read, F. W. 66
Read, Herbert 148, 162, 165
Reagan, Ronald 222, 276
Reed, Rex 157
Reidt, Robert 271
Reliance Insurance 196
Revelle, Roger 116
Reynolds, Arthur 201
Rheingold, Howard 58
Rickenbacker, Eddie 222
Rinehard, John 89
Rinzler, Carol 38, 93, 122
Ripley, Robert 120
Rivera, Geraldo 142
RKO Radio Pictures 150
Roberts, Oral 52
Rodale, J.I. 121, 126
Roddenberry, Gene 143
Rojas, Billy 41, 38, 50, 92, 121, 225
Rolls, Charles Stewart 80
Rolls-Royce 80
Roosevelt, Franklin Delano 219, 242, 251
Roosevelt, Teddy 217
Roper, Elmo 220
Rowan, Margaret 271
Royal Academy 160
Royal Society, England's 113, 114, 134
Rubin, Herman 43
Russell, Charles Taze 270
Russell, T. Baron 22, 27, 32, 79, 124, 160, 184
Russell, Thomas 80
Ruste, R. G. 197
Rutherford, Ernest 103, 104
Saffo, Paul 108
Saint-Etienne, Jean-Paul Rabaut 245
St. Martin of Tours 258
St. Odile 283
Sammons, Ronald 196
Samuel, Arthur L. 107
Saperstein, David 51
Sarnoff, David 104, 139
Sarris, Andrew 151
Sayers, Dorothy L. 175
Schaefer, Natalie 141
Schary, Dore 155
Scott, C. P. 138
Scott, Walter 96
Seaborg, Glenn 21, 37
Secretary of Commerce 137
Secretary of Defense for Strategic and Theater Nuclear Forces 104
Secretary of Defense, Office of the 72
Secretary of State 202, 249
Sedgwick, John B. 245
Segall, Paul 127
Select Committee on Lighting by Electricity, London 61
Select Committee on Lighting, London 101
Selye, Lewis 160
Shapiro, Robert 42
Shaw, Albert D. 44
Shaw, George Bernard 120
Sheppard, Morris 40
Shute, Nevil 81
Siemens, Werner von 101
Simon and Schuster 178
Simon, John 152

Skinner, B. F. 49
Skinner, C. M. 26-27, 35, 132
Slansky, Paul 157
Sloan, Alfred P. 70
Smiles, Samuel 45, 64
Smith Kline and French Laboratories 131
Smith, Adam 193
Smith, Anthony 23
Smith, Bernard E. 201
Smith, Charles Emory 22
Smith, Chuck 277
Smith, E. J. 62
Smith, Ethan 268
Smith, Frederic L. 68
Smith, John 29
Smith, Mary "Mimi" 167
Smith, Roger 196
Smith, Oliver Hampton 134
Smithsonian Astrophysical Observatory 89
Smyth, Charles Piazzi 269
Smyth, John 240
Snively, Emmeline 155
Snow, Samuel 265

Soloviev, Nicolai Feopemplovich 164
Somerville, Mary 139
Southcott, Joanna 264
Southern California Edison 105
Southwest Radio Church 277-278
Spangler, Lee T. 270
Spanish Inquisition 86
Speaker, Tris 184
Sports Marketing Group 188
Sragow, Michael 153
Staffler, Maria 275
Stamford Research Institute 203
State University of New York's Graduate School of Criminal Justice 41
Steel, Danielle 179
Steinbrenner, George 187
Stengel, Casey 185
Stevens Institute of Technology 97
Stevens, Eugene M. 201
Stewart, Basil 272
Stifel, Michael 261
Still, Henry 20, 24-25, 30, 49, 73, 83-84, 126, 128
Stoeffler, Johannes 260
Stover, Lloyd V. 45
Strauss, Lewis L. 104
Strauss, Richard 164
Strong, John 277
Stroudt, Richard 220
Styron, William 177
Sullivan, David S. 226, 235
Sullivan, Mark 218
Summerfield, Arthur 23
Surgeon General 122
Swanson, Gerald 203
Swift and Company 37
Swihart, Stephen D. 277
Swing, David 216
Symonds, William 60
Taborites 259-260
Talmage, Thomas De Witt 120, 124
Tanen, Ned 152
Tarkenton, Fran 188
Task Force on Science and Technology in the Year 2000 126
Taylor, Charles 281
Taylor, Elizabeth 156, 157, 158
Taylor, Zachary 214

Author Index

Tchaikovsky, Peter Ilich 164
Teacher Chen (see Chen, Heng-Ming)
Telegraph Avenue Concerns Committee 223
Terry, Bill 185
Tesla, Nikola 87, 103, 104
Thackeray, Ted 115
Thalberg, Irving 147, 149
Thatcher, Margaret 235
Theobald, Robert 38, 41, 92, 121, 223-224
Thomason, John W. 243
Thompson, William (see Lord Kelvin)
Thomson, George 202
Thring, M. W. 10, 31, 36, 38, 105, 126,
   197, 203
Thurmond, Strom 55
Tiger, Lionel 47
Tillinghast, Charles C., Jr. 91
Today Show, The 226
Todd, Michael 162
Townes, Charles 136
Tracy, Spencer 156
Trahey, Jane 142, 180
Train, Arthur 32-33, 70, 98
Trans-World Airlines 91
Traux, Robert 93
Tredgold, Thomas 66
Trollope, Anthony 61
Trotsky, Leon 233
True Light Church of Christ 276
Truman, Harry 117
Trump, Donald 188
Truscott, Starr 82
Tso, T. C. 31
Tuck, Dick 225
Tucker, Josiah 208
Tupper, K. F. 234
Turner, John 264
Twain, Mark 192
Tyrell, R. Emmett 228
U. S. Air Force 83
U. S. Atomic Energy Commission 37, 104
U. S. Commissioner of Education 216
U. S. Commissioner on Patents 96
U. S. Corps of Engineers 210
U. S. Department of Agriculture 26, 31
U. S. Department of Labor 201
U. S. District Attorney 137
U. S. Foreign Service 247
U. S. Forest Service 51, 84, 188, 194
U. S. Navy 242, 243, 244
U. S. Patent Office 97
U. S. Postmaster General 22, 81
U. S. Secretary of Agriculture 31
U. S. Secretary of the Navy 252
United Artists 156
Universal Pictures 152, 156
University of Louisville 204
University of Texas 186
University of Vienna 113
Valin, Marjorie 11
Van Buren, Martin 65
Van Santvoord, Alfred 62
Van Tassel, George 275
Velpeau, Alfred 128
Verdi, Giuseppe 164
Verne, Jules 19, 96
Vogel, Julius 232
Voliva, Wilbur Glen 272
Von Braun, Werner 90, 92
Von Zeppelin, Eva 168
Vorhees, Russ 111
Waddington, C. H. 56

Wagner, Jane 181
Walker, John H. 33
Walker, Viola 276
Wall Street Journal 37
Wallace, Alfred Russel 97, 115
Wallace, William 186
Wanamaker, John 22
Warner Brothers Pictures 147
Warner, Harry 147
Warner, Jack 149, 154
Washburn, Cadwalader C. 211
Washington, George 208, 209
Waskow, Arthur 223-224
Watkins, John 48, 67, 120
Watson, Thomas 106, 200
Weber, Joseph N. 147
Weber, Vin 227-228
Webster, Daniel 210
Wellesley, Arthur 63
Wells, H. G. 63, 138, 246
Western Union 134
Westinghouse, George 212
Westmoreland, William 254
Weygand, Maxime 251
Wheeler, Andrew Carpenter 196
Wheeler, Wayne B. 40
Whisenant, Edgar C. 280
White, Ellen G. 266
White, Samuel 209-210
Whitehead, Robert 161
Whitson, William 263
Wiener, Anthony J. 57, 235
Wilcox, Ella Wheeler 39, 77
Wilkins, Leslie T. 41
Williams-Ellis, Amabel 86, 123
Wilson, Earl 222
Wilson, Erasmus 101
Wilson, Steve 237
Wilson, Woodrow 217, 247
Winchel, Walter 221
Winstanley, William 172
Wojtyla, Karol Cardinal (see Pope John
   Paul II))
Wolfe-Barry, John 135
Wollaston, William H. 100
Woman in the Wilderness 262
Women's Collective 13
Wood, Bob 141
Wood, Nicholas 65
Woodward, Clark 243
Wooley, Richard van der Riet 89
World's Fair 55, 56, 70, 84
Wovoka 269
Wright, Milton 78
Wright, Orville 80, 81
Wright, Wilbur 16, 78
Wrigley, Phil 184
Wroe, John 264
Wyler, William 149
Xerox Corporation 195
Yale University 195
Yardeni, Edward 109, 112
Yourdon, Ed 110, 111, 112
Yourdon, Jennifer 112
Zablocki, Ray 203
Zambia National Academy of Space
   Research 90
Zanuck, Darryl F. 139
Zimmerman, Johann Jacob 262
Zoglin, Richard 143

Bad Predictions
Subject Index

1812 Overture 164
18th Amendment 40
1984 177
60's legacy 213
Aaron, Hank 185
Absalom, Absalom 176
accessories 25
Adams, Douglas 89
advertising 132, 133, 137
aerophor (instrument) 164
African wars 254
African-Americans 215, 227
aging, physiology of 127
agriculture see farming
AIDS 127
air filtering 44
air-conditioning 30
airplanes 44, 46, 103
  ground travel 70
  aerial navigation 54
Alaska, acquisition 211, 212
alchemy 114 see also gold
alcohol 27, 40, 54, 75
Alice in Wonderland 173
Alice's Restaurant 168
Alien 153
alienation 209-210
aliens 86, 275, 277
  communication 273
alloys 32-33
alphabet 19
aluminum, demand for 198
Amazon.com 12
America 208
American dream 57
American flag 223
American Graffiti 152
American independence 208
American Press Association 196
American Revolution 208, 209
American Telephone and Telegraph
  Company (AT&T) 137
anarchy 272
*And To Think That I Saw it on Mulberry
Street* 176
Andrews, Ellie 148
anesthesia 127
Animal Farm 177
animal sacrifice 266
Ann Veronica 174
Annie Hall 152, 153
antichrist 258, 259, 274
antiseptic 120
Annunciation and Good Friday 258
apocalypse 269
Apocalypse Now 153
appliances, wireless 99
aquaculture 29
Arab-Israeli conflict 277
Arabs 277
architecture (see home design)
armageddon 258, 266-273, 276-277, 280
arms race 246
Arnold, Benedict 209
Arnold, Tom 143
art 160
art appreciation 160
arthritis cure 125

Aryan nation 249
Ashtar 275
assassination 237
  attempt on Pope 278
  presidential 211, 216
  presidential—attempt 226
assembly lines 68
Association of Licensed Automobile
  Manufacturers 68
Astaire, Fred 155
astrology 260, 261, 267-268, 278, 279
astronomy 86
Atari 108
ATM 108
atomic
  batteries 104
  bomb 242, 243, 244
  energy 100, 102, 103, 104, 242, 243
  weapons 253
atoms
  existence of 113
  splitting 100, 103, 104
Attica Prison 40
audio-visual aids/multimedia 49
Australia 233, 234
automated machines 36
automation, industrial 203
automobiles 67, 68, 69
  accidents 71
  Big Three 71
  coin-operated 72
  computer-aided navigation 99
  cost 70
  demand 68, 69, 74
  development of 69
  diesel-powered 73
  electric 69, 73
  gas-powered 73, 74
  market, size 68, 74
  plastic 70
  power stations 73
  production, Germany 70
  production, Japan 71, 74
  radar 72
  rental 72
  safety 71
  self-driving 70, 72, 73, 74
  theft-proof 75
aviation 54, 60, 75-76, 77, 80 (see also flight)
  aircar 83
  aircraft
    private 84
    self-driving 84
    airplanes 75, 78
      size 82
      braking 79
      weight limits 76, 78, 79
    dirigible balloons and balloons 76, 77, 78, 83
    flying canoe 75
    gyrocopter 83 (see also helicopter)
    military 241, 242, 243
Away We Go 162
Axis powers 251
Baby Boom 43
Bach, Richard 180
Bahá'ís Under the Provisions of the Covenant 277
Bain, Barbara 141
baldness 46
Ball, Lucille 154
ball-point pen 193
Baltimore Orioles 186
banking, branch 202

Subject Index

Barney Miller 142
baseball 185, 186, 187
  Hall of Fame 186
  night 184
  popularity 184
Batman 153
Battle of Little Big Horn 245
battleships 242, 243
Baum, L. Frank 173
The Beatles 167, 168
Beatty, Warren 156
beauty 122
Beckett, Samuel 176
Bee Gees 168
Beethoven, Ludwig van 165, 166
Behind the Scenes 181
Bell, Alexander Graham 134, 135, 192
Bening, Annette 157
Berkeley, Busby 151
Berlin Wall 236
The Best Man 156
The Best of Groucho 141
The Bible 277, 283
bilge 89
bioengineering (see food, genetically altered)
biology, molecular 124
birth control 122
birth in space, human 93
Bishop, Joey 143
Black Plague 262
Blacks (see African-Americans)
Blair, Eric Arthur 175
Blair, Tony 109
bleach 192
blood
  circulation 123
  diseases 123
  transfusions 128
bodyguards 41
Bogart, Humphrey 155
bomb attacks 44
bombers 241, 243
Bonaparte, Napoleon 232
Bond, James 150, 151
books
  banned 48
  burning of 48
  disappearance of 48, 180
  self-help 181
Booth, John Wilkes 211
boredom 20, 148
Borgnine, Ernest 156
The Bostonians 173
bow 240
boxing, popularity 184
Brando, Marlon 151
British empire 232
Brooklyn Dodgers 185
Brooks, Mel 141
Brothers and Sisters of Red Death 270
Buck, Pearl S. 175
bureaucracy 252-253
burglary (see crime)
Burton, Richard 157
Butler, Rhett 149
Cain, James M. 176
California acquisition 210
Calvary Chapel 277
camera 98
Cameron, James 154
campaign finance 216
Canada 234

canal system 65
cancer
  cure 56, 124, 125
  lung 120, 121
capital punishment 39, 53
capitalism, death of 199, 202, 235
Capone, Al 142
Capra, Frank 148
Carlson, Chester 99
Carpenters 194
Carrie (book) 180
Carrie (film) 152, 157
Carroll, Lewis 173
cars (see automobiles)
Carson, Johnny 143
Carter, Jimmy 225
cartoons 148
Casablanca 155
cashless payments 41 (see also credit cards)
Casino Royale 150
Castro, Fidel 167, 234, 235, 252
Catholic
  Apostolic Church 270
  Church, Roman 259
  rights 52
Catholicism 235, 276
cavalry 242
CBS 140
censorship 48
Center for Disease Control 127
chauffeurs 68
Chicago 169
Child, Julia 29
childbirth 46
childcare
  child rearing 47
  daycare 34
  machine-fed infants 19
Children of Light 273
China 232-233
The China Syndrome 105
Christian crusade 262
Christianity, unified 276
Clark College 86-87
Cleator, P. E. 88
Cleveland Browns 189
Cleveland Indians 188
climate control 20, 33, 37, 128
Clinton, Bill 109, 227, 228, 229
Clinton, Hillary 228
cloning 27, 244
clothing 19, 21, 25 (see also fashion)
  baby 24
  cleaning of 25, 34
  climate controlled 24
  disposable 24, 194
  illuminated 24
  paper 23, 24
  plastic 24, 56
Coca-Cola's New Coke 194
coffee (see food, synthetic)
Cold War 219, 222, 235
colds, cure for common 124
Coleridge, Samuel Taylor 172
colonies' secession, American 208
Colorado River 210
Comet Kohoutek 93
comets 86
commodities, Japanese 202
communes 275
communication devices 134, 136

Bad Predictions

communism 222, 234, 235
commuting 72, 99
competitiveness 56
computers 30, 32, 105, 106
  market 106, 107
  memory 108
  number of 106
  personal 107
  security 107
  self-monitoring 106
  size 106
  speed 107
  tapes and cards 107
Confederacy of Dunces 178
Congress of Nations 76
Connery, Sean 151
Conrad, Joseph 174
construction materials 199
consumption 124
containers, edible 27
containers, non-polluting 194
cooking 27
Cop Rock 143
Copernicus 86
Coppola, Francis Ford 151, 152, 153
cosmetics 24
cosmic ice theory 116
cowpox 123
credit cards 38, 41 (see also cashless payments)
  as ignition 73
  disappearance of 203
crime 39, 40
  elimination of 40
  fornication 53
  reduction of 124
criminal justice 41
criminals 39, 97, 115
The Crisis Years 181
crucifixion 281
currency (see money)
Curtis, Tony 156
Czechoslovakia 250
DaGuerre, Louis Jacques 96
Daguerrotype 96
Dalton, John 113
dance clubs 148
Darrow, Charles B. 193
Darwin, Charles 114
Darwinism 114 (see also evolution)
Darwin's Theory of Evolution 97
data processing 106
data systems 23
Davidians 274
Davis, John W. 218
Dawn of the Dead 153
Day, Doris 141, 155
DDT 99
De Mille, Cecil B. 151
De Palma, Brian 157
Death of a Salesman 162
Declaration of Independence 208, 209
deforestation 102, 199
delivery, mail 22
democracy 219, 249
destruction 254
  civilization 283
  England 31
  Los Angeles 276
  United States 275
Detroit Lions 186
Dewey, Thomas E. 220, 221
Di Lampedusa, Giuseppe 178

diabetes cure 125
The Diary of Anne Frank 177
Dick Cavett Show 126
Dickinson, Emily 173
diet 122
DiMaggio, Joe 185
Dirksen, Everett M. 211
disease 44, 123, 124
  eradication 56, 124, 127
  reduction 126
dishes, disposable 29, 35, 37
dishwashing 194
disinfectant 124
disintegration of Colosseum in Rome 271
Disney films 149, 150
Disney, Walt 161
disposable bedding 36
District of Columbia 226
divine appearance 281
divorce 39, 156, 158, 192
Dole, Bob 228
doomsday/end of world 110, 111
Dow Chemical Company 192
Dow Jones Industrial Average 204
Down and Out in Paris and London 175
Dr. No 151
Dr. Zhivago 151
Drake, Edwin L. 192
Dream of Fair-to-Middling Women 176
dreams 20
drinking 54
drugs 122
  drugless treatments 126-127
  in hypnosis 126
  intelligence 125, 126
  legalization 41, 125
  psychotropic 125, 127
drunk driving 75
Duchovny, David 143
Duran Duran 169
earnings, cap 213
Earth, flat 116
earthquakes 277, 281, 284-285
  London 263
Eastern front 250
Eastwood, Clint 156
economic disparity 42
economy
  depression 202, 203, 213
  inflation 55, 202
  recession 204, 213
  strength 218
  Y2K 109, 111, 113
Edison Company 69
Edison, Thomas 96, 97, 113
Edsel 71
education 20, 42, 47-52, 97, 126
  adult 49, 52
  classes, customized 49, 50, 51
  collapse 51
  compulsory 50
  costs 48
  curriculum 48
  lifetime learning 49
  school hours 48, 49, 50, 51
  school year length 49, 50, 51, 52
  universities 48
Eiffel Tower 96
Einstein, Albert 115, 116
Eisenhower, Dwight D. 219, 222
Eisenhower, Edgar 222
elections, reform 216, 221

electricity 35, 36, 54, 100, 101
 cars 69
 consumption 69
 currents 101, 102
electromagnetic medical treatments 126
electromobile 72, 99
elevator 19
Elway, John 188
e-mail 12
The Emerald City 173

Emmy awards 151

employment 196, 201
end of all nations (formalized) 272
end of Europe 265
end of France 267
end of London 260
end of the world 258-285
 and cults 270, 273, 275
 comet colliding with earth 263, 269, 272
 earthquake 264
 explosion 274
 fire 270
 flood 260
 Mars colliding with Earth 278
 planetary alignment 284, 285
 sun colliding with earth 261
energy 21, 28, 32, 35, 36, 44 (see also fuel)
 prices 103
 sources, alternative 44
 surplus 54
engines
 gas 69
 reciprocating piston 73
 jet 82
England 233, 237
ENIAC 106
environmental catastrophe 8
environmental destruction 279
epidemics, elimination of 124
Equal Rights Amendment/ERA 47
Erie Canal 65
Eugenics wars 14
evolution 97, 114, 173 (see also Darwinism)
exercise 120
extinction
 flies 20
 horses 64, 67
 housefly 67
 humans 42, 110, 234, 273, 279, 284
 plants and animals 26
 trees 102
extra-terrestrial (see aliens)
fairy tales 173
families, extended 52
famine 26, 31, 232
farmers 30, 48, 65, 218
farming 25, 26, 28, 29, 31, 48
fashion 19, 23 (see also clothing)
costs 23
 female 23, 24
 male 23, 24
Father of Nuclear Physics 103
Father of the Bride 150
Faulkner, William 176
Federal Express 195
feminists 13
Ferraro, Geraldine 138
fertility 122
fertilizer 26
fiber optics 136
fiction 179
Fiddler on the Roof 162

Fields, Debbi 195
firearms 240
fish sandwiches 193
Fitzgerald, F. Scott 175
Fleming, Ian 150, 151
flextime 198
flight 75, 78, 79, 80 (see also aviation)
 commercial 79-80, 82, 84
 expense 80, 84
 heavier-than-air 75-78, 88
 popularity 81
 trans-Atlantic 80, 84
 weight limits 80
flood, London 263
flying saucer 281
food 19, 26, 29, 30, 47, 56
 bacteria steak 30
 genetically altered 28, 30
 preservation 34
 sources, alternative 28-31, 38, 56
 supplements 27
 supply 29, 31
 synthetic 20, 26, 28-30, 47
 tomatoes, square 30
football 186, 187
force, military 209
Ford Motor Company 66, 68
Ford, Gerald 225
Ford, Henry 68, 283
Fortensky, Larry 158
The Fountainhead 176
Franco-Prussian War 240
Frankenstein role 148
freight transport 77
The French Chef 29
fuel
 automotive 50, 69
 alternative sources for 103
Fuji Film 195
Fuller, Buckminster 57
Fulton, Robert 60, 62
furniture, plastic 32-33
Gable, Clark 149, 154
Gagarin, Yuri 89
Galileo 86
Gallup, George 219
gardens, rooftop 46
gases, kinetic theory of 114
Gealeke Xhosa 266
gender roles 13, 40, 45, 57, 187
genetics 113
George, W. G. 184
German expansionism 248, 249
German Reich 248
German reunification 236
germs 120, 128
Get Smart 141

Gettysburg Address 211

Ghost Dance cult 269
Gilligan's Island 151

Gingrich, Newt 225

The Giving Tree 178
glaciers 31
Godard, Jean-Luc 156

Goddard, Robert 86-87, 88, 102

The Godfather 151
Goering, Hermann 249
Going Home 179
gold 114 (see also alchemy)

Bad Predictions

Gold Diggers of 1933 151
gold mines 192
Gone with the Wind 149
The Good Earth 175
Gorbachev, Mikhail 236
Gore, Al 228
government, elective 214
governmental control 199, 209-210
Grammy winners 168
Grand Canyon 210
Grant, Cary 151
gravity
  affecting flight 79
  backscrewing theory of 116
Great Depression 200, 201, 203, 218
The Great Gatsby 175
Great Pyramid 268, 269, 272-273, 277
Great Synagogue 277
greed 54
Green Giant 193
Grenada, U. S. invasion 255
grocery shopping 193, 194
gubernatorial bid 226
Guggenheim Foundation 88
Guggenheim, Harry 88
guns 240
Guyana 275
gymnastics 120
hackers 107
Haig, Douglas 242
hair 24-25
Hall, Arsenio 143
Haloid 99
Handel, George Frederick 165
Harding, Tonya 188
Harleian Museum 268
Harmonists 266
Harrisburg, PA 105
Harrison, Rex 151
Hart, Gary 15, 227
Harvey, William 123
Havilland, Olivia de 149
Hawn, Goldie 157
health 120
health care 55, 121
heart disease cure 124, 125
Heart of Darkness 174
heating 20, 27-28
hegemony 226
helicopters 56, 70, 83
hemophiliacs 127
Henry, Buck 141
Heritage West 2000 111
heroin 124
Hewlett-Packard 108
Heyerdahl, Thor 177
hibernation, human 57
High Sierra 155
high-tension wires 101
highways 20
Hinckley, John, Jr. 226
Hitler, Adolf 14, 247, 248, 249
HIV 127
Holly, Buddy 166
Hollywood 283
Holocaust 249
Holy Land tours 281
home design 32, 33
  architecture 193
  camouflage houses 34
  flying houses 35
  glass houses 34

interior design 34, 35-36
  moveable walls 32, 34
  moveable homes 33, 35, 56, 83
  plastic houses 34, 194
  pre-fabricated houses 34, 35
home schooling 42, 48, 52
homosexuality 143
Hoover, Herbert 201, 218
horses as transportation 67, 68
horseless carriages 96
hospitals 128
  food 128
  rooms, disposable 128
housekeeping 197
housework 35, 36, 194
  computerized home 36
  cooking 36, 37
  cordless appliances 36
  dusting 36
  dishwashing 35, 37
  food preparation 36
  lawn mower 36
  mechanical maids 37
  microwaves 37
  vacuum cleaner 36, 37
housing
  floating cities 45
  life underground 44, 57
  life in the sky 44
  underwater cities 45, 57
hovercrafts 66, 75
Howe, Richard 209
Hughes, Charles Evans 247
Hughes, Howard 150
human survival of the fittest 280 (see also
  Darwinism)
hunting 26
hurricanes 116, 284
Hussein, Saddam 237, 255
Huston, John 155
hydroponics 28
I Dream of Jeannie 140
I Love Lucy 140
IBM 99
illumination 97
immaculate conception 264-265
impeachment 225, 229
imperialism 234
income, guaranteed 50, 197, 203
Independence Day (U. S.) 208, 209
India 232-233
Indians 245
infantry 240
information highway 111, 112
innovation, end of 240
insane, treatment of 115
insects 20, 26
Insull, Sam 97
insurance 199
international trade 202
Internet 107, 108
invention 146
invention, death of 96, 97, 98
inventory 30
investments 192, 195, 204

Iococca, Lee 192
Iraq 237
Irish potato famine 232
Ironweed 180
Ishtar 153
It Happened One Night 148, 149

Subject Index

Ito, Lance 42
J. P. Morgan and Company 74
Jackson, Andrew 65
James, Henry 173
Japan 242
Japanese expansion 234
Japanese power ca. WWII 250, 251, 252
Jaws 153, 179

Jeans West 195

Jefferson, Thomas 214
Jehovah's Witnesses 270
Jenner, Edward 123
jewelry 25
Jews 277
Jonathan Livingston Seagull 180
Jones, Paula 229

Jonestown 275

Judgment Day/doomsday 268
The Jumping Frog 174
The Jungle 174

Jupiter 86, 278

Jupiter Effect 278
justice (see law)
Karloff, Boris 148
Kazan, Elia 162
Keaton, Michael 153
Keats, John 172
Kelpius, Johannes 262
Kennedy, Jackie 222
Kennedy, Joseph P. 223
Kennedy, Ted 226-227
Kennedy, William 180
Kennedys 222, 223
keys 19, 21, 38
kinetic theory of gases 114
King Henry VIII 232
King of Terror 282
King, Stephen 180
Kipling, Rudyard 173
kitchens, automated 13, 27, 31, 38
Kitty Hawk 78, 79, 80
Knowles, John 178
Koch, Edward 222
Kodak 99
Kon-Tiki 177

Kool Aid 275

Kruschev, Nikita 167

labor rights 198
Lady Chatterley's Lover 175
land use 26
Landau, Martin 141
landing fields 82
Landon, Alfred 218
Langley, Samuel 79
language
  phonetic 132
  reform 19, 48
lasers 20, 136
Laugh-In 157
law 39
  international 76
Lawrence, D. H. 175
lawyers 39, 40, 53
Leaves of Grass 174
Led Zeppelin 168
legal system 39
legislation 39, 41, 45

Leigh, Vivien 149
leisure time 29, 48-50, 55, 196-197, 203
Lenin, V. I. 235
Lennon, John 167
The Leopard 178
Lerner, Alan Jay 161
Lesseps, Ferdinand Marie de 61
Letter of Toledo 259
levecars 66
Lewinsky, Monica 228
liberties 52
library usage 136
Life Magazine 274
life span, human 120, 121, 124
  projected for individuals 120, 121, 126, 142
Life With Father 161
light, wave theory of 113
lighting
  incandescent 96
  electric 39, 61, 96, 100-102
  gas 96, 100-101
Limbaugh, Rush 138
Lincoln, Abraham 215, 265
  assassination 211
Lindbergh, Charles 81
Lindsay, John V. 224
Lister, Joseph 120
literacy 51
Little Caesar 154
locks 19, 21
Loewe, Frederick 161
Lolita 177
Lombardi, Vince 187
Lord Byron 172
Lorillard 121

Louisiana Purchase 209-210

Lucas, George 152
Lumiere motion picture camera 146
lunar mining 92, 93
Lust for Life 176
machine gun 241, 242
Madonna 157
magazines, subscription prices 136
magnetic reversal 285
mail
  airmail 81
  delivery 133, 195
  route, establishment of 210
make-up (see cosmetics)
The Maltese Falcon 150, 155
Manhattan 43, 44
Manhattan project 244
marijuana 41
marriage 53, 55, 222, 232, 237
Mars 15, 278, 282
  landing 90, 91, 92
Marty 156
Martz, Sandra Haldeman 181
Marx, Karl 235
masculinity 57
mass ritual suicide 275
mass transit 72, 73, 75, 83, 84
materialism 55
  increase 203
  decline 70, 279
Mattel Toys 195
Matthau, Walter 157
Matthews, Stanley 187
mayoral elections 222
Mays, Willie 185
McCarthy, Joseph 222

Bad Predictions

McCartney, Paul 167
McCormick, Cyrus 25
McDonald's 32, 193
McKinley, William 97, 216, 269
meat consumption 26, 31 (see also
   vegetarian diet)
medicine 48, 121, 123
megalopolis 44, 72
meltdown, nuclear 105, 112-113
Melville, Herman 172
memory aids 98
Mendel, Gregor 113
metric system 75
Mickey Mouse 148, 155
microchips 106
Microsoft 109
Middle East 234, 237, 277
Middle East arms control 227
migration 209-210
military advancements 240, 245
Millennium (see resurrection of Christ)
millennium onset
   millennium bug 109, 110, 111, 112, 113
   preparation 109, 110
Miller, Arthur 162
Miller, William 265
Milton, John 172
mind control 20, 244
Miss America 57
missiles, guided 22
Mission Impossible 141
Moby Dick 172
Model T 68
Mondale, Walter 226-227
Monday Night Football 141
money 32, 41
The Money Game 193
Mongols 282
Monopoly 193
Monroe, Marilyn 155
moon landing 89, 90, 116
moon travel 61, 87, 88, 91, 92
moons, artificial 57
Moore, Roger 151
moral decay 283
morality 54, 56
morphine substitute 124
Morse, Samuel 134
mortgages 52
Most Valuable Player (MVP) 186
Mother Shipton's prophecy 267-268, 283
Mt. St. Helens 117
mountain climbing 189
movies 48, 103, 146, 147
   Civil War 149
   quality of 147
   rental 136
   silent 146, 147
   talking 146, 147
   theaters 136, 148
Mrs. Fields' Cookies 195
musicals 162
musket 240
Muskie, Edmund S. 224
mustard gas 243
mutual funds 204
My Fair Lady 161
Nabokov, Vladimir 177
Namath, Joe 186
nationalism, elimination of 57
Native Americans/Eskimos 211-212
natural resources, depletion of 43, 69, 74,
   104

Nazism 247, 248, 249, 250
New Hampshire 265
New Jersey Generals 188
New Mexico acquisition 210
New York City 43, 44, 110, 203, 222
New York Giants 187
New York Jets 186
New York State 44
New York Stock Exchange 203
New York Yankees 187
news sources 132
newspapers 132-133
   appearance 132
   content 132
Nicholson, Jack 153, 180
Niven, David 151
Nixon administration 253
Nixon, Richard 222
Noah 277
noise pollution 45, 67, 69
Nostradamus 281-282
nuclear
   energy 83, 102, 103, 105
   explosives, industrial use 57
   fallout shelters 275
   fission 100
   nuclear plant accidents 105
   power 31-32, 36, 92
   war 244, 253, 254, 274-279, 284
   weapons 103, 242, 243, 244
nudity 21, 25
O'Hara, Scarlett 149
Ohm, George Simon 100
oil, drilling 192
Oken 97
Oklahoma 162
Onassis, Aristotle 222
opera 165
Orca 153
organ transplants 124, 126
Orwell, George 175, 177
Oscar winners and nominees 148, 149,
   150, 152, 156
Ox-Ho 276
Packard 71
Panama Canal 62
papacy, end 283
paper 36
paper
   carbon 252-253
   paperless office 12, 13, 195, 196
   substitute 98
Pappas, Milt 186
parenting 47
parliamentary system 225
patriotism 222
Pax 165
peace 223, 245, 246, 248, 252
Pearl Harbor 242, 243, 250, 252
People's Temple 275
Percy, Walker 178
Perfect 157
Perkins, George W. 74
Persian Gulf War 255
The Peter Principle 179
Peter Rabbit 174
Peter, Laurence J. 179
Phillip Morris 140
phobias, cures for 127
phonograph 97
photography 96, 97
phrenology 97, 115
physics 115

Subject Index

physiognomy 114
Picasso, Pablo 161
planes (see aviation)
planetary alignment 259-261, 270-271, 279, 284, 285 (see also astrology)
planets 86
plastic 32, 35,105
(see also automobiles, clothing, home design)
plumbing 98
pneumatic tube 22, 77
poetry 179
Poland, invasion of 250
polar shift 284, 285
Polaroid 98
police dramas 143
police surveillance 76
polio vaccine 125
political aspirations 214, 217, 219, 222-227
political parties disappear 222, 223
political revolution 223-224
politicians 253, 269
politics, truth in 221, 223
polling/pollsters 219, 221
pollution 115
  industrial 54
  reduction 73, 83, 84
Pope Clement VII 259
Pope John Paul II 235, 278
Pope Leo 232
population
  growth 26
  trends 42, 43, 56
  U. S. 42, 43
  world 56, 234
Post Office 22
postage 22
postal delivery, air 81
postal service, demand 23
The Postman Always Rings Twice 176
Potter, Beatrix 174
poverty 54, 213
  end 56, 200, 201
  slums, disappearance of 54
power failures and Y2K 112, 113
presidency, U. S. 219, 220, 224
presidential election 214, 215, 217-220, 222, 224-225, 227-228
presidential term of office 216
Presley, Elvis 166
prime minister, England 235
prime minister, India 235
Prince Charles 237
Princess Diana 237
prisons 39, 40
profit sharing 199
prohibition 40, 233
propeller 60
prosperity predictions 200, 201
prostitutes 52
Puccini, Giacomo 166
Pulitzer Prize winners 175, 178, 180
Pygmalion 161
Quebec Act 52
race relations 42, 53, 55
race supremacy 54
racial segregation 55, 223-224
racism 212, 215, 232-233
Rackham, Horace 68
radio 136, 137, 138
radio waves 136

railroads 61, 63-66
  electric trains 66
  obsolescence 77
  passengers 64
  pollution 64
  steam-engine trains 63, 64
  trains 63, 63, 64
  trains, automated 96, 194
  trains, elevated 66
  trains, maximum velocity 65, 66
raising the dead 266
Rand, Ayn 176
Randall, Henry Stephens 215
The Rapture 266-267, 274, 276, 278, 280-281 (see also resurrection of Christ)
ratings 143
Reagan, Nancy 181
Reagan, Ronald 156, 181, 222, 226-227
real estate markets 204
recycling 21, 105
Red scare 222
Red Sox 185
re-election 215
reinforcements, military 245
rejection letters 15
relativity, theory of 116
religion 173,193, 259, 261, 266-267
religious education 49
Rembrandt van Rijn, Harmensz 160
Republican party 225
resignation from office 224, 229
resources 21
resurrection of Christ 258-259, 261-266, 269, 271, 273, 276-277, 280-281
retirement age 197, 198
revolution 233
Reynolds, Burt 156
Rice, Donna 227
Rickey, Branch 185
rifles 240
Rippingille, Mr. 160
The Rise and Fall of the Third Reich 178
ritual sacrifice 266
Rizzuto, Phil 185
roads 67-69
  freeways 73
  pavement 67
  self-cleaning 19
roadside assistance 83
Robinson, Frank 186
Robinson, Jackie 185
robot music 147
robots 32, 35, 37, 38, 48, 99,108
rock 'n' roll 165
rocket fuel 87
rocket mail 22
rockets 82, 86-87, 88, 89
Rockets Through Space 88
Rocky 152
Roddenberry, Gene 141
Rodin, Auguste 160
Roman Empire 240
Romulus 258
Ronalds, Francis 133
Roosevelt, Franklin Delano 43, 216, 219
Roosevelt, Teddy 217
Rose, Pete 187
Rosh Hashanah 280
route planning 72
Russell, Charles Taze 266
Russia/Soviet Union 213, 219, 225, 226, 235, 236, 245, 275, 277

Bad Predictions

Ruth, Babe 184
Ryan, Nolan 100
St. Patrick's day 268
Sajak, Pat 143
Salk, Jonas 125
Salvation Army 53
Samuels, Bernhard 164
sanitation 47, 98
satellite 20
Saturday Night Fever 157
Saturday Night Live 142
Saturn 86
scarcity 57
schools (see education)
seat belt 71
Seaver, Tom 186
Secession 210
Second Adventists 266, 270
second coming (see resurrection of Christ)
The Second Sex 177
Second Temple 277
security 19, 21, 38, 41
seismic activity 284, 285
Selznick, David O. 149
A Separate Peace 178
Seuss, Dr. 176
Seventh Day Adventists 266, 274
sex 53-55, 58
sex roles (see gender roles)
sexual education 50
Sgt. Pepper's Lonely Heart's Club Band 168
The Shadows 165
Shakespeare, William 172
Shanghai Surprise 157
Shaw, George Bernard 161
Shelley, Percy Bysshe (see Lord Byron)
Shirer, William L. 178
shopping 202
silver 25-26
Silverstein, Shel 178
Simpson, O. J., trial 42
Sinclair, Upton 174
skiing 188
Skycar 84
sleep 121
smallpox 123
Smith, Fred 195
Smithsonian Institution 86-87, 160
smog 45, 56
smoking see tobacco
Snow White and the Seven Dwarves 149
soccer 187
social classes, disappearance of 57
socialism 56, 202, 222
software 107
solar energy 93, 105
solar system
  geocentric model 86
  heliocentric model 86
sonic booms 84
South African military defense 254
Soviets (see Russia)
Space Age 91
space
  exploration, timetable 89
  hospital 92
  Russian 89
  stations/colonies 90-93
  travel 61, 82, 86, 89-93
  travel, impossible 87, 88, 89
Spade, Sam role 150, 155
spare time (see leisure time)

spelling 19 (see also language)
Mr. Spock 141
Sports Illustrated 274
sports, violence in 184
stagecoaches 64
Stalin, Joseph 219
Stallone, Sylvester 157
Star Trek 141
Star Trek: the Next Generation 143
Star Wars 152
Starship Titanic 89
starvation (see famine)
statehood 212
Staying Alive 158
steam navigation 61
steamboats 60, 62
  obsolescence 77
  screw-propeller 60
  paddle wheel 62
Stephenson, George 64
stereotypes (see gender roles)
sterilization 34
  reproductive 39
Stevenson, Adalai 224
Stewart, Rod 168
stock market 200, 201, 204
Stone, Irving 176
storms 277
Stravinsky, Igor 165
Streep, Meryl 180
streets, see roads
Studebaker 71
submarine 63
subways 67
Suez Canal 61
suffrage 45, 46, 216
sun 117
super humans 284
Super Money 193
Super Bowl 186, 188
supermarkets 193, 194
superpowers 226, 235
supersonic travel 84
superwoman 13
surgery 98, 124, 128
surprise attack 242
surround screen 148
surround sound 148
suspended animation 121, 127
Swaggart, Jimmy 53
The Swarm 152
Swift, Jonathan 178
swimming, English Channel 184
taboos 21
  profanity 50, 51
Tampax 193
tanks 242, 243
tape 21
Tarkenton, Fran 188
taste, refinement 160
taxes 199, 227
Taylor, Zachary 214
Tchaikovsky, Peter Ilich 164
teachers 48
team relocation 185
technological breakdown 111, 112
technology, assistive 108
teeth 26
telecommunications 136
telegraphs 133, 134
  wireless 135
telemedicine 136

telephone 23, 101, 133-137, 192
  cellular phones 135
  networks 134
telephony 97
telescope 86
television 20, 34-35, 52, 88-89, 138-140
  channels 139
  flat-screen 140
  market 138, 139
  networks 140
  news programs 141, 142
  replacing movies 148
  shows 140, 141
  tastes 139
  three-dimensional 140
The Ten Commandments 151
terminal illness 127
term-limits 216
terrorism 284
testosterone 46
textbooks 49
textile industry 23
theater 146-147, 161-162
Theory of Electricity 100
thermodynamics 114
Thicke, Alan 143
Three Mile Island 105
Thunderball 151
Tilden, Samuel Jones 215
The Time Machine 174
Time Magazine 274
tires 71, 72, 74
Titan (moon) 86
Titanic 62, 154
tobacco 27, 31, 120-122
  cigarettes 120-122
  cigarettes, noncarcinogenic 120-121
  smoking, youth 122
The Tonight Show 142
Toole, John Kennedy 178
track records 184
traffic
  air 67
  jams 54, 83
  underground 67
trains see railroads
trans-Atlantic communication 137
trans-Atlantic travel 60, 66
transpersonal experience 213
transportation 20, 43, 55-56, 60, 99
  free 66
La Traviata 164
Travolta, John 157
Triple Crown (baseball) 186
True Light Church of Christ 276
Truman, Harry S. 220, 221, 244
tsunami 284
Tumulty, Joseph 217
The Turn of the Screw 173
tv see television
Twain, Mark 174
typesetting 192
typewriters replaced 132
U. S. Constitution 40, 209, 214, 215,
  223-224
  replaced 223-224
U. S. expansion, 210, 211-212, 216
U. S. Football League 188
U. S. Navy 252
Underwater! 150
unemployment 65, 203-204, 213
urban expansion 44

urban life 43, 54-55, 67, 6972
  elimination of 54-55
vacations 49, 55, 70
vaccination 123
Van Gogh, Vincent 176
Vatican 276
vegetarian diet 26, 27 (see also meat consumption)
Velikovsky, Immanuel 115
Venus 90
Verne, Jules 89
vice 54
video telephone 10
Vietnam War 252, 253, 254
virgin birth 264-265
Virgin Islands, acquisition 211
voice recordings 132
volcanoes 117, 284
voting rights, D. C. 226
voting, women 45, 46
Wagner, Richard 165, 166
Wall Street 200, 201, 269
Walters, Barbara 140, 142
war 54
  disappearance of 76, 81
  end 56, 245, 247-248
  on foot 240
  preparation for 48
  technology 240
warfare
  chemical 243, 284
  field 240
  machine 240
  naval 241
  submarine 241
Warner Brothers 155
Warren, Earl 220
Washington, D.C. (see District of Columbia)
waste removal/ management 21, 43
water flea 28
water shortage 31
Watergate 224
Waterson, J. J. 114
Wayne, Carol 142
wealth, distribution of 42, 198, 199, 203
weapons 240-244
  shock 240
weather 20
weather control 20, 30, 56, 116
Webb, Matthew 184
weight control 122
Weiss, George 185
Wells, H. G. 174
West Side Story 151
The West 210
Western Telegraph Company 135
Western Union 134, 135
We've Only Just Begun 194
whales, artificial 29
wheels (see tires)
When I am an Old Woman I Shall Wear Purple 181
Whistler, James MacNeil 160
Whistler's Mother 160
Whitman, Walt 174
Whitney, John Hay 161
Whose Body? 175
wigs 25
Wild, Wild West (television) 150
Wilkes, Melanie 149
William Hill Organization 228
Williams, Paul 194
Williams, Robin 158
Williams, Ted 185

Bad Predictions

Williams, Vanessa 57
Wilson, Woodrow 247
Wimsey, Lord Peter 175
Winchell, Walter 162
woman president 216, 217
women (see also gender roles)
  education 45
  in politics 45-47, 216-217, 235
  in the military 254
  in the workforce 45, 47
  masculine traits in 46
  physical changes in 47
  voting rights 45, 46
  woman's place 45
The Wonderful Wizard of Oz 173
Woodstock 165
word processors 108
work force trends 48
work hours 35, 52
workday/week length 196-198
world cooperation 76
World Series 186, 188
World War I 246, 247
  U.S. involvement 247
World War II 202, 247, 248, 249, 250,
  251
  U. S. involvement 251
World War III 252, 278
Wright Brothers 16, 60, 78
Wright, Orville 16, 78
Wright, Wilbur 241
Wuthering Heights 149
xerography 99
Xerox Corporation 99
X-Files 143
x-rays 113
Y2K bug 8
Yankee Stadium 187
year 2000 7, 11 (see also millennium)
You Bet Your Life 141
You Light Up My Life 168
Young, Thomas 113
Youth 174
Zambia 90